SUBMARINE WARFARE.

D. VAN NOSTRAND, Publisher.

DESTRUCTION OF THE U. S. STEAM SLOOP OF WAR "HOUSATONIC."

SUBMARINE WARFARE,

OFFENSIVE AND DEFENSIVE.

INCLUDING A DISCUSSION OF THE

OFFENSIVE TORPEDO SYSTEM,

ITS EFFECTS UPON IRON-CLAD SHIP SYSTEMS, AND INFLUENCE UPON FUTURE NAVAL WARS.

BY

LIEUT.-COMMANDER J. S. BARNES, U. S. N.

WITH ILLUSTRATIONS.

NEW YORK:
D. VAN NOSTRAND, Publisher,
23 MURRAY ST. AND 27 WARREN ST.

1869.

PREFACE.

The Author, in presenting this work to the public, is perfectly well aware that there is much therein open to adverse criticism, and feels very confident that it will not be spared, particularly by his professional brethren of both branches of the service.

He has only designed calling attention to a subject so fraught with consequences to the profession of arms, and to collate the history of the Torpedo, and the various advances made in this new system of warfare, in the hope that it may prove interesting and instructive to those who have not found it convenient or practicable to gather together the scanty scraps of information to be discovered, scattered here and there, among the contributions to military arts and sciences at home and abroad.

Naval Academy,
June, 1868.

LIST OF PLATES.

VIGNETTES.

ERRATA.

On page 154, for Plate XIV., read Plate XII.
" 169, " XV., " XIX.

CONTENTS.

EARLY HISTORY OF GUNPOWDER.

CHAPTER I.

GUNPOWDER.—HISTORY OF ITS APPLICATION TO WAR.—REASONS WHICH RETARDED ITS DEVELOPMENT AND USE.—UTILITY OF THE INVENTION, AND EMPLOYMENT IN WAR HUMANE.—IMPROVEMENTS IN INSTRUMENTS ADAPTED TO ITS USE.—THE TORPEDO.

No invention of man ever created so great a change in warfare, and consequently in the destinies of nations, as the combination of the ingredients which compose gunpowder. Writers upon engines of war have ascribed the origin of the invention to various periods of history, and to different nations. But it would appear that, although the compound had been rudely manufactured by Arabs and Chinese to astonish and delight the curious, the discovery was not promulgated in Europe until the middle of the thirteenth century, when Roger Bacon declared that with "saltpetre, charcoal, and sulphur, one could make thunder and lightning if he knew the art." Certain it is, that what to the Crusaders was known as "Greek Fire" was some imperfect combination of nitre and sulphur; and that as far back as the seventh century the rulers of the Byzantine Empire were acquainted with an incendiary substance of an extraordinary character, the composition of which was ordered to be kept as a state secret, and was so kept until the beginning of the thirteenth century. Then the secret escaped to the Arabs, and the substance was used by them to terrify the superstitious Crusaders, who resorted to prayers and supplications to avoid its effects, and spread throughout the world exaggerated accounts of its terrors.

It was not, however, until the commencement of the fourteenth century that gunpowder was employed as an agent for throwing balls and stones. Although its explosive character was then known to monks and students of Christian nations, the Arabs were the first to avail themselves of its advantages in their wars with the Spaniards, and from Spain its use spread to the other countries of Europe.

Still circumstances tended to check, rather than to develop, the improvement of fire-arms and artillery for a long period after the invention of gunpowder became generally known.

The same sentimentality which in our times has denounced the use of torpedoes as contrary to humanity, prevailed to some extent with reference to gunpowder, and there was a general aversion to the newly invented arms, as calculated to extinguish personal bravery. The ruling classes, who made war their study and sole occupation, saw their armor, lances, and knightly prowess rendered useless, and they vigorously opposed the innovation. It was difficult to overcome the prejudices of the people in favor of ancient engines of war. Fire-arms and artillery were awkwardly constructed, and the gunpowder used in them was so wretched, that its real effects were insignificant when compared with that now in use. The ingredients were imperfectly freed from their impurities, and roughly mixed together on a slab of marble. The compound thus made served better for pyrotechnical displays than for purposes of war, and, at best, formed only a nominal portion of the military engineer's resources, and would seem to have had more of a moral than a physical effect.

There was also a great lack of the mechanical skill necessary to adapt this new agent to purposes of war. Iron and brass were, during the 14th century, costly and scarce; great difficulties were encountered in working them, and in making guns sufficiently strong to stand the explosion of even the powder of that day. Saltpetre and sulphur were also rare and expensive materials. They could only be obtained in small quantities, at great expense and labor.

However, in this invention, as in all arts and sciences,

progress was made. Schwartz discovered that the granulation of gunpowder increased the force of explosion, and soon cannon and small arms figured in every siege and battle.

Men were no longer pitted against each other like gladiators in the amphitheatre, where victory declared itself in favor of the stronger brute. The musket was as powerful in the hands of a pigmy as in those of a giant. Nations as as well as men were put more on an equality as to strength.

While gunpowder is more terrific and destructive in its immediate effects than any of the former instruments of war, there seems to be no doubt that the discovery has been beneficial to the human race. Humanitarians are agreed that while war is the greatest of human calamities, its miseries are ameliorated by every improvement in military art; and, however paradoxical it may at first appear, whoever increases the powers of destruction is engaged in the cause of humanity.

Battles are not more bloody than formerly, but are shorter and more decisive. Submission to force of arms comes only with the exhaustion of one of the combatants, and that means is the best by which this condition of things is brought about in the shortest space of time.

Whatever may be the reluctance of Christian people to employ the modern implements of war, on the score of their "inhumanity to man," "self-defence is the first law of nature and the first duty of nations." Governments act not only in their own interests, but in that of mankind, by supplying their armies and navies with weapons calculated to develop the greatest possible destructive force.

It is needless to trace particularly the progress of improvement in arms and engines of war resulting from the discovery of gunpowder. The mechanical genius of each generation has been constantly directed to the subject, and has left behind it vastly improved cannon and small-arms.

Monster ordnance, incendiary shells, rifled cannon, breech-loading, magazined fire-arms and torpedoes have succeeded simpler and less destructive weapons. Every expedient to destroy life which the ingenuity of an ingenious age can devise, is eagerly adopted, and the originator honored and enriched, until it would seem that the only limit to progress in the art of destruction will be the advent of that period when wars shall cease to be the arguments of contentious humanity.

Of all the inventions by which gunpowder has been adapted to war, the torpedo * is perhaps the most destructive and terrible in its immediate effects when successfully employed, either as a mode of attack upon ships or defence against their operations.

Until the war with Great Britain which secured the independence of the United States, military history furnishes no evidence that the machine now designated torpedo was ever employed as an engine of war, although nearly allied in its operation to the system of mining which followed closely upon the discovery of gunpowder.

It shall be our purpose to show the reasons for this indifference, and, in tracing the history of the torpedo, to account in some measure for the failure to improve and the reluctance to use this truly formidable machine.

---

* Torpedo is the popular name of the electric ray or skate, of the family *torpedinedœ.* It was called ναρκη by the Greeks, and *torpedo* by the Latins; the Germans call it *krampf fisch*, the French *torpille*, and the English *numl-fish.* It is said "to kill its prey as by lightning."

CHAPTER II.

DAVID BUSHNELL, THE INVENTOR OF TORPEDOES.—DESCRIPTION OF HIS ORIGINAL MACHINE.—HIS EXPERIMENTS IN SUBMARINE EXPLOSIONS. ATTEMPTS UPON THE "EAGLE" AND OTHER ENGLISH SHIPS OF WAR IN NEW YORK HARBOR.—BUSHNELL'S FLOATING TORPEDOES.—ATTEMPT TO USE THEM IN DELAWARE RIVER.—GENERAL WASHINGTON'S DESCRIPTION AND OPINION OF BUSHNELL'S TORPEDOES.—CONNECTICUT LEGISLATION IN REGARD TO THEM.—ATTEMPT UPON H. M. S. "CERBERUS."—LETTER OF COM. SYMONS TO R. A. SIR PETER PARKER. —"BATTLE OF THE KEGS."

To David Bushnell* of Connecticut is justly attributed the idea of attacking a ship by applying to its submerged parts a magazine of powder, which, when exploded by devices contrived for the purpose, should disable or destroy her. He

* David Bushnell was born in Saybrook, (now Westbrook) Conn., in the year 1742. He entered Yale College in 1771 and graduated in 1775. During his collegiate career he turned his attention to submarine warfare, and after leaving college devoted his time and patrimony entirely to the subject. He was noted for his studious habits, great inventive genius, and eccentricity. The unfortunate issue of his projects rendered him very dejected. Disappointed by his failures and the neglect of the Government, he went to France at the close of the war, where he remained for a number of years, when he returned and settled in Georgia, under the assumed name of Dr. Bush, desiring thus to conceal his identity and connection with the early efforts of his life. There he was placed at the head of one of the most respectable schools in the State, but subsequently engaged in the practice of medicine, by which he amassed a considerable fortune. He was much beloved and respected by all who knew him, and died at the age of ninety years, in the year 1826. By his will his proper name became known; his executors were required to make inquiries in the town of Saybrook for persons of the blood and family of Bushnell, and whoever in the opinion of the executors was found to be most worthy, on the score of moral worth, should be regarded as the sole legatee. But should none of the kindred be found to fulfil the condition set forth in the will, the estate was to be transferred to Franklin College, Ga. Legatees were found in Connecticut, of whom Mr. Charles J. Bushnell of New York is a direct descendant.—*White's Historical Collections of Georgia*, pp. 404–409; *Howe's American Mechanics*, pp. 136–145; *Transactions of Am. Philos. Soc.*, vol. iv., pp. 303–12; *Clarke's Naval History U. S.*, Sec. ed., vol. i. pp. 63, 64. (2 vols., 1814.)

may also be said to have originated a plan for submarine navigation, in pursuance of which he constructed the first submarine boat capable of locomotion, of which there is any accurate record in history. In its application as a means of warfare, he must have entire credit for originality.

The following account of Captain Bushnell's invention was written by him, and read before the American Philosophical Society June 8, 1798:

"*General principles and construction of a submarine vessel, communicated by David Bushnell, of Connecticut, the inventor, in a letter of October,* 1787, *to Thomas Jefferson, then Minister Plenipotentiary of the United States at Paris.*

"The external shape of the submarine vessel bore some resemblance to two upper tortoise shells of equal size, joined together; the flue of entrance into the vessel being represented by the openings made by the swells of the shells at the head of the animal. The inside was capable of containing the operator, and air sufficient to support him thirty minutes, without receiving fresh air. At the bottom opposite to the entrance was fixed a quantity of lead for ballast; at one edge, which was directly before the operator, who sat upright, was an oar for rowing forward or backward, at the other edge was a rudder for steering. An aperture, at the bottom, with its valve, was designed to admit water for the purpose of descending, and two brass forcing-pumps served to eject the water within, when necessary for ascending. At the top there was likewise an oar, for ascending or descending, or continuing at any particular depth. A water gauge or barometer determined the depth of descent; a compass directed the course, and a ventilator within supplied the vessel with fresh air, when on the surface. The entrance into the vessel was elliptical, and so small as barely to admit one person. This entrance was surrounded by a broad elliptical iron band, the lower edge of which was let into the wood whereof the body of the vessel was made, in such a manner as to give its utmost support to the body of the vessel against the pressure of the water. Above the upper edge of this iron band there was a brass crown or cover, resembling a hat with its crown and brim, which shut water tight upon the iron band. The crown was hung to the iron band with hinges, so as to turn over sideways when opened. To make it perfectly secure when shut, it might be screwed down upon the band by the operator, or by a person without.

"There were in the brass crown three round doors, one directly in front and one on each side, large enough to put the hand through. When open they admitted fresh air. Their shutters were ground perfectly tight into their places with emery, and were hung with hinges and secured in their places when shut. There were likewise several glass windows in the crown for looking through and for admitting light in the daytime, with covers to secure them. There were two air pipes in the crown; a ventilator which drew fresh air through one of the air pipes, and discharged it into the lower part of the vessel.

"The fresh air introduced by the ventilator expelled the impure air through the other pipe. Both air pipes were so constructed that they shut themselves, whenever the water rose near their tops, so that no water could enter through them. They opened themselves immediately after they rose above the water. The vessel was chiefly ballasted with lead fixed to its bottom. When this was not sufficient, a quantity was placed within, more or less, according to the weight of the operator. Its ballast rendered it so solid that there was no danger of its oversetting. The vessel, with all its appendages and the operator, was of sufficient weight to settle it low in the water. About two hundred pounds of the lead at the bottom for ballast, could be let down forty or fifty feet below the vessel. This enabled the operator to rise instantly to the surface of the water in case of accident.

"When the operator desired to descend, he placed his foot upon the top of a brass valve, depressing it, by which he opened a large aperture in the bottom of the vessel, through which the water entered at his pleasure. When he had admitted a sufficient quantity, he descended very gradually. If he admitted too large a quantity, in order to obtain an equilibrium, he ejected as much as was necessary by the two brass forcing-pumps which were placed at each end. Whenever the vessel leaked, or he desired to ascend to the surface, he also made use of these forcing-pumps. When the skilful operator had obtained an equilibrium, he could row upward or downward, or continue at any particular depth, with an oar placed near the top of the vessel, formed upon the principle of the screw, the axis of the oar entering the vessel. By turning the oar in one direction he raised the vessel, by turning it the other way he depressed it. A glass tube, eighteen inches long and one inch in diameter, standing upright, its upper end closed, and its lower end, which was open, screwed into a brass pipe, through which the external water had a passage into the glass tube, served as a water-gauge or barometer.

"There was a piece of cork, with phosphorus on it, put into the water-gauge, condensing the air within, and bearing the cork on its surface. By the light of the phosphorus, the ascent of the water in the gauge was rendered visible, and the depth of the vessel ascertained by a graduated scale.

"An oar formed on the principle of the screw was fixed in the fore part of the vessel; its axis entered the vessel, and, being turned in one direction, rowed the vessel forward; but being turned in the other, rowed backward. It was constructed to be turned by the hand or foot.

"A rudder to the hinder part of the vessel, which commanded it with the greatest ease, was made very elastic, and might be used for rowing forward. The tiller was within the vessel, at the operator's right hand, fixed at a right angle on an iron rod which passed through the vessel. * * *

"A compass marked with phosphorus directed the course above and under water.

"The internal shape of the vessel, in every possible section of it, verged toward an ellipsis, as near as the design would allow; but every horizontal section, although elliptical, was yet as near to a circle as could be admitted.

"The body of the vessel was made exceedingly strong; a firm piece of wood was framed parallel to the conjugate diameter, to prevent the sides from yielding to the great pressure of the incumbent water in a deep immersion. This piece of wood was also a seat for the operator.

"Every opening was well secured. The pumps had two sets of valves. The aperture at the bottom for admitting water was covered with a plate perforated full of holes, to receive the water and prevent anything from closing the passage or stopping the valve from shutting. The brass valve might likewise be forced into its place with a screw. The air-pipes had a kind of hollow sphere fixed round the top of each, to secure the air-pipe valves from injury. These hollow spheres were perforated full of holes for the passage of air through the pipes ; within the air-pipes were shutters to secure them, should any accident happen to the pipes or the valves on their tops. All the joints were exactly made, and were water-tight.

"Particular attention was given to bring every part necessary to performing the operation, both within and without the vessel, before the operator, so that everything might be found in the dark. Nothing required the operator to turn to the right hand or the left.

"*Description of a magazine and its appendages designed to be conveyed by the submarine vessel to the bottom of a ship.*

"In the fore part of the brim of the crown of the vessel was a socket, and an iron tube passing through the socket ; the tube stood upright, and could slide up and down six inches. At the top of the tube was a wood-screw, fixed by means of a rod, which passed through the tube and screwed the wood-screw fast upon the top of the tube. By pushing the wood-screw up against the bottom of a ship, and turning it at the same time, it would enter the planks. When the wood-screw was firmly fixed, it could be cast off by unscrewing the rod which fastened it upon the top of the tube.

"Behind the vessel was a place, above the rudder, for carrying a large powder magazine. This was made of two pieces of oak timber, large enough, when hollowed out, to contain an hundred and fifty pounds of powder, with the apparatus used in firing it. A rope extended from the magazine to the wood-screw above mentioned ; when the wood-screw was fixed, and to be cast off from its tube, the magazine was to be cast off likewise, leaving it hanging to the wood-screw. It was lighter than water, that it might rise up against the object to which the screw and itself were fastened.

"Within the magazine was a clock, constructed to run any proposed length of time under twelve hours ; when it had run out its time, it unpinioned a strong lock, resembling a gun lock, which gave fire to the powder. This apparatus was so pinioned that it could not possibly move till, by casting off the magazine from the vessel, it was set in motion.

"The skilful operator could swim so low on the surface as to approach very near a ship in the night without fear of being discovered, and might, if he chose, approach the stem or stern with very little danger. He could sink very quickly, keep at any necessary depth, and row a great distance in any direction he desired without coming to the surface. When he rose to the surface he could soon obtain a fresh supply of air, and, if necessary, he might then descend again and pursue his course.

" *Experiments made to prove the nature and use of a submarine vessel.*

"The first experiment I made was with about two ounces of powder, which I exploded four feet under water, to prove to some of the first personages in Connecticut that powder would take fire under water.

"The second experiment was made with two pounds of powder, enclosed in a wooden bottle, and fired under a hogshead, with a two-inch oak plank between the hogshead and the powder; the hogshead was loaded with stones, as deep as it could swim. A wooden pipe, descending through the lower head of the hogshead and through the plank into the powder contained in the bottle, was primed with powder. A match put to the priming exploded the powder with a very great effect, rending the plank into pieces, demolishing the hogshead, and casting the stones and ruins of the hogshead, with a body of water, many feet into the air, to the astonishment of the spectators. This experiment was likewise made for the satisfaction of the gentlemen above mentioned.

"I afterwards made many experiments of a similar nature, some with large quantities of powder.

"In the first essays with the submarine vessel, I took care to prove its strength to sustain the great pressure of the incumbent water, when sunk deep, before I trusted any person to descend much below the surface; and I never suffered any person to go under water without having a strong piece of rigging made fast to it, until I found him well acquainted with the operations necessary for his safety. After that I made him descend and continue at particular depths without rising or sinking; row by the compass; approach a vessel; go under her, and fix the wood-screw into her bottom, etc., until I thought him sufficiently expert to put my design into execution. I found, agreeably to my expectations, that it required many trials to make a person of common ingenuity a skilful operator. The first I employed was very ingenious, and made himself master of the business, but was taken sick in the campaign of 1776, at New York, before he had an opportunity to make use of his skill, and never recovered his health sufficiently afterwards.*

"After various attempts to find an operator to my wish, I sent one who appeared more expert than the rest from New York, to a fifty-gun ship, lying near Governor's Island.† He went under the ship and attempted to fasten the wood-screw into her bottom, but struck, as he supposes, a bar of iron. * * * Not being well skilled in the management of the vessel, in attempting to move to another place, he lost the ship, and after seeking her in vain for some time, he rowed some distance and rose to the surface of the water, but found daylight had advanced so far, that he durst not renew the attempt. * * * * On his return from the ship to New York, he passed near Governor's Island, and thought he was discovered by the enemy; he cast off the magazine, as he imagined it retarded him in the swell, which was very considerable.‡

"After it had been cast off one hour, the time the internal apparatus was set to run, it blew up with great violence.

"Afterwards, there were two attempts made in Hudson's River, above the city, but they effected nothing. * * * Soon after this the enemy went up the river, and pursued the vessel which had the submarine boat on board, and sunk it with their shot. Though I afterwards recovered the vessel, I found it impossible to prosecute the design any further. I had been in a bad state of health from the beginning of my undertaking, and

---

* This person was Mr. Ezra Bushnell, the brother of the inventor.—*Thacher's Mil. Journal, p.* 63.

† This is a mistake. The ship was the "Eagle," of 64 guns, commanded by Captain Duncan, bearing Lord Howe's flag. The operator was Sergeant Ezra Lee.—*Vide Silliman's Journal, vol. ii. No.* 1, *pp.* 95–100 (*April,* 1820).

‡ For a detailed account of this adventure, see *Silliman's Journal, April,* 1820, *pp.* 95–100, where will be found a statement of the operator, Mr. Ezra Lee, taken from his own mouth by Mr. Griswold, and communicated to the Journal by him.

was now very ill. The situation of public affairs was such, that I despaired of obtaining the public attention and assistance necessary. * * * I therefore gave over the pursuit for that time and waited for a more favorable opportunity, which never arrived.

"In the year 1777, I made an attempt from a whale-boat against the "Cerberus" frigate, then lying at anchor between Connecticut river and New London, by throwing a machine against her side by means of a line. The machine was loaded with powder to be exploded by a gun-lock, which was to be unpinioned by an apparatus, to be turned by being brought alongside of the frigate. This machine fell in with a schooner at anchor, astern of the frigate, and concealed from my sight. By some means or other it was fired, and demolished the schooner and three men, and blew the only one left alive overboard, who was taken up very much hurt.*

"After this, I fixed several kegs under water charged with powder, to explode upon touching anything as they floated along with the tide. I set them afloat in the Delaware, above the English shipping at Philadelphia, in December, 1777. I was unacquainted with the river and obliged to depend upon a gentleman very imperfectly acquainted with that part of it, as I afterwards found. We went as near the shipping as we durst venture. I believe the darkness of the night greatly deceived him, as it did me. We set them adrift, to fall with the ebb upon the shipping. Had we been within sixty rods, I believe they must have fallen in with them immediately, as I designed; but as I afterwards found, they were set adrift much too far distant, and did not arrive until after being detained some time by the frost; they advanced in the daytime in a dispersed situation and under great disadvantages.

"One of them blew up a boat with several persons in it, who imprudently handled it too freely, and thus gave the British that alarm which brought on the 'Batttle of the Kegs.' The above vessel, magazine, etc., were projected in the year 1771, but not completed until the year 1775.

D. Bushnell."

---

* See copy of Commodore Symons' letter to Rear-Admiral Sir Peter Parker, *infra*.

The following is an extract from a letter of General Washington's to Mr. Jefferson, dated Mount Vernon, 26th September, 1785, two years previous to the foregoing communication :

"I am sorry that I cannot give you full information respecting Bushnell's projects for the destruction of ships. No interesting experiments having been made, and my memory being bad, I may in some measure be mistaken in what I am about to relate. Bushnell is a man of great mechanical powers, fertile in inventions and master of execution. He came to me in 1776, recommended by Governor Trumbull and other respectable characters, who were converts to his plans. Although I wanted faith myself, I furnished him with money and other aids to carry his plan into execution. He labored for some time ineffectually, and, though the advocates for his schemes continued sanguine, he never did succeed. One accident or another always intervened. I then thought, and still think, that it was an effort of genius, but that too many things were necessary to be combined to expect much from the issue against an enemy who are always upon guard.

"That he had a machine so contrived as to carry him under water at any depth he chose, and for a considerable time and distance, with an appendage charged with powder, which he could fasten to a ship, and give fire to it in time sufficient for his returning, and by means thereof destroy it, are facts, I believe, which admit of little doubt. But, then, where it was to operate against an enemy, it was no easy matter to get a person hardy enough to encounter the variety of dangers to which he would be exposed—first, from the novelty ; secondly, from the difficulty of conducting the machine and governing it under water, on account of the current ; and thirdly, from the consequent uncertainty of hitting the object devoted to destruction, without rising frequently above water for fresh observations, which, when near the vessel, would expose the adventurer to discovery, and to almost certain death. To these causes I always ascribed the failure of his plans, as he wanted nothing that I could furnish to insure the success of it.

"This, to the best of my recollection, is a true statement of the case ; but Humphreys, if I mistake not, being one of his converts, will be able to give you a more perfect account of it than I have done." *

That the Connecticut authorities were converts to Mr. Bushnell's plans will appear more fully from the following extracts from the acts of the Governor and Council of Safety, or the Committee of War, called by the Governor, and held at different places, from the 7th day of June, 1775, until the 6th day of May, 1778 :

"1776. In session, February 2 (New Haven).—Mr. Bushnell, by request of the Governor and Council, appeared before them, and gave an account of his machine for blowing up ships, etc., which he explained. After he retired, the Governor and Council voted that they were under obligations of secrecy respecting the machine, and that the Deputy-Governor should reward Mr. Bushnell for his trouble and expenses for attending, and inform him that the Governor and Council fully approved of his plan, and would like to have him proceed, and make every necessary preparation and experiment about it, with expectation of proper notice and reward."

"1777. In session, April 22 (Lebanon).—David Bushnell, with Colonel Huntington, appeared before the Governor and Council, and exhibited a specimen of a new invention for annoying ships, etc. (torpedo). The Governor and Council gave him an order on officers, agents, and commissaries, to afford him assistance of men, boats, powder, lead, etc., as he might want, delivered him without stint."

The latter invention was probably the one with which, a few months afterwards, he made the attempt upon the "Cerberus," the result of which is described in the following letter from Commodore Symons to Rear-Admiral Sir Peter Parker, dated August 15, 1777 :

"Wednesday night, being at anchor to the westward of New London in Black Point Bay, the schooner I had taken, at anchor close by me, astern, about eleven o'clock at night, we discovered

* Sparks' Washington, vol. ix., pp. 134-5.

a line towing astern that came from the bows ; we immediately conjectured that it was somebody that had veered himself away by it, and began to haul in ; we then found that the schooner had got hold of it (who had taken it for a fishing line), gathered in near fifteen fathom, which was buoyed up by little bits of sticks at stated distances, until he came to the end, at which was fastened a machine, which was too heavy for one man to haul up, being upwards of 100 cwt. ; the other people of the boat turning out, assisted him, got it upon deck, and were unfortunately examining it too curiously, when it went off like the sound of a gun, blew the boat to pieces, and set her in a flame, killed the three men that were in the stern ; the fourth, who was standing forward, was blown into the water ; I hoisted out the boat, and picked him up much hurt ; as soon as he could recollect himself, he gave me the following description, as near as he could remember. It was two vessels shaped like a boat, about twenty inches long, and a foot broad, secured to each other at the distance of four feet, by two iron bars, one at each end, and an iron tube or gun-barrel in the centre, which was loose (as he had himself turned it round with his hand); they swam one over the other, the upper one keel upwards; the lower swam properly, but was so under water as just to keep the upper one a few inches above the surface ; to the after iron bar hung a flat board, to which was fixed a wheel about six inches in diameter, and communicated itself to one on the upper side of the boat, of a lesser diameter ; opposite to these was another wheel, on the flat of the under one or loaded vessel, which had likewise communication with the wheels of the upper boat ; it was covered with lead, and the keel heavily loaded in order to keep it down in the water.

" The fatal curiosity of the seamen (who unfortunately had been bred in working in iron) set this wheel agoing, which it did with great ease backwards and forwards, and during their looking at it, which was about five minutes from the time of its being first put in motion, it burst. Upon examining round the ship after this accident, we found the other part of the line on the larboard side buoyed up in the same manner, which I ordered to be cut away immediately for fear of hauling up another machine, which I concluded was fast at the end, and might burst when near the ship.

"The mode these villains must have taken to have swiftered the ship, must have been to have rowed off in the stream a considerable distance ahead of the ship, leaving one of their infernals in shore, and floating the other at the distance of the line, which, from the quantity that we have got on board (near 70 fathoms), and what the man tells me they saved in the schooner, which was upwards of 150 fathom more, must have been near 300 fathom; they at the length of this line put the other in the water, and left it for the tide to float down, which in this place runs very strong.

"As the ingenuity of these people is singular in their secret modes of mischief, and as I presume this is their first essay, I have thought it indispensably my duty to return and give you the earliest information of the circumstances, to prevent the like fatal accident happening to any of the advanced ships that may possibly be swiftered in the same manner, and to forbid all seamen from attempting hauling the line, or bringing the vessel near the ship, as it is filled with that kind of combustible that burns though in the water.

"I am, sir, etc.,

"J. Symons.

"To Rear-Admiral Sir Peter Parker.

"P. S. Having made a model as near as I could, from the description of the man who was saved, and sending for him to inquire if the model represented the machine he saw, he informed me the large wheel on the flat of the upper board was made of wood, with iron spokes, sharp at the end and projected about an inch without the gunwale of the boat, in order to strike into the side in hauling up, and by that means set the wheels in motion, which in five minutes after it had been moved by the people, burst; it is therefore very fortunate I ordered the other to be cut away, for had it touched under the hollow of the counter, in hauling up, so as to set the wheels in motion, there is no knowing what damage it might have done, either to the ship or people."*

---

* For further information concerning Bushnell's apparatus and experiment, see *Lendrum's Am. Rev., vol. ii., pp.* 163–164*; Thacher's Mil. Journal, ed.* 1817, *pp.* 63, 121–124, 361–362*; Morse's Am. Geog., ed.* 1805, *vol. i., p.* 454*; Allen's Am. Biog. Dict.,* 3d *ed.* 1857, *p.* 174*; Hinman's Histor. Collections of*

The following winter we find Mr. Bushnell engaged in fresh adventures with a third contrivance, of which we have no particular description. We only know that it was a floating torpedo in the shape of a keg, and designed to explode by contact. According to some accounts, one of these kegs demolished a vessel near the Long Island shore. About Christmas, 1777, he set out from Bordentown and proceeded down the Delaware, casting adrift a great number of his kegs, in order to annoy the British shipping at Philadelphia. Unluckily, the very night of his enterprise the vessels were hauled into the docks to avoid the ice. The enemy were sufficiently alarmed, however, to man the wharves and shipping, and open a brisk fire upon every floating object. This engagement was made the subject of a humorous song, entitled "The Battle of the Kegs," by the Honorable Francis Hopkinson, the author of "Hail, Columbia," which is an amusing relic of the times, and will be found in the works of that author.

Mr. Bushnell served throughout the war under a commission as Captain in the corps of Sappers and Miners. At his death, an unfinished model was found amongst his effects, which was evidently intended for a torpedo. It serves to show that, notwithstanding his failures, his mind still clung to the great project of his life.

Connecticut; Works of David Humphries, pp. 298–303; *Memoirs af Gen. Heath, p.* 69; *Lossing's Field Book Rev., vol. ii., p.* 814; *Cutter's Life of Putnam, pp.* 227, 232; *Howe's Am. Mech., p.* 136.

CHAPTER III.

ROBERT FULTON PROPOSES THE TORPEDO SYSTEM TO THE FRENCH GOVERNMENT.—PROCEEDINGS UNDER THE AUTHORITY OF THE FRENCH CONSULATE.—DESCRIPTION OF HIS FIRST MACHINE, THE "NAUTILUS." —EXPERIMENTS.—M. ST. AUBIN'S REPORT.—FULTON IN ENGLAND.—CATAMARAN EXPEDITION.—DESTRUCTION OF THE DOROTHEA.—ALARM OF THE ENGLISH AT THE RESULTS.—FULTON'S PLANS ABANDONED IN ENGLAND.—PAYMENT TO HIM OF £15,000.—HIS RETURN TO THE U. S. AND EXPERIMENTS THERE.—RECEIVES GOVERNMENTAL ASSISTANCE.—DESCRIPTION OF HIS TORPEDOES.—ATTEMPT UPON THE U. S. S. "ARGUS." —OPPOSITION ENCOUNTERED FROM COM. RODGERS, AND HIS OFFICIAL REPORT.—REPORTS OF THE COMMISSIONERS.—FULTON'S EXPLANATIONS. —ATTEMPT UPON ENGLISH SHIPS DURING THE WAR OF 1812.

The subject seems to have slept and been forgotten for a period of twenty years, when Robert Fulton, sojourning in France, revived the system, and proposed it to the Government of that country. He seems to have had a correct idea of the vast power of submarine explosions, and his busy and inventive genius was wholly given to the development and recognition of the system as a legitimate means of warfare.

In the year 1797 Fulton constructed a machine by which he designed "to impart to carcasses of gunpowder a progressive motion under water to a given point, and there explode them." The French Government, to which he applied for aid to carry on his experiments, rejected his plans as entirely impracticable, although he held out to it the seductive prospect, "To deliver them and all the world from British oppression" by their adoption.*

The change in the government, by which Napoleon became its head, with the title of First Consul, gave him new hope, and he renewed his application for assistance with such suc-

* Admiral Dacres, to whom Fulton explained his plans, is reported to have treated the proposition and the proposer with great contempt, saying, as he turned him out of his office, "Go, sir, your invention may be of use to the Algerines and corsairs, but learn that France has not yet abandoned the ocean."

cess that a commission was appointed to give him the desired means, and to witness and report the result of his experiments.

Fulton immediately built a plunging-boat, which, like all new and strange inventions, was very far from perfect in its arrangements, and, with a daring rarely equalled, he commenced a series of experiments, which cannot be stigmatized as failures. His faith in his invention is evinced by the boldness with which he risked his life.

On the 3d of July, 1801, in the harbor of Brest, with several companions, he descended in his boat to the depth of twenty-five feet from the surface, where he remained for one hour in utter darkness. He then ascended, and, provided with candles, again descended, remaining, however, but a short time, as the burning candles made great inroads upon his stock of air, of which he had no other supply than that contained in the boat itself.

Having demonstrated to his satisfaction that he could descend to any given depth and reascend to the surface at will, and that he could live for a considerable time without fresh supplies of air, he improved his machine by the addition of windows of thick glass, a wheel and crank to give the boat locomotion above as well as below the surface, and masts and sails capable of being struck in a few moments, when he desired to plunge. He also added an air chamber of copper of a cubic foot capacity, into which he compressed two hundred atmospheres, intended as a reserve supply of air.

With the machine thus improved, Fulton repeatedly descended to various depths, and succeeded in moving about under water in any desired direction at the rate of about one mile per hour; and upon one occasion remained beneath the surface for the space of four hours and twenty minutes, when he came to the surface without experiencing any inconvenience from so long a stay.

Satisfied with the performance of his boat, he next made numerous experiments with his "submarine bombs," to which he now gave the name "torpedoes," and baptized the boat "Nautilus."

By the direction of the Commissioners a small vessel was provided, and Fulton directed to destroy it. He placed under the vessel a torpedo containing but twenty pounds of powder, by means of the "Nautilus," which speedily blew her into fragments. This seems to be the first instance on record of the effect of submarine explosions upon ships. It occurred in August, 1801.

M. St. Aubin, a member of the Commission gives, in the *Journal de Commerce* of the 20th of January, 1802, an account of Fulton's experiments, from which the following curious extract is taken :

"The diving-boat, in the construction of which M. Fulton is now employed, will be capacious enough to contain eight men and provisions for twenty days, and will be of sufficient strength and power to enable him to plunge one hundred feet under water, if necessary. He has contrived a reservoir of air which will enable eight men to remain under water eight hours. When the boat is above water it has two sails, and looks like a common sail-boat; when it is to dive, the masts and sails are struck. In making his experiments, M. Fulton not only remained a whole hour under water with three companions, but kept the boat parallel with the surface at any given depth. He proved that the compass points as correctly under water as on the surface, and that while under water the boat made way at the rate of half a league an hour, by means contrived for the purpose.

"It is not twenty years since all Europe was astonished at the first ascension of men in balloons; perhaps in a few years they will not be less surprised to see a flotilla of diving-boats, which, on a given signal, shall, to avoid the pursuit of an enemy, plunge under water, and rise again several leagues from the place where they descended! But if we have not succeeded in steering the balloon, and even were it impossible to attain that object, the case is different with the diving-boat, which can be conducted under water in the same manner as upon the surface. With these qualities, it is fit for carrying secret orders, to succor a blockaded port, and to examine the force and position of an enemy in their harbors. These are sure and evident benefits which the diving-boat at present promises. But who can foresee all the consequences of this discovery, or the improvements of which it is susceptible? M. Fulton has already added to his boat a machine, by means of which he blew up a large boat in the harbor of Brest; and if by future experiments the same effects can be produced upon frigates and ships of the line, what will become of navies, and where will sailors be found to man ships of war, when it is a physical certainty that they may at any moment be blown into the air by means of diving-boats, against which no human foresight can guard them?" *

It must be borne in mind that all Fulton's experiments with plunging-boats were made with the machine originally constructed, improved from time to time, as new ideas suggested themselves or difficulties arose. Owing to lack of means and encouragement, the boat St. Aubin refers to was never completed.

Failing in inducing the French Government to adopt or further his schemes, and, it is alleged, at the solicitation of friends in England, Fulton withdrew to that country, in the hope of obtaining the countenance and assistance he needed to demonstrate the value of his system and put it into practical operation.

Fulton arrived in London in May, 1804, and proceeded at once to lay his torpedo and plunging-boat schemes before the British Ministry.† He assumed the name of *Francis*, in

* *Niles' Register*, vol. iv., p. 366; also, *European Magazine*, April, 1812, p. 245.

† LONDON, Dec. 13, 1808.—About three years ago, a man of grave and mysterious carriage of body made his appearance in a certain class of fashionable society in London, under the name of *Francis;* it was shortly whispered about that he was a Yankee American, whose real name was Fulton, expatriated for reasons of State. He was undoubtedly an intelligent and ingenious man, which recommended him to the notice of several scientific persons in the metropolis, under whose patronage he was encouraged to lay certain projects before this Government; among the rest was the *submarine bomb*, which he palmed upon his official patrons as an original invention of his own, to be transferred exclusively to the use and behoof of the English nation. * * Mr. Francis, *alias* Fulton, received a very liberal gratuity, and took himself off. He had hardly gone when it was discovered that he had been hawking his *secret* at Paris. * * * The invention is at least ten years old, and is attributed to a Mr. Bushnell; so that unless Mr. F. can make out a right to that name by an additional *alias*, he is liable to the imputation of having received our money under false pretences.—*Nav. Chron.*, vol. xx., p. 452.

order, as was supposed, to conceal his identity from the French. Mr. Pitt, then Prime Minister of England, was greatly impressed with the importance of the proposed system, and exclaimed, when the force of submarine explosions were explained to him, that "Such a system, if successfully introduced into practice, could not fail to annihilate all military marines." Lords Mulgrave, Melville, and Castlereagh all manifested great interest in the plans of Fulton, and determined upon a course of experiments which should test their value. A commission was accordingly appointed in June to examine and report upon the torpedo and plunging-boat system. The commissioners were Sir Joseph Banks, Mr. Cavendish, Sir Home Popham, Major Congreve, and John Rennie.

It was a long time before they met, and when they did they at once pronounced the plunging-boat scheme entirely impracticable.

In October, 1804, an expedition against the French shipping lying at Bologne, called the "Catamaran Expedition," was fitted out with a view to test Fulton's torpedoes. Owing to a variety of causes, it failed of results.* A year afterwards another attempt was made, Fulton himself accompanying the expedition. Two officers—Captain Siccombe and Lieutenant Payne, of the navy—succeeded, with their boats, in placing two of Fulton's torpedoes, united by a coupling-line, between the buoys and cables of two French men-of-war lying in the harbor of Boulogne. In both cases the torpedoes exploded without inflicting any damage upon the vessels.† Fulton accounted for the failure to destroy them

* The Catamaran Expedition was proposed by Fulton, and carried out, under his superintendence, by Admiral Lord Keith, commanding the English squadron off the coast of France, whose official report will be found in the *Naval Chron.*, vol. xiv., p. 314. The "coffers" or catamarans, were shaped like a coffin, were made of plank lined with lead, and exploded by clock-work. A reward was given for bringing off the pin which started it in motion. They were towed in amongst the French ships at night by boats, and cast adrift so as to foul the hawses of the ships. Many exploded, but no serious damage resulted.

† For the French official report of this attack, see *Nav. Chr.*, vol. xiv., p. 339.

by the fact that the torpedoes exploded on the surface and *alongside* the vessels, instead of beneath them, and to insure thereafter this necessary condition, he united the coupling-line to the torpedoes by means of a span, asshown in Pl. II., Fig. 3. This arrangement, he averred, would cause the torpedo to dive beneath the bottom of the ship when influenced by the tide. Pl. II., Figs. 2, 3, and 4, illustrates this idea. *

These failures, however well accounted for, threw great discredit upon the proposed system. Mr. Pitt alone still believed in Fulton, and encouraged him to persevere. He caused a stout Danish brig, the "Dorothea," to be provided and anchored near his own country seat at Deal, which, after repeated experiments with his new coupling-line, Fulton succeeded in blowing to atoms with a torpedo containing 170 pounds of powder. This occurred on the 15th of October, 1805, in the presence of a large concourse of spectators, amongst whom were the commissioners and a number of naval and military officers of high rank, one of whom, Captain Kingston, loudly asserted, a few minutes before the "Dorothea" was blown up, that "If one of the machines were placed underneath his cabin while he was at dinner, he should feel no concern for the consequences." †

* Fulton's Torpedo War.

† DEAL, *Oct.* 16, 1805.—On Monday, Mr. Francis, who last year contrived the Catamaran Expedition, and constructed the machines which Sir Home Popham ran among the enemy's flotilla at Boulogne, arrived here from Dover, to blow up a brig of 300 tons with his newly-invented catamarans. * * * Great crowds assembled on the beach near Walmer Castle, opposite which the brig lay. I saw several people working about her, but till dark the brig remained unhurt, and the people, much disappointed, very liberally cursed Mr. Francis and his catamarans. On Tuesday he appeared on the beach with Lady Stanhope, niece to Mr. Pitt, and tied his pocket-handkerchief to his cane, made a signal to the brig. A galley darted out from the brig and threw something into the water. Mr. Francis drew out his watch, and turning to the lady, said: "Fifteen minutes is her time." In sixteen minutes the explosion took place. * * * It is impossible to conceive of a more complete decomposition of a vessel, or a more dreadful crash of materials. It was the most curious experiment of modern times, for who would not have concluded that the powder would spend its force

Fulton was highly elated with his success, and, in a letter to Lord Castlereagh, thus describes the experiment:

"Yesterday, about four o'clock, I made the intended experiment on the brig, with a carcass of one hundred and seventy pounds of powder. Exactly in fifteen minutes after drawing the peg and throwing the carcass into the water, the explosion took place. It lifted the brig almost bodily, and broke her in two. The ends sunk immediately, and in one minute nothing was to be seen of her but floating fragments. In fact, her annihilation was complete, and the effect most extraordinary. The power, as I had calculated, passed in a right line through her body, that being the line of the least resistance, and carried all before it. At the time of her going up, she did not appear to make more resistance than a bag of feathers, and went to pieces like a shattered egg-shell."

The success of this experiment, showing as it did the vast power of submarine explosions, alarmed the English, and particularly the naval authorities. The Earl St. Vincent, when Fulton explained the torpedo, and the result of the "Dorothea" experiment, reflected for some time, and then said: "*Pitt was the greatest fool that ever existed, to encourage a mode of war which they who commanded the seas did not want, and which, if successful, would deprive them of it.*"

England at this time was mistress of the seas, a distinction gained by many a hard battle fought upon the ocean. Her fleets scoured the seas, attacked the fortified harbors, and destroyed the commerce of her enemies. Her navy was, as now, the pride and first object of solicitude of her rulers and people, and, more than all else combined, gave to her the position she held amongst the nations of Europe.

It is natural that she should have viewed with dislike a project which by any possibility would weaken or tend to neutralize the power she enjoyed by virtue of the strength

---

upon the water, which is movable, and not pass through the strong bottom of a ship? Why was the report so inconsiderable when the effect was so great?—*Nav. Chron.*, vol. xiv., p. 342.

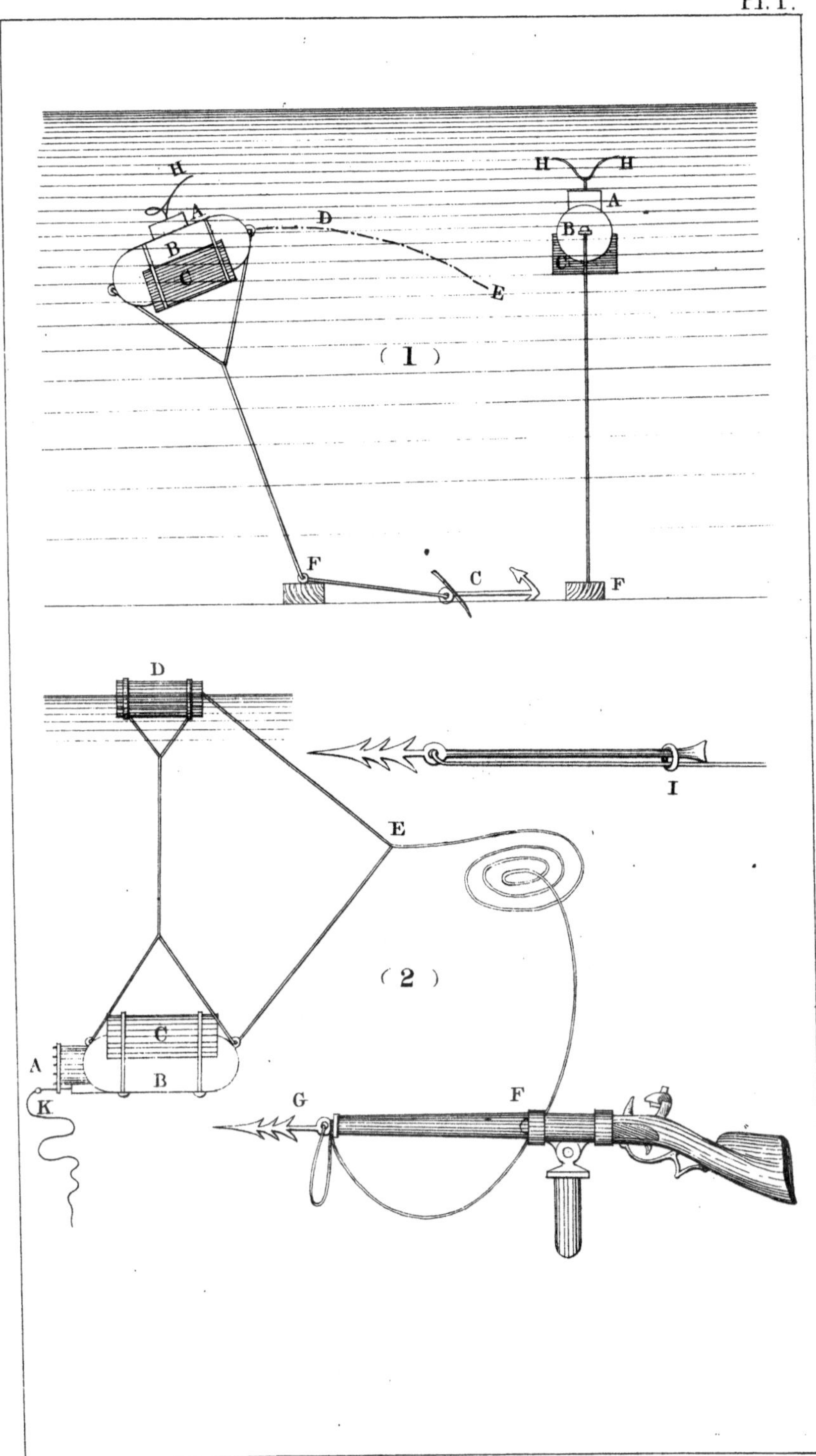

D. VAN NOSTRAND, Publisher.

of her navy and the seaman-like qualities of her people, and it is asserted that propositions were now made to Fulton, for a sum of money, to suppress his inventions, so that none should derive any advantage from them, and that he refused the offer with great indignation.*

At all events, no one could now be found to listen to him, and Fulton at last turned his attention to his own country for the material aid and encouragement so necessary to the prosecution of his plans.

He returned to New York in December, 1806, and immediately presented his schemes for submarine war to the Secretary of State, Mr. Madison, and the Secretary of the Navy, Mr. Smith. A certain sum was authorized to be expended under Fulton's direction. A vessel was prepared to be submitted to his operations, which, after many fruitless efforts and great disappointment, he succeeded in blowing up on the 20th of July, 1807, in the harbor of New York, with results similar to those in the "Dorothea" experiment.

This experiment was advertised to come off at a certain hour, and a large number of spectators assembled to witness it. For reasons afterwards explained, it was not until several

---

* IMPERIAL PARLIAMENT, HOUSE OF LORDS, *Tuesday, June* 5, 1810.—Earl Stanhope adverted to the experiments tried some years back off the French coast, and since then in America, by a Mr. Fulton, for the ascertaining of a mischievous and horrid mode of destroying vessels of any size while floating in the water. He then went through the history of these terrible inventions. * * * This person (Fulton) was invited over here, and his Lordship had seen an engagement between him, Mr. Pitt, and Lord Melville, agreeing, in certain events, to give him £40,000. After the failure of the trial at Boulogne, his claim was referred to certain scientific umpires, who awarded him £15,000. Since then he has made experiments in America, where both Jefferson and Madison were present. His Lordship was led, at the present moment particularly, to this motion, by a pamphlet he had just received from America, containing the particulars, with plates illustrative of the nature and effects of the invention. [Fulton's Torpedo War.] What he wanted to know was this—what had been done by Government in the way of providing a remedy, and to what extent? For the purpose of ascertaining this, he had framed a motion, which he read, describing an account of the measures taken to counteract the effects of these submarine carcasses and explosions, and of the torpedo triggers, etc., etc. The motion was lost by a majority of seventeen votes.

hours after the time announced for the explosion, and repeated trials, that the result was accomplished. The experiment was generally denounced as a failure, although it afforded additional proof of the annihilating effects of submarine explosions.

In a letter addressed to the authorities of New York, Fulton explained the imperfections of his torpedoes to be purely mechanical, and easily overcome. In this letter he asserts that the weight of the gun-locks capsized the torpedoes when placed in the water, and threw out the primings in the pans; and added:

> "Having now clearly demonstrated the great effect of explosions under water, it is easy to conceive that, by organization and practice, the application of torpedoes will, like every other art, progress in perfection. Little difficulties and errors will occur in the commencement, as has been the case with all new inventions; but where there is little risk, little expense, and so much to be gained, it is worthy of consideration whether this system should not have a fair trial. Gunpowder has, within the last three hundred years, totally changed the art of war, and all my reflections have led me to believe that this application of it will, in a few years, put a stop to maritime wars, give that liberty on the seas which has been so long and anxiously desired by every good man, and secure to America that liberty of commerce, tranquillity, and independence which will enable her citizens to apply their mental and corporeal faculties to useful and humane pursuits, to the improvement of our country and the happiness of our whole people."

Not discouraged by the seeming indifference of the people, or deterred by failures, Fulton addressed himself with renewed energy to the task of arousing interest and confidence in his plans. He published a pamphlet entitled "Torpedo War; or, Submarine Explosions," with the motto, "The liberty of the seas will be the happiness of the earth." It was addressed to the President and to both Houses of Congress, and it contained a description of his torpedoes, the manner of using them, and an account of all his experiments.

The result of his unwearied importunities was an act of

Congress, passed March 30, 1810, authorizing the expenditure of $5,000, under the directions of the Secretary of the Navy, in trying practically the use of torpedoes.

A commission was duly appointed to witness the experiments and report results.* Commodore Rodgers and Captain Chauncey, of the Navy, were also directed to assist in every way in giving the system a fair trial.

In the month of September, 1810, the commissioners met Mr. Fulton in New York, who proceeded to explain his torpedoes and methods of operating them.

The following are the descriptions of these machines:

Pl. I., Fig. 1, represents the anchored torpedo, so arranged as to blow up the vessel which should run against it. *B* is a copper case, two feet long, twelve inches diameter, containing one hundred pounds of powder. *A* is a brass box containing a lock similar to a gun-lock, with a barrel two inches long, to contain a musket charge of powder; the box, with lock cocked and barrel charged, is screwed to the copper case. *H* is a lever attached to the lock and holding it ready to fire. *C* is a deal box filled with cork, lashed to the case (*B*). The cork renders the torpedo about 15lbs. lighter than water; it is held by the weight (*F*) and anchor (*G*). During flood tide it will rest as represented; at slack water it will stand at *D*, at ebb tide at *E*.

Fulton proposed an arrangement to be attached to the box (*C*), which would hold the torpedo under water for a day, week, or month, and then lock the lever (*H*) and permit the torpedo to rise to the surface and to be handled with safety.

Pl. I., Fig. 2, represents a clock-work torpedo, as prepared for the attack of a vessel while at anchor or under sail, by harpooning her in the bow. *B* is a copper case for 100lbs. of powder. *C*, cork cushion bored with holes to make it sink rapidly. *A*, a cylindrical brass box 7 inches in diameter, 2 inches deep, in which is a gun-lock and barrel for charge and wad, which is to be fired into the powder. In the

* The commissioners were Chancellor Livingston, Morgan Lewis, Cadwallader D. Colden, John Kemp, Oliver Wolcott, John Garnett, and Jonathan Williams.

brass box (*A*) there is a piece of clock-work which, being wound and set, will let the lock strike fire at any desired interval after drawing out the pin at *K*. *D* is a pine box ten or fifteen pounds lighter than water, and floats on the surface. The line from it to the torpedo is the "suspending line," in length equal to the estimated draft of the ship to be attacked, or eight or ten feet longer than that draft, so that it may bend around her sides. A span connects the float and torpedo, and is united to the harpoon line at *E*. The harpoon line should be about fifty feet long, to bring the torpedo underneath the bottom when the ship is harpooned in the bow. The harpoon (*K*) is of iron, two feet long, half an inch in diameter, made large at one end to fit the bore of the gun. The line is spliced into the eye of the harpoon; a link runs on the shaft to which the line is fastened, so that when in the gun it makes a loop as at *H*. When fired, the line straightens and acts as the tail of a rocket and guides the harpoon straight. *F* is the harpoon gun, to work on a swivel fixed in the stern sheets of a boat. The object of harpooning the ship in the bow is to fix the end of the torpedo line, so that the tide, or her action through the water, will draw the torpedo under her.

This was the form of torpedo used against the "Dorothea" and the hulk in New York bay; the gun and harpoon were after-thoughts of Fulton's.

Pl. II., Fig. 1, represents the boat, torpedo and gun, arranged for attack, and sufficiently explains itself.

Pl. II., Fig. 5, illustrates Fulton's ideas of the use of the span, and the position the torpedo would assume when attached by the harpoon and line to the bow of the ship.

Pl. II., Fig. 6, represents the torpedo boats rowing to attack a ship with torpedoes and harpoons, which Fulton explained to be an entirely practicable scheme. He entered into a comparison of the force and cost of a frigate, and his boats manned and armed; and, estimating the frigate equal in the number of her crew to fifty boats, demonstrated to his own complete satisfaction that the torpedo boats must prevail in a contest between them and the ship, while the cost would

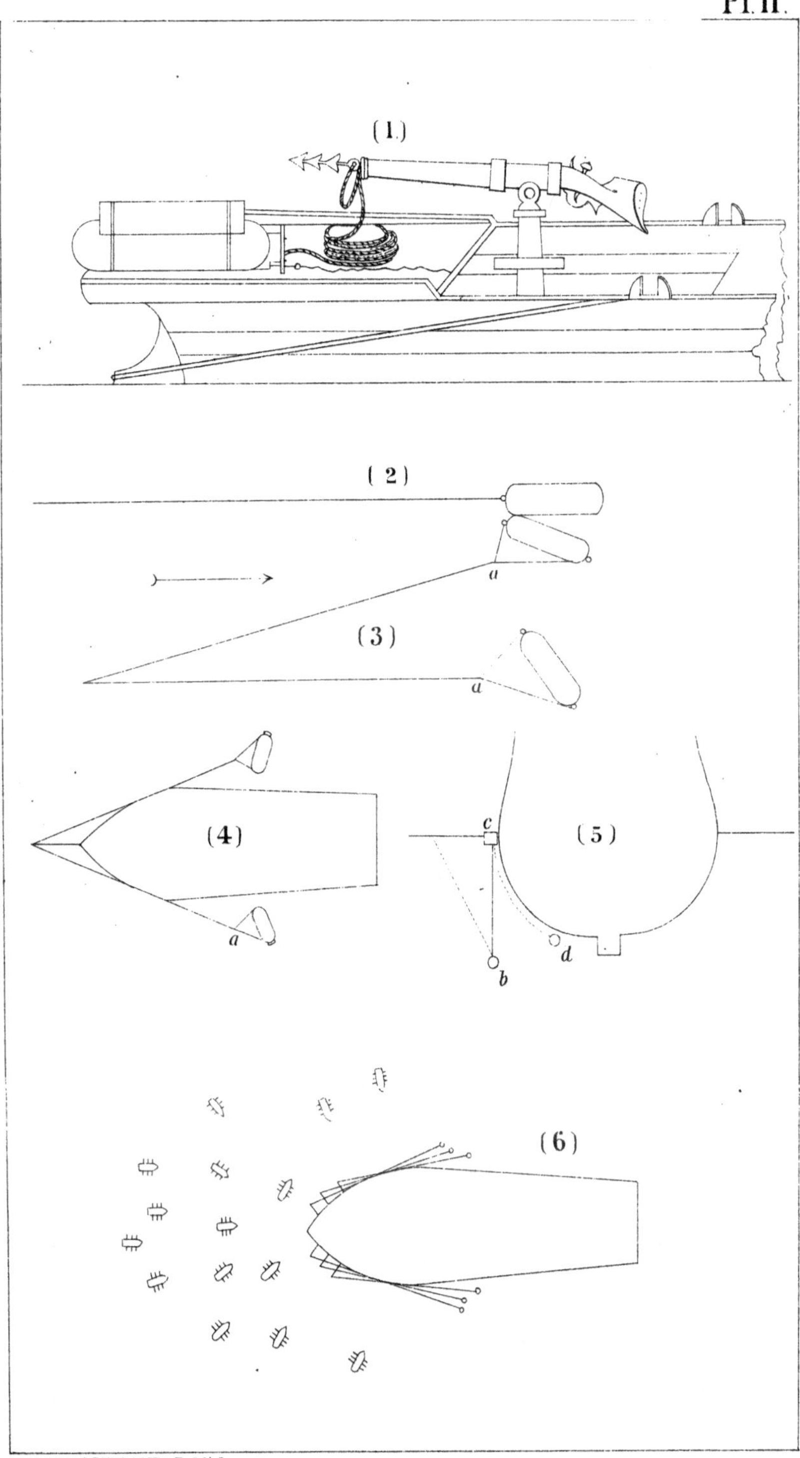

D. VAN NOSTRAND, Publisher.

be $24,000 for the boats, and $400,000 for the frigate. Fulton proposed himself to lead such an attack, if occasion offered, and the boats were provided. He estimated the number of boats, etc., necessary for the defence of the ports of the United States as follows: 650 boats, 1400 anchoring torpedoes, 1300 clock-work torpedoes, the total cost of which would be $531,000. "Here," said Fulton, "we have perfect security of our ports and harbors at a cost but little greater than a single frigate!"*

The particulars above enumerated embody the plans laid by him before the commissioners. The plunging-boat project was by this time entirely abandoned by him, and he substituted for it an arrangement much more practicable, which will be alluded to hereafter.

For the purpose of fully testing these plans, the sloop-of-war "Argus," then lying off the New York Navy Yard, under the command of the gallant Lawrence, was directed to be prepared to receive an attack from Fulton's machines, Commodore Rodgers assuming charge of the preparations. He had expressed great incredulity as to the value of the inventions, but made such arrangements to meet the attack as argued a greater belief in their power than he was willing to admit. He surrounded the "Argus" with nets to the ground, booms, swinging spars armed with scythes, to sweep off the heads of persons approaching in boats, and hung heavy weights to the yard-arms and rigging; in fact, he so encumbered his vessel with defensive preparations, that her efficiency as a man-of-war was materially interfered with.

When all was ready, the commissioners met, and Fulton endeavored in vain to operate his machines. He finally abandoned the attempt, and acknowledged that the ingenuity of the Commodore in defending his vessel was greater than his in attacking it; but argued that a system, then only in its infancy, which compelled a hostile vessel to guard herself by such extraordinary means, could not fail of becoming a most important mode of warfare.

* The drawings which are here used are copies from Fulton's designs in his "Torpedo War."

Fulton tried his harpoon-gun at a target with but poor success, and showed his stationary torpedoes anchored in a tide-way; he also made a few experiments with a "cable-cutter," which resulted in nothing.

Commodore Rodgers was particularly active in his endeavors to defeat Fulton's plans, and met him at all points with objections and bluff ridicule of his inventions. He showed to the commissioners the effect of grape and canister upon boats, by firing carronades at one within range, and particularly ridiculed Fulton's boat attack and cable-cutter. He disliked the whole system, while his sensitiveness and pride in his profession seem to have been wounded by Fulton's pretensions to do away with navies with his cheap contrivances.

During the course of the investigation, Fulton proposed a torpedo-boat, which particularly called forth the Commodore's animadversions. In his journal of the proceedings of the commissioners, he thus describes it:

"Mr. Fulton exhibited a model of a vessel of three hundred tons, in the presence of Colonel Williams, Captain Chauncey, and myself, and some other gentlemen of similar curiosity, which he called a 'torpedo block-ship,' the sides of which were calculated (he said) to be cannon-proof, and the decks proof against musket-shot, the former being six feet thick and the latter six inches.

"This vessel is intended to be armed with two torpedoes on each side, which are to be applied by means of a spar ninety-six feet long, projecting from the vessel's side, supported at the inner end by a double circular swivel, and at the outward end by guys leading from the mastheads. For the particulars of this singlar vessel (which to my mind deserves the name of 'Non-descript'), I leave the reader to make his own conclusions from the figure annexed, and by which alone he will be enabled to judge whether such *torpid, unwieldy, six-feet sided, six-inch decked, fifteen-sixteenths sunk water-dungeons* are calculated to supersede the necessity of a navy, particularly when the men who manage them are, as is intended, confined to the limits of their holds, which will be under water, and in as *perfect darkness as if shut up in the Black Hole of Calcutta!*"

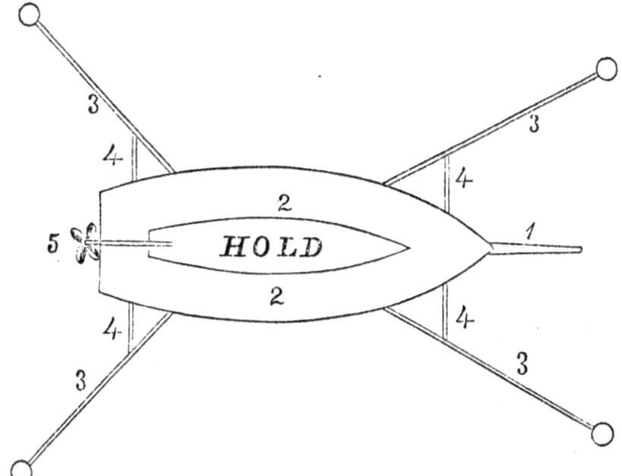

"REFERENCES: 1. Bowsprit. 2. Hull of vessel. 3. Four long booms, with a torpedo on each. 4. Bumpkins, on which the booms are supported 5. A skull wheel, which is intended to propel this vessel against the tide."

The gallant but apparently disgusted Commodore takes leave of the subject by stating: "His (Fulton's) torpedoes, so far from being of the importance which he had considered them, were, on a more thorough examination of their principles, assisted by all the practice of which he himself had supposed them susceptible, found, to say the least, comparatively of no importance at all; consequently they ought not to be relied on as a means of national defence."

The commissioners were differently impressed by the few experiments made—Messrs. Livingston, Lewis, and Colden each making separate reports, the others uniting in a joint report. All agreed that the experiments were failures, and attributed the results to the active, determined opposition of Commodore Rodgers. Chancellor Livingston, in a long and interesting paper, thus concluded his remarks:

"*Upon the whole, I view this application of powder as one of the most important military discoveries which some centuries have produced. It appears to me to be capable of effecting the absolute security of your ports against naval aggression, provided that in connection with it the usual means necessary to occupy the attention of the enemy be not neglected.*"

Mr. Lewis in his report says:

"*The submarine use of gunpowder will, at no distant day, be entitled to rank among the best and cheapest defences of ports and harbors.* Torpedoes will certainly meet with opposition from adverse interests, deep-rooted prejudices, and perhaps foreign attachments. Their advocates will have to encounter the pertness of the witlings of the day. Still, I trust the system will not be deserted while even a distant prospect of its becoming useful shall remain."

Mr. Colden thought Fulton's experiments failed for want of experience, and on account of the energy of the "nautical gentlemen;" but was confident that "this application of gunpowder might produce greater changes in the world than have been made by it since its introduction into Europe."

The others expressed no decided opinions as to the value of Fulton's plans, but united in urging the necessity of a Government institution to which such subjects could be appropriately referred.

These reports, forwarded to the Secretary of the Navy, had the effect of arresting all further investigation, the opinions of Commodore Rodgers, more than all others, operating to destroy what little confidence existed in the public mind in regard to the system. Fulton, wearied with his unsuccessful efforts, took leave of the subject of torpedoes for ever, in a characteristic letter to the Secretary of the Navy, from which the following extracts are taken.

Having reviewed the reports of the commissioners, he says:

"It is proved and admitted, first, that the water-proof locks will ignite gunpowder under water. Secondly, it is proved that seventy pounds of powder exploded under the bottom of a vessel of 200 tons will blow her up; hence it is admitted that if a sufficient quantity—and which I believe need not be more than 200lbs.—be ignited under the bottom of a first-rate man-of-war, it would instantly destroy her. * * * With these immensely important principles proved and admitted, the question naturally occurs, whether there be within the genius or inventive faculties of man, the means of placing a torpedo under a ship in defiance of her powers of resistance.

"He who says there is not, and that consequently torpedoes never can be rendered useful, must of course believe that he has penetrated to the limits of man's inventive powers, and that he has contemplated all the combinations and arrangements which present or future ingenuity can devise, to place a torpedo under a ship.

"I will now do justice to the talents of Commodore Rodgers. The nets, booms, kentledge, and grapnels, which he arranged around the "Argus," made at first sight a formidable appearance against *one torpedo-boat and eight bad oarsmen.* I was taken unawares. I had explained to the navy officers my means of attack, they did not inform me of their measures of defence; the nets were put down to the ground, or I should have sent my torpedoes under them. I might be compared to what Bartholomew Schwartz, the inventor of gunpowder, would have appeared had he lived at the time of Julius Cæsar, and presented himself before the gates of Rome with a four-pounder, and endeavored to convince the Roman legions that with such a machine he could batter down the walls and take the city: a few catapultas, casting arrows and stones, would have caused him to retreat; a shower of rain would destroy his ill-guarded powder, and the Roman centurions would therefore call his machine a useless invention, while the manufacturers of catapultas, bows, arrows, and shields, would be the most vehement against further experiments!

"I had not one man instructed in the use of the machines, nor had I time to reflect on this mode of defending a vessel. I have now, however, had time, and I feel confident that I have discovered a means which will render nets to the ground, booms, kentledge, oars with sword-blades through the port-holes, and all such operations, totally useless."

However, despite Fulton's energy and enthusiasm, and his thorough belief in the system, other more important projects connected with steam navigation, forced him to abandon his schemes, and public interest in them ceased.

The war of 1812 afforded many opportunities for testing practically the value of torpedoes as a means of attack upon ships, and it is not, therefore, surprising that attempts should have been made by individuals, not authorized by Government, to blow up English ships which held control of many of our bays and harbors. These efforts were fruitless of results, and in the main contributed to produce a feeling of distrust in the efficacy of submarine warfare as a means of attack or defence, although it is curious to note the fear which this species of warfare produced in the minds of the English.

The most noted of these attempts was made by a Mr. Mix, a citizen of Norfolk, who, with a torpedo constructed after Fulton's original designs, made repeated attempts to blow up H. M. S. "Plantagenet," lying in Lynn Haven bay, which created great alarm on board of the ships of the squadron then controlling those waters.*

At New York an attempt was made by private parties to destroy the frigate "Ramilies," which, although it may not be classed as belonging to torpedo warfare, nevertheless grew out of Fulton's experiments with torpedoes. On the 15th of June, 1813, the schooner "Eagle" was prepared with a magazine of powder, over which boxes and barrels of merchan-

---

* For a long account of Mr. Mix's efforts against the "Plantagenet," see *Niles' Register*, vol. iv, p. 366. He made six different attempts to float his torpedoes upon the vessel. The last was successful. The torpedo exploded under the bow of the ship, blew off her fore channels, and destroyed a boat lying alongside. The following extract from an Alexandria paper, September 1, 1813, shows the nature of the discussion that arose from this attempt:

"TORPEDOES.—It appears to be acknowledged on board Admiral Cockburn's ship, that Mr. Mix's torpedo had marked near the cathead, although it had no ways injured the line-of-battle ship 'Plantagenet;' and that in the whole fleet there is plentiful abuse of the American Government, although it was merely the effusion of an enterprising, active young man in the naval service. They unfairly condemn it as a villanous, invidious, improper, and cowardly means of warfare, never reflecting that their ruling administration had paid Mr. Fulton a very handsome stipend for his invention. They also forgot Lord Grey's recent statement in Parliament as to the commuted payment, as the then Lord of the Admiralty, which he made Mr. Fulton upon it (vide *London Morning Chron.*, May 15, 1813), nor reflecting either that the British ministry had induced the trial of torpedoes upon the French flotilla at Boulogne."—*Niles' Reg.*, vol. v., p. 6.

dise were placed, so connected by lines with gun-locks attached to the magazines, that any attempt to remove them would fire the charge. The schooner was sent off New London, where she was captured by barges of the "Ramilies," Commodore Hardy, the crew abandoning her as the enemy's boats approached.

Having towed their prize near to the frigate, the captors commenced discharging her, when the magazine exploded, killing a number of men.

The precise amount of destruction from this attempt was never ascertained. The journals of the day were filled with extravagant statements on both sides—some averring that one hundred men lost their lives, while the English statements put the loss at less than ten. The one being apparently desirous to magnify the results in order to stimulate others, the other seeking to diminish the effect for opposite reasons.*

The design of the originators was that the schooner should be placed alongside the frigate for discharge, as was customary, when it was hoped that the explosion would destroy her.

The occurrence caused the English to be exceedingly suspicious of all craft seen near their ships, and brought out severe orders of retaliation from the British naval commanders, for what they termed "inhuman and savage proceedings."†

---

* *Niles' Register*, vol. iv., pp. 293, 308.

† The following is a copy of an indorsement upon the papers of the schooner "Sally":

"H. M. SHIP 'LA HOGUE,' AT SEA, 8 *July*, 1813.

"I have warned the schooner 'Sallie,' of Barnstable, to proceed to her own coast, in consequence of the depredations of the 'Young Teazer,' . . . but more particularly from the inhuman and savage proceedings of causing the American schooner 'Eagle' to be blown up, after she had been taken possession of by H. M. ship 'Ramilies'—an act not to be justified on the most barbarous principle of warfare. I have directed H. B. M. cruisers on the coast to destroy every description of American vessels they may fall in with, flags of truce only excepted.

"Given under my hand, etc.,

"THOS. P. CAPEL, Captain."

—*Niles' Reg.*, vol. iv., p. 337.

Torpedoes were also stretched across the Narrows, "so as to blow up the most, if not all the vessels passing by Forts Richmond and Hudson."*

Various notices also appear in the journals and records of the war, showing that torpedo boats of different kinds were devised, and attempts made to bring them into service. None were under the sanction or authority of the Government, and although they excited great apprehension on the part of the English, and made them very wary of approaching our harbors, nothing was ever accomplished by them.

In Niles' Register there is an account of a submarine boat, and a description of a chase in which the vessel escaped her pursuers by diving "like a porpoise." From the description given, this vessel does not appear to differ much from Captain Bushnell's boat, although it is so general in its character that no accurate conclusions can be drawn from it.

In Vol. VI., p. 318, of the same, appears the following notice of another torpedo boat:

"Torpedo Boat.—A boat, of which the following is a description, was lately built at New York. It unfortunately happened that while proceeding to the expected scene of action, by some accident she went ashore near Southold, L. I. The enemy being at hand, immediately manned his barges to destroy her. The people collected, and for some time resisted them, and having removed the spiral wheel (by which the boat was moved), the rudder crank, etc., they blew her up.

"*Description.*—She resembles a turtle floating just above the surface of the water, and sufficiently roomy to carry nine persons within, having on her back a coat of mail, consisting of three large bombs, which could be discharged by machinery, so as to bid defiance to any attacks by barges. She left this city one day last week to blow up some of the enemy's ships off New London. At one end of the boat projected a long pole under water, with a torpedo fastened to it, which, as she approached the enemy in the night, was to be poked under the bottom of a

---

* *Niles' Reg.*, vol. iv., p. 337.—The British send us Congreve rockets to burn our towns and habitations; we, in return, despatch some of our torpedoes *to rub the copper off their bottoms.*

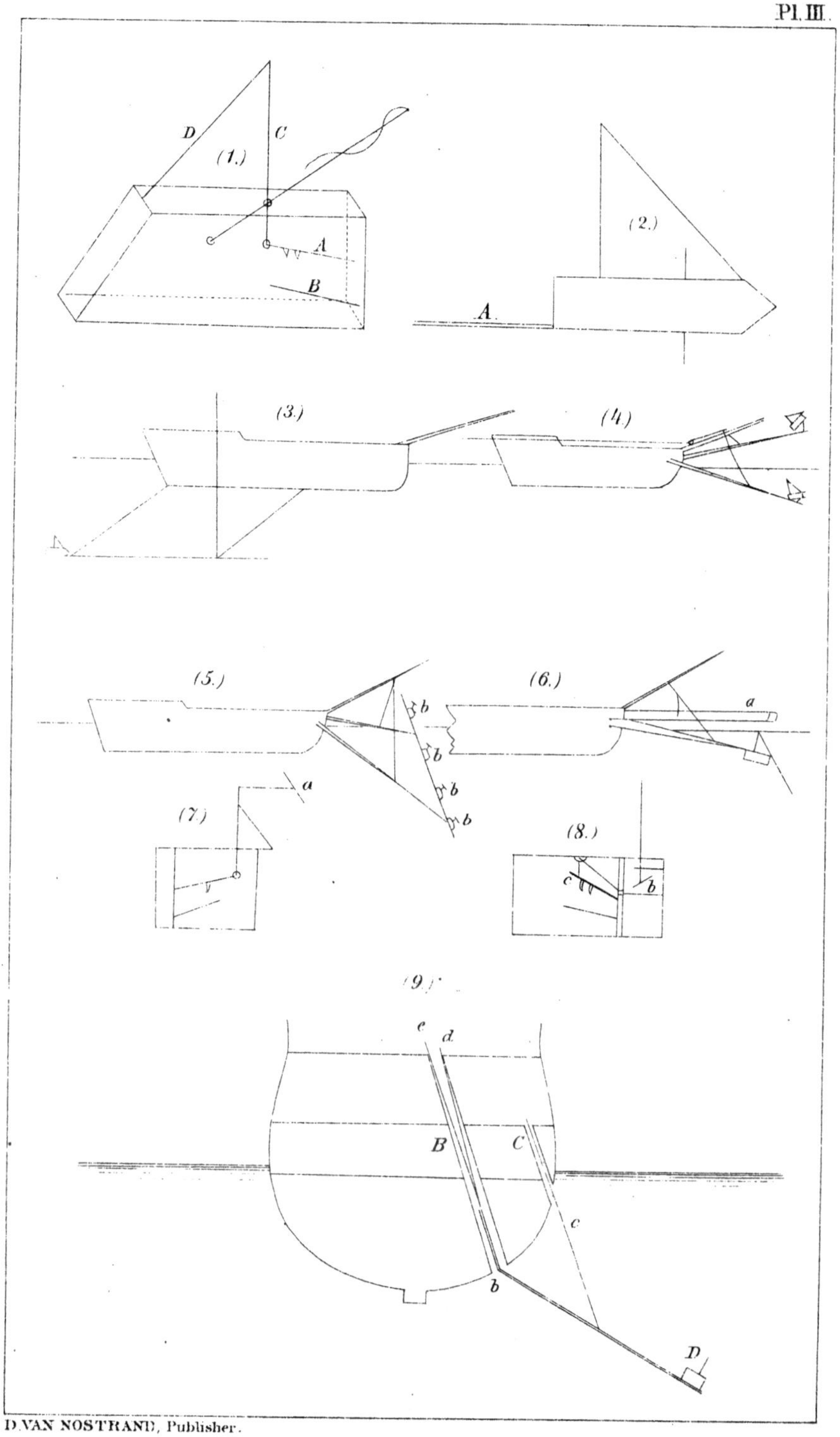

D. VAN NOSTRAND, Publisher.

74, and then let off. The boat is, we understand, the invention of an ingenious gentleman by the name of Berrian."

It is proper here to note the fact that Fulton had thought of employing electricity as an agent to ignite sunken torpedoes, but considered the plan entirely impracticable, and so expressed his views in an interesting letter to William Brents, Jr., Esq., a resident of Aquia, Virginia, in the possession of the writer.

Before taking leave of this early history of torpedo devices, at the risk of wearying the patience of the reader, we desire to call his attention to a few of the plans proposed in a treatise, entitled "Hints relative to Torpedo Warfare, by a gentleman of the State of New York," published in 1815, as an appendix to "Machiavelli's Art of War." By reference to Pl. III. the ideas of this gentleman may be understood, and which we describe nearly in his own words. The drawings are also copies of the illustrations of his text.

Fig. 1.—The torpedo. *A*, A steel spring fixed with flints. *B*, The steel for it to strike on. *C*, Horn of the torpedo. *D*, A slender cord to keep the horn from being thrown back until the right time. This is to arm the end of a spar with which to stab the ship, as in Fig. 4.

Fig. 2 is a torpedo to tow under and behind a "torpedo ship," having a tail, *A*, to make it run steadily under water, as in Fig. 3.

Fig. 5 shows an arrangement of torpedoes (*b*, *b*, *b*, *b*), brought in a line to blow away nets, which being done, the "torpedo ship," to destroy the enemy, follows. Fig. 7 is the form of torpedo to blow away nets. It has a broad cross-piece (*a*) in advance to push against the net. Fig. 6 is another way to get rid of nets. The torpedo has a board slanting downwards to make it dive under water when pushed, and is carried under two shafts (*a*), joined at the fore ends by a cross-piece, which is to push the net aside and press upon the horn of the torpedo, arranged, as in Fig. 8, with a knife (*b*), to cut the string holding the spring (*c*).

"This plan, on further reflection, bids defiance to net-work," says the gentleman, and adds: "You may supply the want of wind to manœuvre your torpedo boat by a water-wheel, turned by horses, and steer her from a small boat towed astern, having two dabs of phosphorus on the stern and foremast respectively, to enable you to keep her head straight."

The horses are supposed to be sufficiently desperate to keep going until the object is accomplished.

Fig. 9 "shows how when ships grapple and come side to side, it is *extremely easy* for one to explode the other." . . .

"Now, when you wish to fix the torpedo, *D*, to the end of the shaft, pull on the rope, *c*, until the end of the shaft is out of water, there being a pivot at *b*: fix the torpedo, and lower the shaft, pulling up on the rope, *d*, which brings the shaft into the well, *B*. When you wish to apply the torpedo to the ship near you, let down the shaft from the well, *B*, and pull up briskly on the rope, *c*, which brings the torpedo up with a force sufficient to drive in the horn——and the work is finished!"

A multitude of other equally ingenious and practicable plans for submarine warfare are suggested by this gentleman, who evidently intends his "Hints" to be taken by individuals at localities where the British shipping was exposed to such attacks, whose means were small and patriotism unlimited.

CHAPTER IV.

FULTON'S APPARATUS INCOMPLETE.—PREVAILING SENTIMENT OPPOSED TO THE USE OF TORPEDOES AS INHUMAN.—COL. COLT'S EXPERIMENTS.—FIRST APPEARANCE OF THE ELECTRIC TORPEDO.—COL. COLT'S LETTER TO PRESIDENT TYLER.—DESTRUCTION OF A VESSEL UNDER WAY.—RUSSIAN TORPEDOES.—JACOBI'S FULMINATE.—GEN. DELAFIELD ON TORPEDOES AND HARBOR DEFENCE.

It must be acknowledged that the apparatus of Fulton was crude, imperfect, and unreliable. The review of his experiments is only valuable or interesting, as it shows how, in the infancy of this new device of war, one man at least, despite failures, criticism, and ridicule, conceived fully the importance of the system, and labored unweariedly in the prosecution of ideas requiring further advancement in kindred arts for practical proof of their value. He was simply in advance of his time. Commodore Rodgers would undoubtedly have ridiculed and condemned more heartily the plan of a "Monitor" had it been presented to him, than he did Fulton's "Nondescript." Steam iron-clad navies, monster ordnance, and revolving turrets, the instruments by which the art of maritime warfare has since been revolutionized, would have excited towards their originators then, even more adverse criticism and discouragement than Fulton encountered with his torpedoes, and would have been infinitely more difficult to sustain by experiment.

No authority or attainments, however great or respected, could have saved the person daring enough to have predicted such a revolution in naval warfare, from being regarded as laboring under mental derangement. They have been born of circumstances, as it were, forced upon the world at a time when mechanical arts and sciences were in a condition to make experiments fruitful in vast results.

Fulton's flint gun-locks, clock-work, and row-boats were altogether inadequate to his purposes. Fulminates, steamships, and electricity were then barely conceived of. The power of the torpedo was there, terrific and annihilating in its effects. How to ignite and place it so that its power could be directed to its object, were the questions Fulton failed to answer. Later discoveries and a higher degree of mechanical skill have so far solved the problem, that the torpedo system, although still imperfect, is clearly destined to fulfil most, if not all, of Fulton's high anticipations.

Sir Howard Douglass, as all know, denounced the use of shells as an "inhuman system prepared for naval warfare in an age of enlightened humanity, * * * a merciless, barbarous idea, the object of which is to set fire to the ship at heart, and if possible blow her up!"*

Such ideas, benevolent and humane as they are, reiterated with double vehemence in reference to torpedo warfare, are arguments against war, not against the means by which it must be carried on. They are quite in the vein of him who said:

"It was in sooth, great pity, so it was,
This villanous saltpetre should be digged
Out of the bowels of the harmless earth,
Which many a good tall fellow had destroyed
So cowardly, and but for these vile guns
He would himself have been a soldier."

To defend a nation's honor and right, is by every one admitted to be justifiable. The sole purpose of military and naval armaments, is killing and destruction, and when the art of war is so perfected that war ceases to be

* *Naval Chronicle*, vol. xxi. p. 408.—The writer in an article devoted to the consideration of Fulton's schemes, which he stigmatizes as "revolting to every noble principle," and their projector as a "crafty, murderous ruffian," and his patrons as "openly stooping from their lofty stations to superintend the construction of such detestable machines, that promised destruction to maritime establishments," protests against the policy of encouraging inventions that tend to innovate on the triumphant system of naval warfare, in which England excels. He exclaims that "Guy Fawkes is got afloat," and adds, "battles in future may be fought under water; our invincible ships of the line may give place to horrible and unknown structures, our frigates to catamarans, our pilots to divers, our hardy dauntless tars to *submarine assassins*; coffers, rockets, catamarans, infernals, water-worms, and fire-devils! How honorable! how fascinating is such an enumeration! how glorious, how fortunate for Britain are discoveries like these! How worthy of being adopted by a people, made wanton by naval victories, by a nation whose empire are the seas!"

the umpire of disputes by its bringing certain annihilation to all parties resorting to it, then will peacable arbitration become the resort in all cases of international controversy.

The close of the war with England put a stop to further experiments with torpedoes, and until the year 1829 no writer or inventor seems to have given any attention to the subject; there seemed to be a tacit understanding, that its practice was inhuman, impracticable, or impolitic, and it was left where the war left it—a failure.

But it was revived, and public interest again excited by the experiments of Col. Samuel Colt, the inventor of the revolver, who, in the year 1829, although but a boy in years, commenced a series of experiments with torpedoes that excited the attention of older and more experienced heads. It seems that Col. Colt's pet idea was not the revolver, but rather his submarine battery, and he labored unweariedly from the time above mentioned up to the year 1845, as he writes to President Tyler, "employing his time in study and experiments to perfect his submarine explosives."

"His earnings had been swallowed up in abortive arm factories," says his biographer,* "and he therefore solicited governmental aid for trying submarine experiments which were beyond his private means, and which, if successful, were sure of redounding to the public good." The following letter to the then Chief Magistrate, shows how identical were his views with those who had preceded him in the path of invention, and how earnestly and confidently he gave himself to plans which were ridiculed by many.

LETTER FROM COL. COLT TO PRESIDENT TYLER.

"WASHINGTON, *June* 19, 1841.

"SIR,—It is with no little diffidence that I ventured to submit the following for your consideration, feeling as I do that its apparent extravagance may prevent you from paying it that attention which it merits; and but for the duty I owe my country in these threatening times, I should still longer delay making this communication.

---

* Rev. Dr. Barnard. Armsmear, p. 277.

"For more than ten years past I have employed my leisure in study and experiment to perfect the invention of which I now consider myself master; and which, if adopted for the service of our Government, will not only save them millions of outlay for the construction of means of defence, but in the event of a foreign war it will prove a perfect safeguard against all the combined fleets of Europe, without exposing the lives of our citizens.

"There seems to prevail at this time with all parties a sense of the importance of effectually protecting our sea-coast; and, as economy is a primary consideration in the present exhausted condition of our treasury, I think I have a right to expect a favorable consideration of the propositions which I have determined to make.

"By referring to the Navy State papers, page 211, you will discover that Robert Fulton made experiments which proved that a certain quantity of gunpowder discharged under the bottom of a ship would produce her instant destruction. That discovery laid the foundation for my present plan of harbor defence; and, notwithstanding the failure of Fulton to use his invention to much advantage, in its imperfect condition, during the last war, one glance at what he did perform is sufficient to convince the most incredulous that if his engine could be brought under easy and safe control, it must prove an irresistible barrier to foreign invasion.

"Discoveries since Fulton's time, combined with an invention original with myself, enable me to effect the instant destruction of either ships or steamers at my pleasure on their entering a harbor, whether singly or in whole fleets, while those vessels to which I am disposed to allow a passage are secure from the possibility of being injured. All this I can do, while myself in perfect security, and without giving an invading enemy the slightest sign of his danger.

"The whole expense of protecting a harbor like that of New York would be less than the cost of a single steam-ship; and when the apparatus is once prepared, one single man is sufficient to manage the destroying agent against any fleet that Europe can send.

"With the above statements as an intimation of what can be done, I will mention, in as brief a manner as possible, the terms on which I will make an exhibition to prove to yourself and your Cabinet that a sailing vessel or steamboat cannot pass (without permission) either in or out of a harbor where my engines of destruction are employed.

"To make the exhibition will require an expenditure of $20,000, which sum I will employ for that purpose from my own means, on condition that the Government will lend me such aid as I shall require, and that when I get through my exhibition the Government shall refund to me all money I shall have expended, and pay me an annual sum as a premium for my secret.

"I hope I may be excused for mentioning that, as any hint of my plans at this time must prove prejudicial, it is my wish that the present communication may be kept from the view of all persons, excepting the members of your Cabinet.

"I have the honor to be, Sir, most respectfully,

"Your Excellency's devoted and obedient servant,

"SAMUEL COLT."

In the *New York Herald* for March 17, 1842, it is stated that Mr. Colt had been engaged in experimenting under the authority of the Secretary of War, and it was asserted that he could ignite a destructive shell under water at the distance of ten miles, in a few seconds, its principle being founded on the electric fluid.

On the 4th of June that same year he exploded a torpedo in New York harbor with a galvanic battery; and on the 4th of July following he produced a tremendous explosion just opposite Castle Garden, and completely destroyed the old gunboat "Boxer," creating great excitement amongst the spectators and public generally.

The Government immediately offered him a schooner on the Potomac river to destroy "if he could." On the 20th of August, 1842, in the presence of the President, Heads of Departments, and Gen. Scott, he utterly destroyed the schooner, while stationed at no less than five miles from her. Before the end of that month, so great was the impression produced by his experiments, Congress voted him a grant of $17,000 to still further perfect his apparatus, and for new experiments, despite the determined opposition of John Quincy Adams, whose disfavor seemed based on his disbelief in the practicability of Col. Colt's schemes, which he publicly declared he would not use if he could, because it was a "cowardly, and no fair or honest warfare."

On the 18th of October, 1842, the brig "Volta," of 300 tons, was blown up in New York by Col. Colt's battery. This experiment was conducted under the patronage of the American Institute and was witnessed, says the *N. Y. Tribune*, by 40,000 spectators, amongst them the Secretary of War, who was stationed on board the "North Carolina," while Col. Colt applied the electric spark from a battery on board the Revenue cutter "Ewing."

So far, all the vessels destroyed were at anchor; but on the 13th of April, 1843, on the Potomac river, a brig of 500 tons was blown to pieces while under way and sailing at the rate of 5 knots an hour, while Col. Colt, the operator of the battery, was stationed at Alexandria, five miles away. Congress adjourned to witness this experiment, and its success seemed to be complete. The vessel thus destroyed was abandoned by her crew a few moments before she was blown up, so that her consequent uncertain course precluded the possibility of collusion on the part of Col. Colt and any other operator. This was the last recorded experiment of Col. Colt with torpedoes. Col. Totten, then the eminent head of the Engineering Bureau, as well as most of the naval authorities, discountenanced any further proceedings looking to the further development of Colt's plans, and it appears that no official reports in regard to the results of the experiments, or the method of arranging the batteries and wires, can now be found at the Navy or War Department. From a resolution of inquiry passed by Congress in April, 1844, and the replies thereto by the Secretaries of War and of the Navy, it appears that the money appropriated ($17,000) was wholly expended, but that Col. Colt's invention and the results of experiments were *secrets* to both of those departments.

From Col. Colt's private papers and memoranda, it appears that he claimed to possess a further secret which died with him; but that his invention consisted principally in the arrangement of groups of torpedoes connected by insulated wires with each other and with the galvanic battery, and that one of his projects was to compel a vessel to tell her proximity by telegraph as she touched certain parts of his apparatus, or, by a method since adopted by the Austrians, the vessel's contact caused the circuit to close, and thus insured the explosion at the proper instant. To Col. Colt certainly is due the credit of being the first to conceive of the project of igniting deposits of powder, placed in harbors for their defence, by means of galvanic electricity; and the cable employed by him in this connection was the first submarine cable ever invented for conducting the electric fluid, only differing from the most approved forms of present telegraphic submarine cables in the substitution of asphaltum and beeswax instead of gutta-percha, then unknown.

The Russians employed torpedoes very extensively in their defensive systems at Sebastopol and Cronstadt; but, owing rather to the wariness of their enemies than to their ineffectiveness, no direct results came from their employment—that is to say, no ships were destroyed by them. How far they contributed to the security of their great naval ports from attacks by the allied fleets can only be a matter of conjecture; but it is very apparent, from a review of the history of the war, that they entered largely into the calculations of the English and French naval commanders in their discussions of the chances of success in their enterprises against those harbors.

The Russian torpedoes were great improvements upon previous inventions in the method of igniting the charge. General Delafield, in his "Art of War in Europe," thus refers to them:

"Torpedo mines, if I may use this name, given by Fulton to self-acting mines under water, were among the novelties attempted by the Russians in their defences about Cronstadt as well as at Sebastopol. Around and about the Island of Cronstadt, and the anchorages that the allied fleets would probably occupy, as well as the channels of approach, and anchorages abreast of the castles defending these channels, numerous submerged mines—or as Fulton calls them torpedoes—were placed, to explode by the contact of any vessel running against them. Their peculiar arrangement was entirely new, and, as I believe, the conception and idea of Professor Jacobi, an eminent Russian chemist and philosopher."

The General does not describe the submarine torpedo, as when he was at Cronstadt the principles upon which they were operated were known to the few Russian officers whose duty it was to apply them, and of whom no inquiry could be made. Subsequently, however, the allies raised numbers of them, and their mode of ignition was found to be identical with the land mines employed about the fortifications, which General Delafield describes as follows :

Fig. 2.

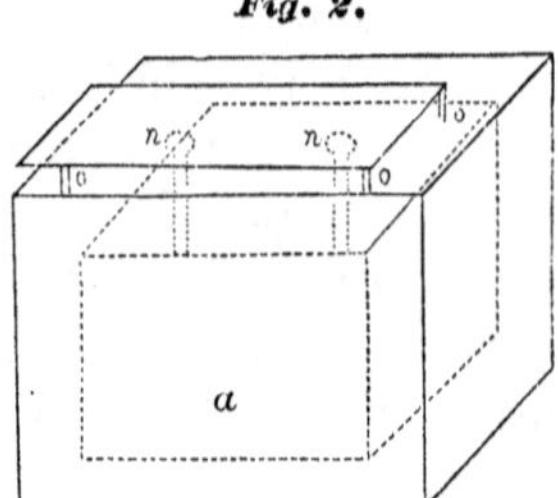

Fig. 2 is a box (*a*) of eight inches cube, contained within another box, leaving a space of two inches between them filled with pitch. Upon the top of the exterior box rested a piece of board supported by four legs of thin sheet iron (*o*). Upon any pressure upon the board the iron supports yielded, and it came into contact with a glass tube (*n*) containing sulphuric acid, breaking it and precipitating the acid upon chloride of potassa, causing instant combustion and explosion of the powder.

Fig. 3.

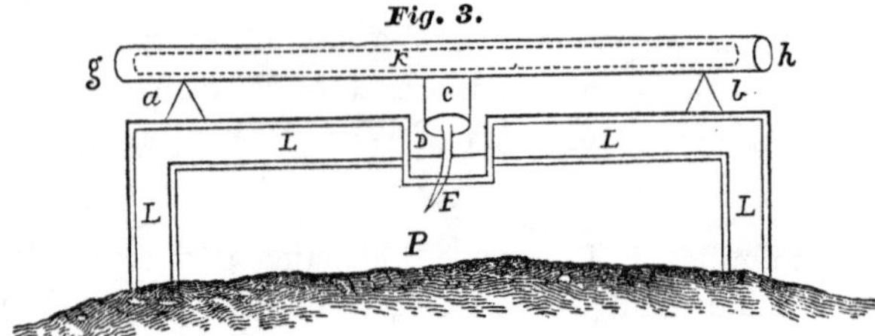

Fig. 3 is another arrangement, found at Sebastopol, and was used for submarine mines as well as on land. The acid was contained within a glass tube (*k*). This was placed within a tin or soft thin leaden tube (*g h*), which rested on the box at (*a*) and (*b*). The tube had a branch (*c*), opening downward into an apartment (*D*) in which was the chloride of potassa and the fuze (*F*). The manner of its operation is evident from the drawing. Barrels were often substituted for the box for submarine mines.

General Delafield remarks, that the explosive mixture was not carefully analyzed, but there was no doubt of the certainty of Prof. Jacobi's arrangement to explode powder, and recommends the combination to our attention as certain in its effects, and as little liable to accidental influences as any other.*

Electric torpedoes were also used most extensively by the Russians. At Yenikale the allies found off the fort a hulk filled with a most complete series of galvanic apparatus, attached to vessels full of powder. Russel, the *Times*' correspondent who saw the arrangements, describes them as follows:

> "The submarine machines, with their strange caps and exploding apparatus, have been recognized by Mr. Deane as portions of the instruments he employs in submarine operations. They were all regularly numbered, and, as there is a break in the series, there is reason for believing that some of them are actually sunk, but the wires connecting them with the battery on board the ship were cut, and the vessel itself foundered subsequently. There were many miles of wire, and the number of cells indicated a very powerful battery."

Admiral Napier, in the Baltic, had a very great respect for the torpedoes of the Russians, which rumor informed him were much depended on by his enemy. He was ridiculed and abused for his fear of their effects, and, as he never encountered any, they were declared myths created by his imagination. Admiral Dundas, who supplanted him in the

* General Delafield omits from the mixture the proportion of white sugar, which aids combustion, and was undoubtedly employed by the Russians, as well as by the rebels at a later day.

command of the Baltic fleet, not only proved their existence, by finding and raising great numbers, but also what might be expected from them in the event of attacking with his fleet the defences of Cronstadt. Two of his ships—the "Merlin" and "Firefly"—while reconnoitering the fort, narrowly escaped destruction from the explosion of floating torpedoes. An officer on board the "Merlin," in a letter to be found in "Nolan's Russian War," thus describes the occurrence:

"The ship was steaming slowly along when a tremendous shock was felt; the portion of the crew below rushed wildly on deck, and for some moments great confusion prevailed. Bulkheads were thrown down, the ship's side was bulged in, girders and beams broken, crockery smashed, and the contents of the hold inextricably mixed together. The vessel was nearly dismasted, and escaped destruction as by a miracle. The effects upon the 'Firefly' were similar."

His consideration of the torpedo defences of the Russians induced General Delafield to conclude his remarks upon the system with the opinion that "it is a most powerful auxiliary to harbor defence;" and is undoubtedly the cause of the interest which he, almost alone of all our army engineers, has taken in the subject. Of a large number of officers of rank in the navy as well as in the army, who were invited by Secretary of War Conrad to give their views upon the sea-coast defences of the United States, General Delafield is the only one who in any way mentions submarine defences as available, although the request brought out long and learned treatises on harbor defence from each of the officers appealed to for an opinion.

CHAPTER V.

CAUSES OF THE FINAL ACCEPTANCE OF THE TORPEDO AS A LEGITIMATE ENGINE OF WAR.—THE SOUTH THE FIRST TO CREATE A REGULAR SYSTEM OF TORPEDO WARFARE.—FIRST APPEARANCE OF TORPEDOES.—THEIR FORM AND ARRANGEMENT.—ACTS OF THE REBEL CONGRESS AUTHORIZING A TORPEDO CORPS.—FRAME TORPEDOES.—FUZES.—BUOYANT TORPEDOES.—LOSS OF THE REBEL VESSELS "ETTIWAN," "MARION," AND "SCHULTZ."—SINGER'S TORPEDO.—HIS PERCUSSION SYSTEM.—SPAR TORPEDO AND "DEVIL CIRCUMVENTOR."—SLOW MATCH TORPEDO.—CURRENT TORPEDO.—HYDROGEN GAS TORPEDO.—OBSTRUCTION TORPEDO.—CLOCK-WORK TORPEDO.—COAL TORPEDO.—PLATINUM FUZE.—BATTERIES.

Having traced the history of the torpedo from its first inception to its use in recent European wars, we shall now advance into a more interesting period of its history, when its employment was accompanied by results so unexpected and extraordinary that it seems to have sprung with one bound into the foremost rank of the novel and tremendous engines of war which have so completely changed the aspect of modern battle-fields and scenes of naval conflicts.

This sudden and astonishing development of a previously derided and apparently insignificant theory, has been due, first to the naval superiority of one of two parties to a stupendous contest, which called for all the ingenuity and boldness of which the weaker side was capable, to counteract; and secondly, to the appearance upon the scenes of conflict of iron-clad ships impenetrable by ordinary artillery, and indestructible by the usual machinery of war.

Whatever may be the result of the strife between the builder and the gunner—the one increasing the thickness and strength of his iron shield, as the other hurls heavier and swifter bolts to penetrate and destroy it—it is plain that so long as there is left a vulnerable part exposed to the arts of military science, so will that part become the target to which the aim of the naval engineer will be directed.

Achilles is represented to have been vulnerable only in the heel, and we are told that savages in their contests with the scaly, thick-coated monsters of African waters, plunge their knives into their soft and penetrable bellies, experience having taught them to seek thus their speedier destruction. So may it be said to be with ships—their vulnerable parts are submerged, but open to a species of attack which gains fresh importance with every additional layer of iron which coats them above.

The general recognition of the torpedo as a legitimate engine of war, which has followed the results of its use during the Rebellion, may be said to be the natural result of the iron-clad system, although the other cause, as already stated, had much to do in securing its introduction into this, as in the Russian war.

With a vast extent of coast peculiarly open to attack from sea; with a great territory traversed in every part by navigable streams, the rebels of the South had no navy to oppose to that of the Union—a condition which, from the very commencement of the struggle, stood in the way of their success, and neutralized their prodigious efforts on land. Their seaports were wrested from them, or blockaded; fleets of gunboats, mostly clad with iron, covered their bays and ascended their rivers, carrying dismay to their hearts, and success to the Union cause. The few feeble efforts they were enabled to make to dispute this naval supremacy, resulted almost without exception in utter discomfiture.

Under such a pressure, the pressure of dire distress and great necessity, the rebels turned their attention to torpedoes as a means of defence against such terrible odds, hoping by their use to render such few harbors and streams as yet remained to them inaccessible, or in some degree dangerous to the victorious gunboats.

Notwithstanding the previous history of the torpedo, the sentiment against it was so decided and prevalent that they sought an excuse for its use, and found it in their feebleness and necessity. Within a very short period after the inception of the design, a system was formed so far perfect and complete that our progress upon the water was materially checked. The channels of approach to the ports of Wilmington, Charleston, and Mobile, which then remained to them, were lined with sunken torpedoes of many different forms, and capable of ignition by a variety of agencies and clever devices. Rivers and bays, through which our vessels had passed freely and with impunity, now became dangerous ground, to be navigated with caution. Carrying out the original design of Fulton, which, as we have seen, so excited the derision of Commodore Rodgers, they armed the bows of their hitherto insignificant craft with these cheap and diminutive contrivances, converting them at once into tremendous engines of destruction, against which, when boldly handled, no amount of armor could prevail. Casting aside all high-flown sentiment, forgetting or ignoring the execrations with which its introduction was at first saluted, our Government adopted the system thus forced upon it, and the torpedo became with us, as it has since become with other nations, an acknowledged instrument of war.

At the naval actions at Hatteras, Port Royal, and New Orleans, and throughout all the movements afloat which resulted in our occupation of the entire sea-coast except Wilmington, Charleston, and Mobile, no torpedoes were found, nor was their presence suspected.

Admiral Foote, in command of the Mississippi flotilla, appears to have heard rumors that the rebels proposed to use them, but reports to the department, Jan. 7th, 1862, that such rumors were unfounded in fact. On the 18th of February, 1862, our gunboats, endeavoring to force a passage into the Savannah river, above Fort Pulaski, to assist in the reduction of that post, encountered at the mouth of Mud River, an arrangement of torpedoes which virtually initiated this system of rebel defence. Although unproductive of results, save delay to our fleet, this incident is worthy of notice, as marking the first appearance of these machines in a practical form.

Fig. 4.

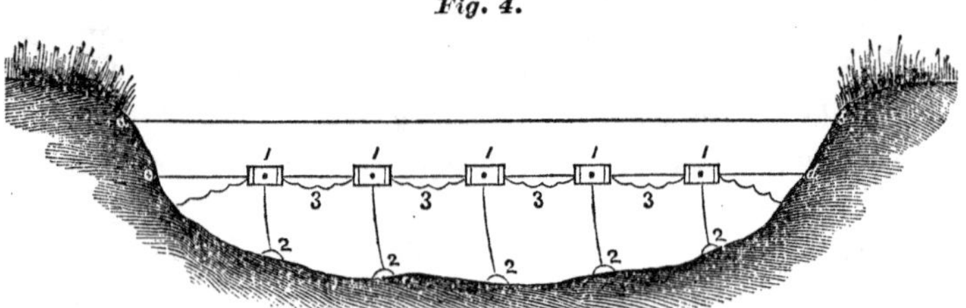

Fig. 4 shows their arrangement. 1 1 1 1 1, Torpedoes; 2 2 2 2 2, Anchors; 3 3 3 3, Spiral wires connecting the torpedoes, one end of which is fastened to the primer; *a b*, high-water mark; *c d*, low-water mark.

Fig. 5.

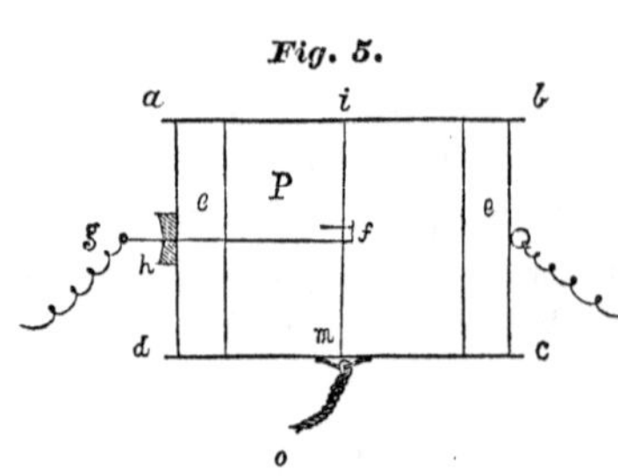

Fig. 5. Section of torpedo; *a b c d*, water-tight tin case; *e e*, air-chambers; *P*, powder-chamber containing 70 lbs. of powder; *F*, ordinary cannon friction primer, held at centre of charge by strip of tin, *i m*; attached to it is the wire *g f*, passing through a box, *h*, filled with wax and tallow; *m o*, mooring line.

Commodore John Rodgers, commanding the expedition, reports that these torpedoes were covered with water at all stages of the tide practicable for gunboats; but were visible at low water. The connecting spiral wire was intended to be drawn by the impact of a passing vessel, and the torpedoes being beneath her, the charge was ignited by the primer.

Having discovered them, they were exploded and sunk, one being secured as a specimen. Similar devices were found in great numbers in most of the narrow streams of the Atlantic coast during that year.

Commodore Rowan, in ascending the Neuse to attack the defences of Newbern, found thirty torpedoes, each containing 200 lbs. of powder, with a percussion arrangement and trigger lines connected with the piling, which obstructed the channel of the river.

These efforts were apparently the desultory acts of individuals, at or near the localities in which the torpedoes were found, rather than the result of any carefully organized system. In the month of October, 1862, however, the rebel Congress passed an act, authorizing the formation of a secret service corps, to be composed of persons not otherwise liable to military duty, who were to be considered as belonging to the provisional army of the Confederate States, and entitled, when captured, to all the privileges of prisoners of war.* Various other acts were soon after passed, having special reference to "engineering operations" upon the water, under which was formally organized what was termed "the Confederate States Submarine Battery Service."† A bureau was established in Richmond, called the "Torpedo Bureau," at the head of which was placed Mr. M. F. Maury, formerly of the U. S. navy.

The men enlisted in this special service were sworn to secrecy as to their duties, and granted many privileges on account of the supposed hazardous nature of their employment. Prize-money was also allowed them for successful operations, as a reward for daring enterprise.

Officers of the old navy, of high standing and ability, were appointed by special commissions to the duties of organizing and drilling the men and perfecting the system of operations. Inventions multiplied, experiments on a large scale were carried on, and emissaries were sent abroad to acquire in Europe necessary information, and to procure there the skilled labor and the material requisite to accomplish their designs.

The effect of thus systematizing this mode of defence was soon apparent. The crude machines, uncertain in their action, and defective in principle, which up to this time had been found so harmless as to cause a feeling of contempt for their originators, and disregard of their possible effects, were thrown aside, and in their places were substituted torpedoes which were so certain and well devised that the most incredulous and daring began to respect and fear them.

During the summer of 1863 the rebels were busily and systematically engaged in improving and adding to their torpedo

---

* Secretary of Navy Rept., 1864, p. 567.

† *Id.* pp. 26, 31.

defences. The "Department of Submarine Defences" in Charleston alone numbered from fifty to sixty officers and men, whose sole duty was to prepare, put down, examine, and keep in order the torpedoes of Charleston, while all the material requiring skilled labor was furnished by the Bureau at Richmond. At other points the same system prevailed.

Three distinct forms of defensive torpedoes seem to have been adopted, and henceforward extensively used.

First, *Frame Torpedoes.*—Second, *Floating or Buoyant Torpedoes.*—Third, *Electric Torpedoes.*

These were each specially adapted to different localities, and were found necessary to the complete defence of a harbor and its approaches, and will be particularly described.

First. Frame torpedoes (Pl. IV., Fig. 1) were placed only in narrow and quite shallow channels, the entrances to rivers and creeks, and upon bars traversable by monitors and light-draft gunboats. They performed the double function of obstruction and torpedo. Each frame or section consisted of four heavy timbers parallel to each other (*a, a, a, a*) and a few feet apart, tied together by cross timbers (*b, b, b*). At the head of each timber was bolted a cast-iron torpedo (*c, c, c, c*), of the shape shown in Fig. 3, containing about 27 lbs. of gunpowder, with a fuse so presented that it would come into contact with the bottom of any advancing vessel. The frame being securely anchored at one end, its specific gravity caused the other end bearing the torpedoes to rise towards the surface. It was kept inclined at the proper angle and depth by weights, anchors, and chains, and from sinking when water-soaked by supports (*e, e*). Each torpedo weighs 400 lbs., and will contain about 27 lbs. of powder. The four projections at the base are perforated for bolting the torpedo to the timber head. The sides of the torpedo are decreased internally to about $\frac{3}{4}$ of an inch at nine inches from the apex, in order that the first effects of the explosion may break it at that point, and force the upper or fuzed part of the torpedo through the bottom of the vessel.

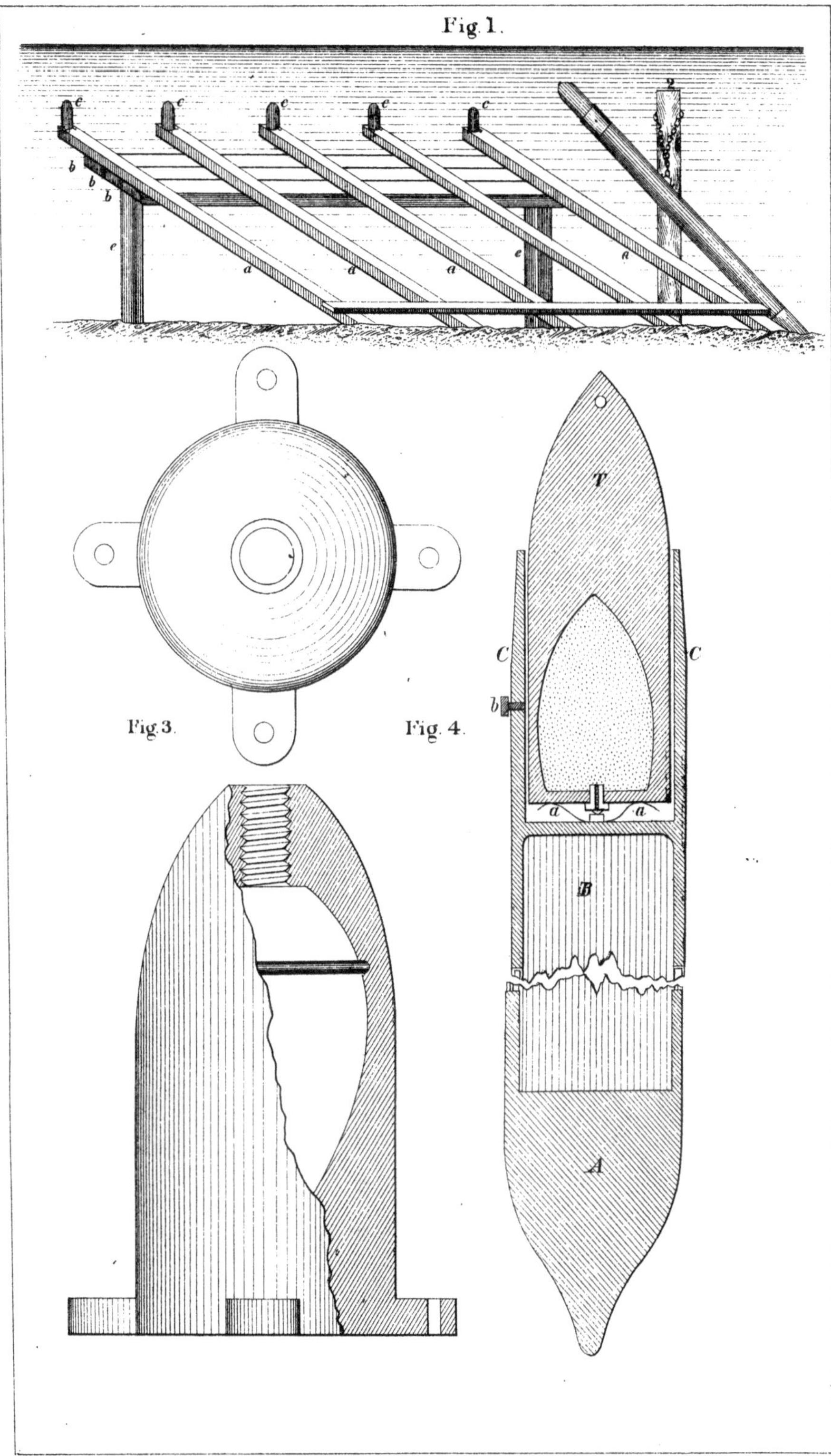

D. VAN NOSTRAND, Publisher.

Pl. V., Fig. 5. *The fuze* is of composition metal, and is composed of an inner cylinder 1½″ diameter and 2½″ long, a thread cut on the outside; the upper end is solid for one inch and perforated by three holes to receive each a percussion primer. A bouching 2″ long and 2¼″ diameter, having a sextagonal projection for applying a wrench, and an external and internal thread. Thin, soft, and well-annealed copper is soldered to the upper end of the bouching to keep moisture from the primers, and is so thin that a slight blow will crush without breaking it, and explode the primer beneath. The external thread above the projection is intended for screwing on a metallic safety-cap, to prevent the explosion of the primers by an accidental blow.

The contact of the primers with the covering copper cap is secured by screwing up the internal cylinder which holds them, until they touch the cap. A piece of shellac paper was usually glued or tied over the lower opening of the primer cylinder to still further protect the primers from moisture. Thus prepared, the torpedo being filled with powder, the whole is firmly screwed into the fuze hole of the torpedo, a little white lead being introduced into the thread of the screw, and a leather or gum washer or collar placed under the head to render the joint water-tight.

The sensitive primer used in this exploding arrangement, as well as in all the later contact fuzes for offensive and stationary buoyant torpedoes, was invented by and was manufactured immediately under the eye of General Rains, Chief of the Torpedo Bureau at Richmond, who succeeded Mr. Maury, and who carefully preserved from publicity all information concerning its manufacture. So sensitive was the detonating composition, that the pressure of seven pounds weight applied to the head of one of the primers would explode it.*

This primer was not, however, the original device for exploding contact torpedoes, which was an ingenious adaptation

* The writer is not aware of any chemical analysis ever having been made of this composition; but from inspection merely, the detonate is simply a combination of fulminate of mercury mixed with *ground glass*, to which the detonate probably owes its extreme sensitiveness.

of Prof. Jacobi's preparation, already noticed in describing the Russian torpedoes, and is shown in Plate V., Fig. 2. It consisted of a small glass tube *(a)* of sulphuric acid contained in and resting against the head of a soft cap of thin lead *(b)*. Surrounding the tube and holding it in position is a mixture of chlorate of potash and white sugar; a primer filled with mealed powder, or other quick burning preparation (*c*), is in contact with the charge of the torpedo. Upon striking any solid body the soft lead cap is crushed, breaking the glass tube of sulphuric acid, causing it to come into contact with the chlorate of potash and sugar, thus producing fire which is communicated to the charge by the primer. The action of this composition is as follows: When sulphuric acid, in its concentrated state, is allowed to fall upon chlorate of potash, a yellowish gas is evolved, which is very explosive, and becomes decomposed by a very moderate temperature when in contact with combustible matter.

This action is instantaneous when a mixture of nearly equal parts of chlorate of potash and fine white sugar are finely pulverized, and a single drop of strong acid is allowed to fall upon it. The first contact of the acid develops the explosive gas, and at the same time sufficient heat is evolved to cause the sugar to take fire, and the combustion once started goes on with a rapidity equal to that of gunpowder.

Plate IV., Figs. 2 and 4, represents another form of frame torpedo. The specimen from which the drawing is made was found, with a large number of others, attached to the obstructions in front of Fort McAllister, after its capture by Gen. Sherman's army. It consists of a heavy cast-iron shell (*T*) enclosed in an iron case (*C*), bolted to a timber (*B*). The heel of this timber is heavily weighted by a pointed cast-iron shoe (*A*).

The weight of the shell is supported by a spring (*a a*) and a set screw (*b*), which yield to pressure so as to permit the base of the torpedo shell, in which is fixed a sensitive fuze, to come into contact with a piece of metal in the bottom of the case, and thus produce the desired explosion.

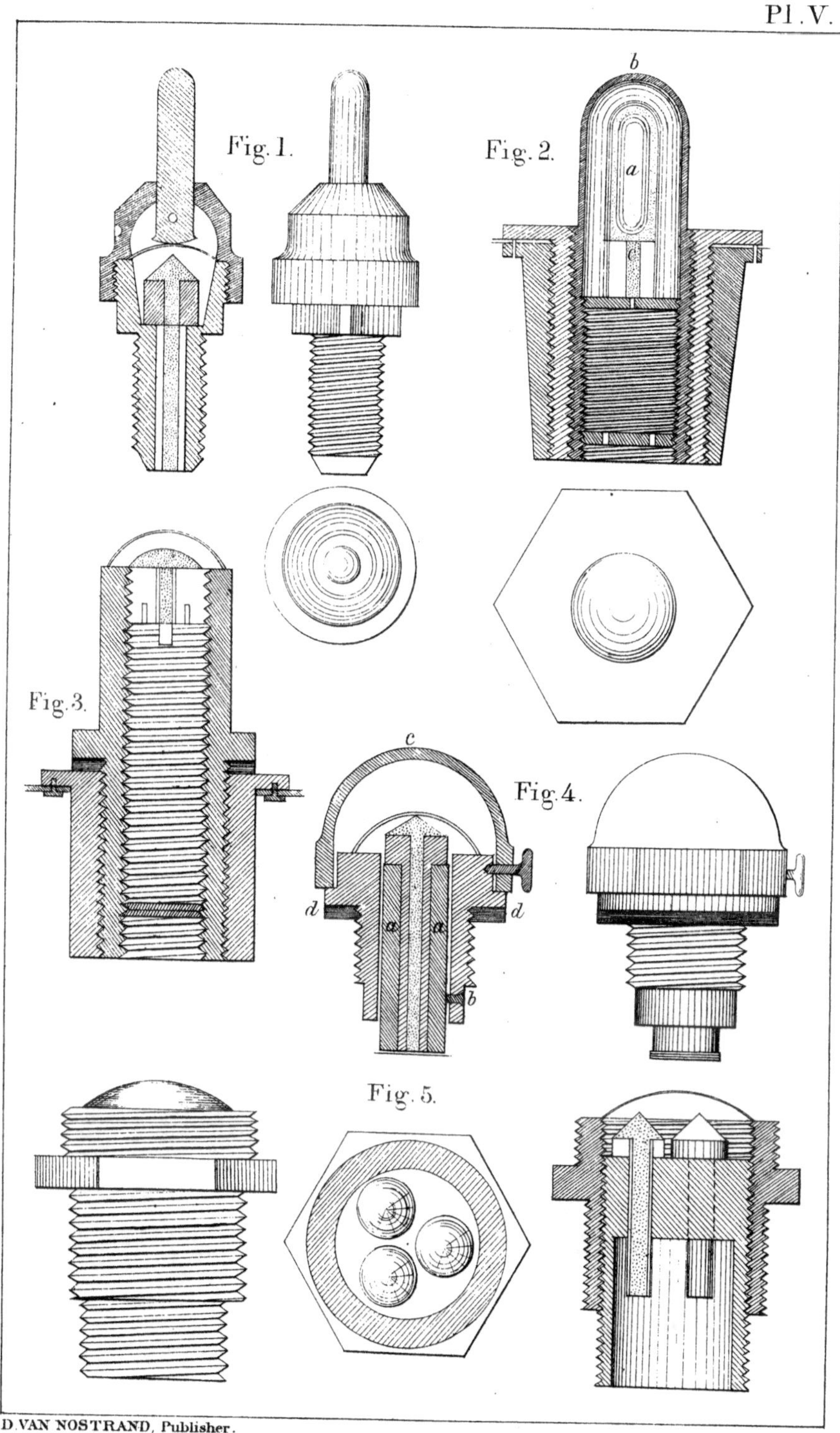

D. VAN NOSTRAND, Publisher.

Fig. 2 shows the manner of connecting it with the piling by slinging it near the upper end with heavy chains passed over the pile head.

The frame torpedoes were usually placed in double rows, with intervals between the sets, the second row being so distributed as to cover the interval between the sets of the first row.

In Charleston harbor this form of torpedo was very extensively used, and formed a most formidable barrier to the advance of our light-draft vessels through the streams leading to the city, as well as over the bars in the harbor. After the fall and occupation of the city, the naval force was for many days engaged in removing them. Four sets were found at the entrance to Ashley river, mounting 15 torpedoes each; six sets were placed in the narrow pass of Hog Island channel, and as many more in the neck of the middle channel near Castle Pinckney. In attempting to remove them, although they had been two years under water, the U. S. gunboat "Jonquil" was nearly destroyed by the accidental explosion of one of the torpedoes.

Our gunboats never, during the war, attempted to force a passage through a channel defended by this form of torpedo, and it would have been impossible to have passed either to Charleston, Mobile, or Wilmington, without encountering them.

Second.—Floating or Buoyant Torpedoes.—Plate VI., Fig. 1. This torpedo was usually made of a strong small barrel or breaker; lager beer barrels were preferred and were everywhere seized by the rebel authorities for this purpose. Pitch was poured into it through the bung-hole, and the barrel rolled about until the interior was evenly covered. It was then thoroughly coated with pitch on the outside.

Two cones of pine (*c c*) about seventeen inches long were securely fastened to each end of the barrel to prevent the current from tumbling it over, and to insure the fuze coming properly into contact when touched by the bottom of a vessel. Five and sometimes more sensitive fuzes (*a a a*), like those already described, were screwed into the barrel, two on each side, and one on top of its bilge. These torpedoes contained from 70 to 120 lbs. of gunpowder. The barrel was strapped with rope, and to a span underneath were attached a weight (*b*) to keep it upright, a mooring line (*e*) to keep it the proper depth below the surface, and a line (*f*) to connect it with another torpedo.

This kind of torpedo was the most convenient, cheap, and, in some respects, the most dangerous one employed during the war; unless very carefully and securely anchored they were apt to give trouble to the parties using them, the current sometimes causing them to shift their positions. From this cause two rebel steamers—the "Marion" and "Ettiwan"—were "hoisted by their own petards" in Charleston harbor, the former being totally destroyed. A similar accident happened to the rebel flag-of-truce boat "Shultz" on the James river, when a number of exchanged rebel prisoners were killed as they were being carried to Richmond.

The practice of the rebels was to keep large numbers of these torpedoes always on hand and ready for use. Whenever an attack was threatened, or an emergency arose, they were rapidly put down in places likely to be passed over by our gunboats. They were encountered everywhere, sometimes exploding with full effect, and, as we shall see, creating great havoc and destruction. Several hundred were found in and about Charleston, after its occupation by our troops, ready for immediate use. A small boat with two men could easily plant four of them in an hour.

Singer's Torpedo.—Plate VI., Fig. 2, shows the form and arrangement for exploding this, perhaps the most successful torpedo used by the rebels during the war. It made its appearance simultaneously upon the Western waters and along the Eastern coast. The case is made of tin, and contains from 50 lbs. to 100 lbs. of powder, according to the size desired. It may be understood by the following description: *A*, air chamber; *P*, powder magazine; *B*, *C*, a heavy cast-iron cap, resting upon the top of the case, and prevented from falling off by a low rim of tin entering an aperture in the cap as shown at *D*; a wire connects the cap with a trigger at *E*,* which holds a plunger ready to strike when liberated; directly beneath the plunger, and inside the magazine, there is a rod of iron, its end resting in a cup formed in the lug (*a*), where there is a screw by which the rod is forced gently against the interior surface of the bottom of the case. In this cup is placed a fulminating substance. When the cap is struck or pressed by a passing vessel, it is knocked off, and its weight in falling pulls out the trigger, and the plunger, forced by the spiral spring, is driven against the interior iron rod, which explodes the fulminate and the charge.

The torpedo is lowered by a slip rope wove through the eye at *D*, which also prevents the cap from slipping off accidentally while planting it. A "safety-pin" (*e*) was also used to secure the plunger in case the trigger should be accidentally withdrawn. It was hauled out by a small line after the torpedo was in its place.†

---

* In some specimens captured, three triggers connected by spans to the wire were used, as shown in the drawing; the object being to secure the explosion in the event of failure of one trigger to do its work, and to ignite the charge at its centre in three different places, and thus secure the entire combustion of the powder. By adding one more lug to the spindle, and connecting it by rods to the lower ones, the charge could be exploded at six different points, or, by placing fulminate at the lower end of the first set of rods, at nine points.

† The following rebel document was captured by Admiral Porter, and forwarded for the information of the Navy Department:

Report of a Commission on Singer's Torpedo.

"ENGINEER HEADQUARTERS,
"DEPARTMENT NORTHERN VIRGINIA, *July* 14, 1863.

"COLONEL,—In accordance with your order of the 13th, appointing the undersigned a commission to examine and report upon the merits of Mr. E. C. Singer's torpedo, we beg to state that we have carefully examined the same, and submit the following report:

"*First.* 'As to the plan for exploding the charge.' In this plan or lock, in our opinion, consists the great merit of the invention. The lock is simple,

Plate VI., Fig. 3, shows another form of buoyant torpedo, designed with the special purpose of preventing its discovery or removal by dragging or sweeping. It consists of a copper chamber (*A*) attached to the extremity of a spar, the other end of which is secured by a universal joint to a mud anchor (*B*). Into the top of the chamber are screwed five or more fuzes, of the form known as the "Sensitive Fuze," or of that already described as the "Chemical Fuze."

It is evident that the bight of a rope or chain, or a grappel hook, would slip over without being arrested by this torpedo, and that even if its presence were discovered, its

---

strong, and not liable at any time to be out of order; and as the caps which ignite the charge are placed within the powder magazine, they are not likely to be affected by moisture; while the percussion is upon the exterior of the magazine, actual contact with the rod which acts as a trigger is necessary, but by mechanical contrivances the contact may be obtained in various ways.

"*Second.* 'The certainty of action' depends, of course, upon contact, but by the peculiar and excellent arrangement of the lock and plan of percussion mentioned above, the certainty of explosion is almost absolute. One great advantage this torpedo possesses over many others is, that its explosion does not depend upon the action or judgment of any individual; that it is safe from premature ignition, and at the same time is cheap and portable, while its position in river or harbor cannot readily be ascertained by an enemy's vessels.

"*Third.* 'The efficiency of its explosion, if made in deep channels,' cannot well be ascertained without experiment, but would be the same as submarines fired by any other contrivance. We are of the opinion, however, from the best information accessible, that if the powder, say 100 pounds in quantity, is within the distance of fifteen feet from the keel of the vessel when exploded, its efficient action is not materially affected by the depth of channel. Of course the quantity of powder required would have to be determined by experiment. Rifle powder, from its more rapid combustion, would be preferable in deep water to cannon powder, while some of the detonating compounds would doubtless effect certain destruction to vessels passing over torpedoes at even much greater depth.

"The peculiar arrangements for firing the batteries would have to be determined by the circumstances of position and draught of vessels and motion of currents, depth, and width of channels, and would require the exercise of great judgment on the part of those intrusted with the duty of placing them.

"We are so well satisfied with the merits of Mr. Singer's torpedo that we recommend the engineer department to give it a thorough test, and, if prac-

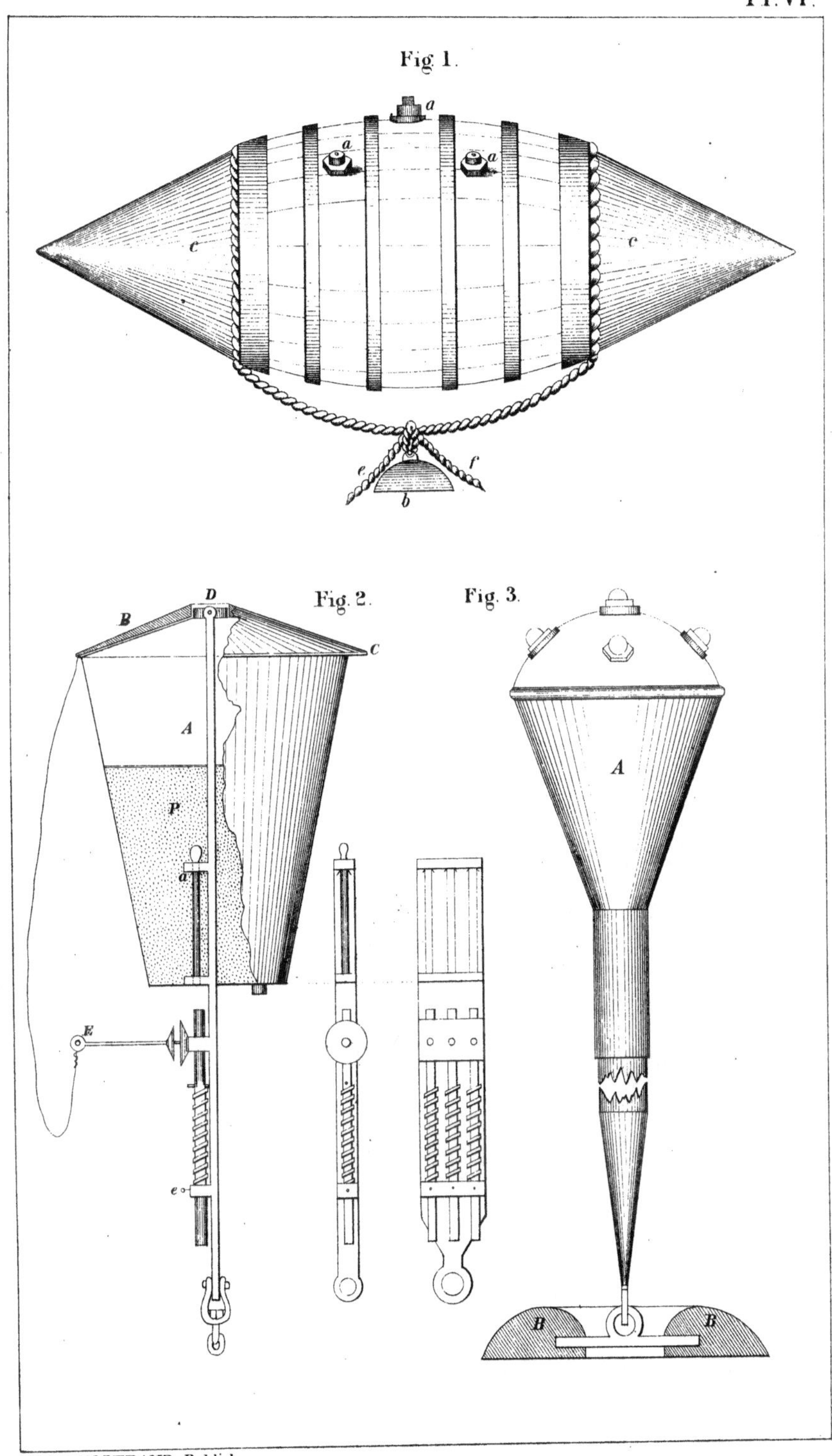

D. VAN NOSTRAND, Publisher.

removal would be exceedingly difficult. To render such an attempt still more uncertain and hazardous, the extremity of the spar was frequently attached by a wire to another form of torpedo, as shown in Plate VII., Figs. 1 and 2. This was yclept "the devil circumventor." It is of boiler iron, and contains about 100 lbs. of powder.

The wire from the torpedo spar, just described, enters the case through a water-tight joint *(a)*, and is attached inside to a friction primer. The object of the arrangement is, that in the event of making fast to the spar torpedo, and raising or dragging it aside, the attached torpedo may be exploded underneath the boats engaged in the duty. The "circumventor" was placed about fifty yards from its companion. It

---

ticable, to have some of them placed at an early day in some of the river approaches of Richmond.

"*General Remarks.*—The mode of loading this torpedo dispenses with any connection through the case of the magazine, involving no packing of any kind.

"The risk of the lock fouling by sand or mud, if on the bottom of a stream, we think can be prevented by enclosing it in a metal case, which would be nearly water-tight. In narrow streams these could be placed in *quincunx*, so that a vessel attempting to pass would be sure to come in contact with some one.

"We consider the employment of submarines as a legitimate mode of defence, and, as officers connected with the defence of Richmond, feel it our duty to recommend torpedoes as a powerful accessory to our limited means. The moral effect of an explosion upon an enemy would be incalculable, and would doubtless deter them from attempting to bring troops, by transport, to points accessible to the city, as White House or Brandon.

"Respectfully submitted.

"W. H. Stevens,
"*Col. Engineers.*

"I. A. Williams,
"*Maj. Engineers.*

"W. G. Turpin,
"*Capt. Engineers.*

"To Col. J. T. Gilmer,
"*Chief Engineer.*

"*(Official copy.)*

"A. L. Rives,
"*Acting Chief Bureau.*"

is not known that this combination was effective, but the torpedo first described was considered as one of the most dangerous used by the rebels. They were found in considerable numbers at Charleston, Richmond, and elsewhere.

Fig. 2 shows the apparatus for exploding the "circumventor."

Fig. 3 is another form of floating torpedo, sent down in the current of James river in great numbers. It is exploded by slow match, and is provided with a tin lantern, kept above the water by a board as a "float;" a tin tube protects the match while burning down to the charge. None of them were ever known to explode, although they were frequently found in the nets, and alongside our vessels, the slow match extinguished before reaching the charge.

Plate VII., Fig. 4, shows a "current torpedo" used by the rebels, but never with success. This is intended to be carried by the current against a vessel; when arrested in its course, the propeller wheel is revolved by the tide, releasing a hammer, which, forced by the spiral spring, drops upon the percussion rod and cap, arranged as in the Singer torpedo, and thus explodes the charge. It is supported at the proper depth by a buoy.

Plate VIII., Fig. 1, is a torpedo which, although never effectively employed, shows the ingenuity of rebel devices. It is exploded by throwing a jet of hydrogen gas upon a small mass of spongy platinum, which, becoming incandescent, sets fire to the charge. A number of atmospheres of gas are compressed into the globe *(A)*; when the arm *(B C)* is struck by a vessel, it turns a cock at *D*, which permits the gas to flow through the pipe to *d*, where it meets the platinum, surrounded by fulminate of mercury; this is exploded in the centre of the charge. The cords from the arm keep it from turning, unless struck by a blow sufficiently heavy to rupture them.

Fig. 2 is a torpedo which caused our vessels, passing up and down the James, great annoyance. It consists of a tin case, containing about 70 lbs. of powder. A stiff wire *(fb)*

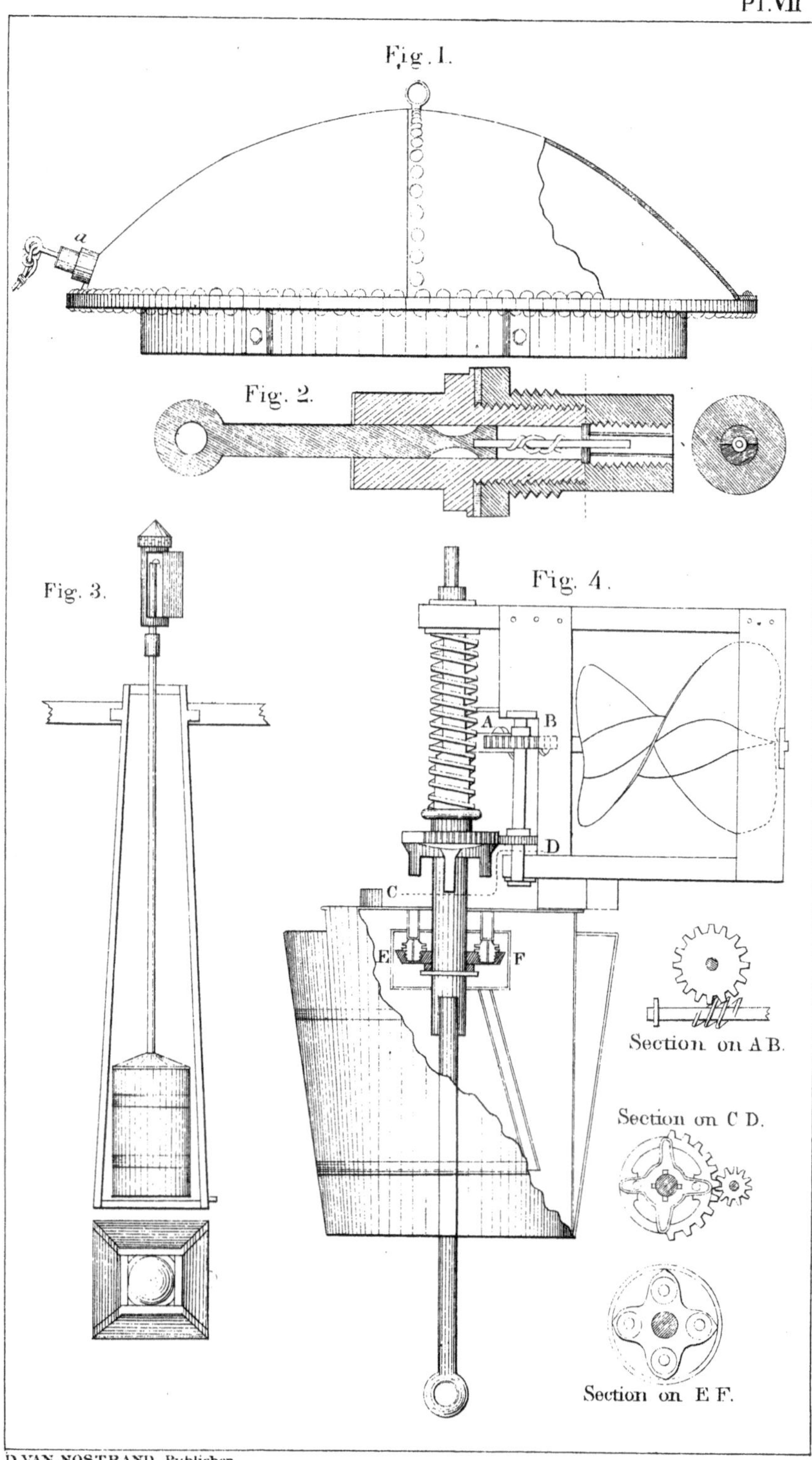

D.VAN NOSTRAND, Publisher.

passes through a hole punctured through a strip of tin at *f*, and a box filled with beeswax at *b;* the end *(f)* is covered with fulminate, like an ordinary friction parlor match. A number of wires lead from *b* to pieces of drift-wood on the surface, and the case is supported at the right depth by a line attached to a section of log. The apparatus is set adrift at night, in the hope that the trigger lines will foul the propellers of passing steamers—an anticipation more than once realized, although the explosion which ensued usually took place astern of the vessel entangled.

Fig. 3 is a form of torpedo used to remove obstructions by the United States authorities. Clock-work is contained in the tin case *A*, which at the desired moment permits a hammer to fall upon a percussion cap, which by its explosion ignites a quick match passing through a rubber tube into the case *B*, containing about 200 lbs. of powder. It is intended to be cast into the water when the tide sets in the direction of the obstruction.

Fig. 4 is the form of a clock-work torpedo employed by the rebels to blow up storehouses, magazines and transports, and was used by them in two instances with appalling effect. It consists of a common wooden box containing clock-work and about 50 lbs. of powder. The reader will remember the tremendous explosion which occurred at City Point in 1864. The quartermaster's force was there engaged in unloading several ordnance boats of their cargoes of powder, shell, and prepared ammunition. A man was noticed to approach one of the vessels with a box upon his back. He was dressed like an ordinary laborer, passed the sentries without being questioned, and deposited his load upon the deck of a barge filled with powder, and disappeared. A few moments after, the explosion occurred, which destroyed the wharves, storehouses, and vessels near it; a number of men were killed and injured by the falling fragments.

The wharf boat at Mound City, containing the reserve supplies of ammunition and stores for Admiral Porter's fleet, was also destroyed by a similar contrivance.

Fig. 5 is a "coal torpedo" which may be truly designated an "infernal machine." It appears to be an innocent lump of coal, but is a block of cast-iron with a core containing about ten pounds of powder. The rebels had an organized body of men whose duty was to deposit these machines in coal-piles or barges, from which our vessels took their supplies—or even in the coal-bunkers of the vessels themselves.* Covered with a mixture of tar and coal-dust, it was impossible to detect their character. A great number of unaccountable explosions of our vessels, principally transports, have been traced to these devices; the most notable of which was that of the "Greyhound" on the James river, a magnificent steamer employed by General Butler as his "headquarters boat." She was totally destroyed, and the General and Admiral Porter, who happened to be on board at the time, escaped with difficulty from the burning vessel.

The third and the most approved form of torpedo for

---

* The following captured document explains itself:

"RICHMOND, VIRGINIA, *January* 19, 1864.

"MY DEAR COLONEL,—I hope you have received all my letters. I wrote two to Mobile, one to Columbus, and two to Brandon; I now send this by a party who is going to Shreveport, and promised to learn your whereabouts, so as to forward it to you.

"I have met with much delay and annoyance since you left. The castings have all been completed some time, and the *coal* is so perfect that the most critical eye could not detect it. The President thinks them perfect, but Mr. Seddon will do nothing without Congressional action, so I have been engaged for the past two weeks in getting up a bill that will cover my case. At last it has met his approval, and will to-day go to the Senate, thence to the House in secret session. It provides that the Secretary of War shall have the power to organize a 'secret service corps;' commission, enlist, and detail parties who shall retain former rank and pay; also give such compensation as he may deem fit, not exceeding 50 per cent., for property partially and totally destroyed; also to advance, when necesary, out of the secret service fund, money to parties engaging to injure the enemy.

"As soon as the bill becomes a law I have no doubt I shall get a suitable commission, and means to progress with, and that all the appointments you or I have made will be confirmed. * * * * *

"Your friend,

"T. E. COURTENAY.

"Colonel H. E. CLARK,

"*7th Missouri Cavalry, Maj.-Gen. Price's Headquarters, Arkansas.*"

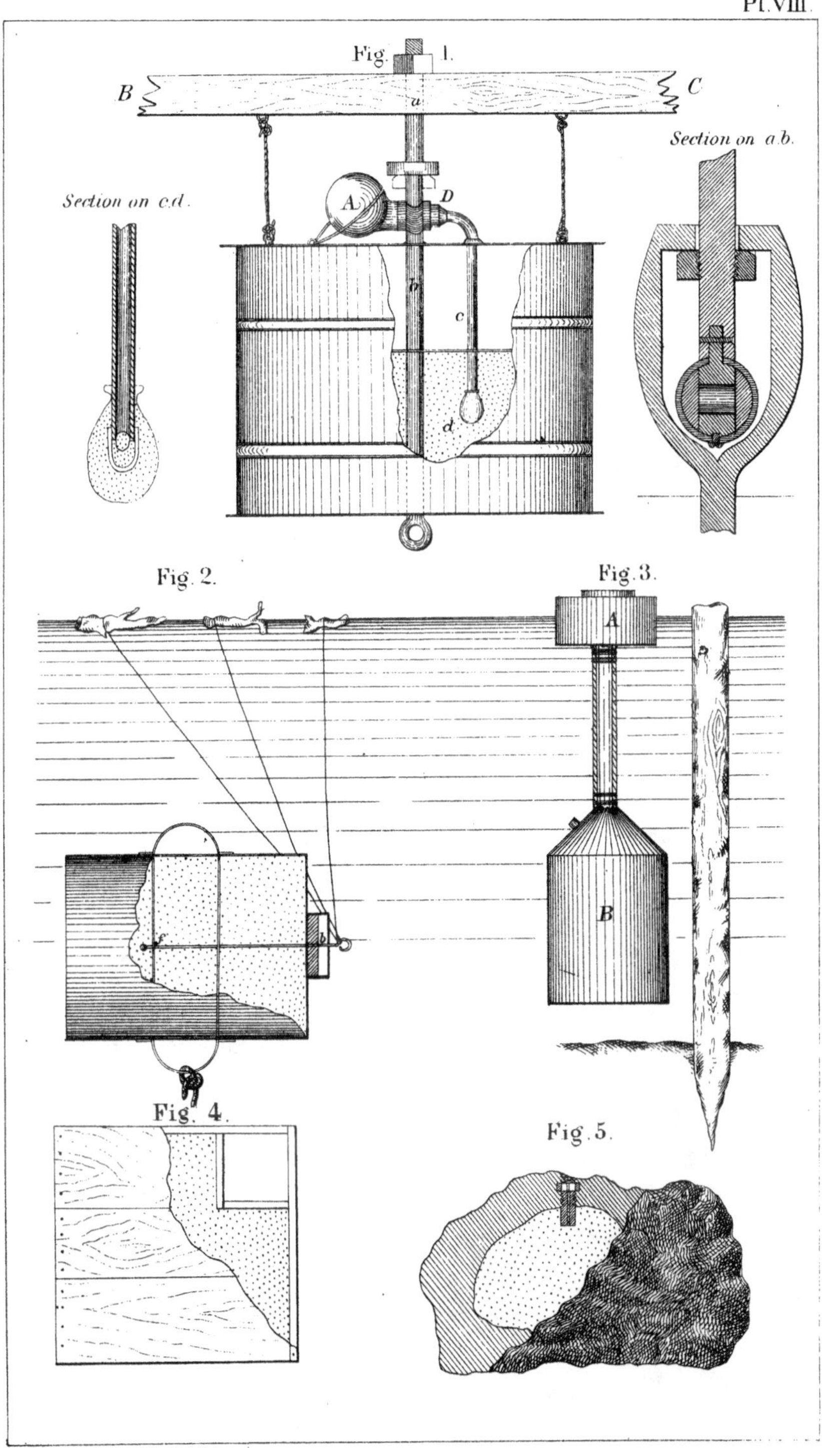

D. VAN NOSTRAND, Publisher.

harbor defence is that exploded by an electric battery, and termed the "Electric Torpedo."

After the attack upon Charleston of the 7th of April, the rebels planted in that harbor a number of gigantic torpedoes of this character; they also constituted the most formidable part of the defences in the James river, at Fort Fisher, and Mobile, where they were raised by our forces in great numbers, after the fortifications in which the electrical batteries or machines were placed came into our possession. Several were used with appalling effect upon our ships.

They rarely contained less than a ton of powder, and were usually placed in the narrow and deep channels to which passing vessels were necessarily confined.

Boilers of useless steamers were at first used to contain the charges, but the rebels soon commenced the fabrication of cases expressly designed for the purpose, the work upon them being done in a skilful and thorough manner; each case being submitted to the test of a powerful water pressure before being submerged.

Plate IX. Fig. 1 represents the form of the electric torpedo established by the Bureau at Richmond, as affording the best protection to the wires, and to bring the charge as near the object to be destroyed as possible. The case is made of $\frac{3}{4}$-inch boiler iron closely riveted. Heavy composition castings are bolted to the ends *A* and *B*, the former to cover and protect the circuit wires. Two wires were usually employed, each connected with the poles of the electric battery. The conductor was the ordinary gutta-percha-covered No. 16 copper wire used in telegraphy, the submerged parts being additionally protected by a covering of tarred hemp, and weighted with chain. The torpedo was anchored by heavy masses of kentledge, attached by chain cable to a span shackled to bolts (*C*, *D*).

Fig. 2. represents the stuffing-box for the conductors and the fuze employed with the voltaic batteries. The box consists of three pieces: 1. A screw-cap (*E*), open on its face. 2. A cylindrical disc (*F*), in which are two round holes, with brass tubes soldered into them to receive the conducting, wires; 3. A metal stock (*H*), which screws into the bouching at the opening of the torpedo case.

The fuze consists of a slip of pine, grooved at the sides for the wires, which, bared of the insulating material and scraped, are turned back at the end (*a*). A small section of goose quill is filled with fulminate of mercury, and secured by thread to the end of the stick; through this fulminate is passed the fine platina wire, which acts as a secondary conductor between the terminals of the conductors. The wires are then passed through the metal stock, and the end of the stick is wedged into the bore of the stock. The disc is then slipped on over the wires. The hollow space in the stock (*K*) is packed with tallow and cotton waste and the disc is pressed down upon the packing, the screw-cap is then screwed firmly upon the disc, and the whole is then screwed into the torpedo case, as shown in Fig. 1. The case is filled from the opposite end.

The batteries employed were, until the last year of the war, ordinary voltaic piles of Grove or Bunsen. They were, however, found to be uncertain in their action, cumbersome, and difficult to keep in effective condition. A beautiful instrument, called "Wheatstone's Magnetic Exploder," was subsequently imported from England, where it was made for the special use of the rebels. This battery, and "Abel's Fuze," used in connection with it, are described on pp. 169 and 171. A sketch of the fuze is shown in Fig. 3.

Range stakes were established in front of the batteries, for the purpose of determining the position of the vessel in regard to the torpedo, and thus enable the operator to fire it at the proper time.

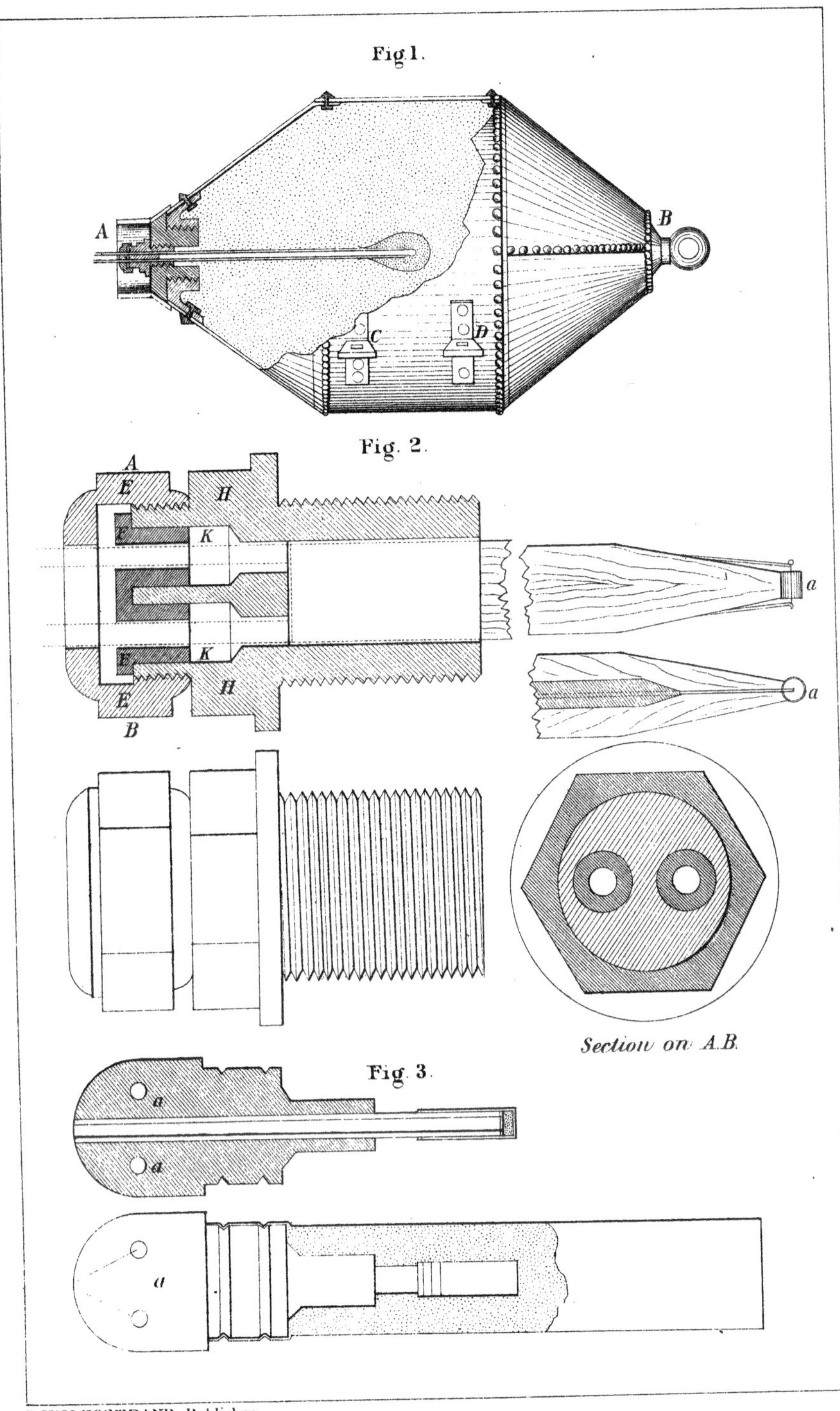

D. VAN NOSTRAND, Publisher.

CHAPTER VI.

LOSS OF THE U. S. S. "CAIRO."—REPORT OF ADMIRAL PORTER.—INJURY TO THE U. S. MONITOR "MONTAUK"—REBEL CONFIDENCE IN TORPEDOES AT CHARLESTON.—U. S. GOVERNMENT ARE WARNED OF THEIR PRESENCE.—MR. ERICSSON'S TORPEDO AND OBSTRUCTION REMOVER.—ADMIRAL DUPONT'S PREPARATIONS TO PROTECT HIS FLEET.—ATTACK ON CHARLESTON.—ESCAPE OF "NEW IRONSIDES" AND "WEEHAWKEN."—"ESSEX" TORPEDO.—LOSS OF IRON-CLAD "BARON DE KALB."—REPORTS OF ADMIRAL PORTER.

Having described the forms of defensive torpedoes employed by the rebels, we return to the course of events which illustrate the value of these devices.

As has been noticed, the rebels formed their torpedo corps, and commenced the systematic use of torpedoes, during the fall of the year 1862; and in the month of December, 1862, reaped the first fruits of their organization, in accomplishing the total destruction of the iron-clad "Cairo," one of the most powerful vessels of the Mississippi squadron. The following official reports of her commander, and Admiral Porter, convey the particulars of this disaster:

Report of Lieutenant Commander Thomas O. Selfridge.

"United States Gunboat 'Signal,'
"Off Yazoo River, *December* 13, 1862.

"Sir,—It becomes my painful duty to announce to you the total loss of the gunboat 'Cairo,' while under my command, from the explosion of two torpedoes under or near her, placed in the Yazoo river, some sixteen miles from its mouth.

"I left our anchorage at about eight o'clock A.M., December 12, in company with the gunboats 'Pittsburg,' 'Marmora,' 'Signal,' and ram 'Queen of the West,' under orders from Captain Walke to proceed carefully up the Yazoo to where torpedoes had been discovered the day before, and to effect the destruction of as many as possible. It was understood that the light gunboats were to go ahead, followed by myself and the 'Pittsburg,' to protect them by shelling the woods on the river bank.

"Arriving near the spot indicated, when the leading gunboat, the 'Marmora,' was partially hidden by a bend in the river, a heavy fire of musketry opened; the steamer commenced backing at the same time, leading me to suppose she was attacked from the shore. I hastened up to her support, when I found the firing was from the 'Marmora,' at an object, a block of wood floating in the water.

"I ordered her to cease firing and to lower a boat to examine. They either did not hear my order or were loth to obey it, and showing no signs of executing it, I lowered one of my own boats. They fished it up, and found it to be a portion of a torpedo which had exploded the day before.

"In the meanwhile, the head of the 'Cairo' having got in towards the shore, I backed out to straighten up stream, and ordered the 'Marmora' to go ahead slow. I had made but half a dozen revolutions of the wheel, and gone ahead perhaps half a length—the 'Marmora,' a little ahead, leading—when two sudden explosions, in quick succession, occurred—one close to my port quarter, the other apparently under my port bow; the latter so severe as to raise the guns under it some distance from the deck. She commenced to fill so rapidly that in two or three minutes the water was over her forecastle. I shoved her immediately for the bank, but a few yards distant; got out a hawser to a tree, hoping to keep her from sliding off into deep water. The pumps, steam and hand, were immediately manned, and everything done that could be. Her whole frame was so completely shattered that I found immediately that nothing more could be effected than to move the sick and the arms. I ordered the 'Queen of the West' alongside, and passed what articles I could get at into her, with a portion of the crew, the remainder taking to our boats. The 'Cairo' sunk in about twelve minutes after the explosion, going totally out of sight, except the top of the chimneys, in six fathoms of water. I am happy to say that, though some half a dozen men were injured, no lives were lost.

"I cannot speak too highly of the officers' and men's behavior; there was perfect discipline and order to the last. The crew remained at their quarters until ordered away, and did what little could be done under the circumstances.

"The most of the bags and hammocks were saved, as was everything that floated from the wreck. In the meanwhile I directed Captain Hoel, of the 'Pittsburg,' to send boats up the shore, under cover of his guns, to destroy and discover the mode of firing these torpedoes. Several of them were destroyed, but I leave the particulars to his report.

"Having accomplished all that was in our power, and destroyed what vestige of the unfortunate 'Cairo' that remained above water, it was with deep regret that I felt obliged to return down the river.

"I have nothing to add in justification of myself that does not appear in this report.

"Though I found we were in the vicinity of torpedoes, there were no signs to show, at the time, that any were in my immediate neighborhood, the 'Marmora' having passed ahead of me.

"Very respectfully, your obedient servant,

"THOMAS O. SELFRIDGE,
"*Lieutenant Commander.*

"Captain HENRY WALKE, U. S. N.,
"*Commanding Naval Forces off Yazoo River.*"

Acting Rear-Admiral Porter's Detailed Report of the Loss of the "Cairo."

No. 251.] "UNITED STATES MISSISSIPPI SQUADRON,
"*December* 17, 1862.

"SIR,—When I sent you my despatch notifying you of the loss of the 'Cairo,' I had not examined carefully all the accompanying reports, being pressed for time, and I left it to the department to judge where the blame lay. My own opinion is that due caution was not observed, and that the vessels went ahead too fast. These torpedoes have proved so harmless heretofore (not one exploding out of the many hundreds that have been planted by the rebels), that officers have not felt that respect for them to which they are entitled. The torpedo which blew up the 'Cairo' was evidently fired by a galvanic battery, as in some of them, which were afterwards taken up, the officers followed the wires over four hundred yards from the river bank, and would have followed them up but for fear of surprises. Lieutenant Commander Selfridge was proceeding with proper caution *before* the accident, and the 'Marmora' was proceeding ahead of him some distance, while the boats were cutting the wires and dragging the torpedoes to the bank. Several had been safely disposed of when the 'Signal' commenced firing musketry; and as the river bank was full of sharpshooters, Lieutenant Commander Selfridge went to assist her, supposing she was attacked. It appears she was firing at floating torpedoes. Not obeying the signal made to her to return, Lieutenant Commander Selfridge went up to hail her, and in doing so lost his vessel. The boats were doing their work very effectually, and had the orders of Captain Walke been carried out no accident could have occurred. The torpedoes were known to be there in numbers, and every precaution should have been observed. Lieutenant Commander Selfridge, however, did not go ahead with his vessel until his pilot assured him that everything was clear. In my orders to Captain Walke I directed him as follows: 'Send on the "Signal" and "Marmora," with some good marksmen, besides their crews; let them hold on to all they can until you can get your large vessels in. We must make a landing for the army at all hazards, and prevent the rebels from raising batteries,' etc., etc. The first part of the order was executed, and the 'Signal' and 'Marmora' proceeded thirty miles up the river until stopped by the batteries. They were attacked by guerillas, whom they easily drove off, but they returned again to Captain Walke, and enabled the rebels to plant the torpedoes between that time and the return of the second expedition, when the 'Cairo' was lost. What was the cause of the return of the light-draught vessels in the face of my order, I have yet to learn. I do not see any thing to reprehend in the course of Lieutenant Commander Selfridge, except being rather incautious. His vessel was a great loss to us; she was in splendid order, and had just been made shot-proof with railroad iron where she was before vulnerable. He is too good an officer to lose his services just now, and I have put him in command of the 'Conestoga,' which was vacant, trusting that he may be more fortunate hereafter, this being the second time during the war his vessel has gone down under him. The conduct of the officers and crew was admirable;

everything was conducted with perfect coolness, and not a man was lost, although so short a time elapsed between the explosion of the torpedo and the sinking of the vessel, that nothing was saved except a few hammocks and bags, belonging to the men, which floated off. In a few minutes after the 'Cairo' sunk, nothing could be seen but the top of her pipes, which the ram 'Lioness' hauled out and sunk, to prevent the rebels from finding the spot. This affair will give me some extra trouble, but I hope to succeed, nevertheless, though this leaves me only six vessels which can go under a battery.

"Very respectfully, your obedient servant,

"David D. Porter,

"*Acting Rear-Admiral, Com'd'g Mississippi Squadron.*

"Hon. Gideon Welles,

"*Secretary of the Navy, Washington, D. C.*"

Acting Rear-Admiral Porter's instructions to Captain Walke.

"United States Mississippi Squadron,

"*November* 21, 1862.

"Sir,—On receipt of this communication you will take with you all the iron-clads, except the 'Benton' and the 'General Bragg,' and proceed down as near the mouth of the Yazoo as you can get, and, if possible, enter it. The object is to prevent the erection of batteries at the mouth of the Yazoo river, or as far as our guns will reach, and in case you see anything of the kind, your duty wiil be to destroy the batteries if you can; if the rebels have not covered them in, there will be no difficulty in driving them away and destroying the guns. The best time to do that kind of business is about daylight in the morning."

Upon the 28th of February, 1863, the monitor "Montauk," aided by some wooden gunboats, destroyed the rebel privateer "Nashville" lying under the protection of Fort McAllister, on the Ogeechee river, Georgia. As she was returning to her anchorage, and when at a point about 1,000 yards below the fort, she struck a torpedo, which, by its explosion, materially injured the vessel. Nothing but the favoring stage of the tide, and the close vicinity of a mud-bank, upon which she was immediately run, saved her from sinking. The mud partially closed the hole made in her bottom, and permitted it to be temporarily closed from within so as to enable her commander, Captain Worden, to navigate her safely to Port Royal.

The following order and report explain the extent of the injury received by the "Montauk":

"FLAG SHIP 'WABASH,'
"PORT ROYAL HARBOR, S. C., *March* 5, 1863.

"GENTLEMEN,—You will hold a strict and careful survey on the hull of the United States iron-clad 'Montauk,' and report to me in triplicate what damages she has sustained from the explosion of the torpedo on the 28th ultimo, the best mode of repairing the same, and the time required for that purpose.

"Respectfully, your obedient servant,
"S. F. DUPONT,
"*Rear-Admiral, Commanding S. A. B. Squadron.*

"Chief Engineer ALBAN C. STIMERS,
"Chief Engineer R. McCLEERY,
"*U. S. steamer 'Wabash,'*
"Mechanical Engineer EDWARD FARON."

"PORT ROYAL, SOUTH CAROLINA, *March* 5, 1863.

"SIR,—In obedience to your orders of this date, we have examined the bottom of the iron-clad 'Montauk' with reference to the injury sustained by the explosion beneath it of a torpedo in the Ogeechee river, and we beg leave very respectfully to report:

"The explosion took place beneath the back end of the port boiler, under a part where the ship's bottom is very flat.

"We found the cast iron portion of the boiler—blow-off pipe—which in all iron ships it is considered necessary to place between the copper pipes and the wrought iron of the ship's bottom to prevent galvanic action, which would otherwise take place—broken off; the bottom permanently indented two and a half inches; the indentation extending five feet athwartship and three feet fore and aft. The greatest force of the explosion was directly under a twelve-inch floor, along beneath which the plating of the ship is cracked a distance of two feet four inches (2′ 4″); thence diagonally aft and toward the keel one foot ten inches (1′ 10″), its direction being indicated by saying that it extends aft nine inches (9″), and athwartships one foot eight inches (1′ 8″,) the diagonal portion of the crack being in the next streak to garboard. This twelve-inch (12″) floor, and the sixteen-inch (16″) one forward of it, are warped and torn somewhat from the frames.

"We would respectfully recommend that the ship be beached, and a soft patch tap bolted to the inside of the cracked plate; that the floors be straightened and refastened to the frames, and that a wrought-iron pipe be put in place of the cast-iron one which broke.

"In making this last recommendation, we are aware that we are departing from what is considered the best practice in iron ship-building where copper pipes are used, and that a torpedo may never again explode with that nice adjustment of locality and force which may break a cast-iron pipe and not break through entirely into the ship. Yet we prefer to assume that this may occur, and to suffer the certain inconvenience of the galvanic action, than to replace a broken part with material which will certainly be broken upon an exact repetition of the accident.

"We estimate the time required as follows:

"To make the necessary preparations................	4 days
"To remain on the beach..........................	2 "
"To complete all that it is proposed to do............	4 "
"Total time from date................	10 days

"We are, very respectfully, your obedient servants,

"Alban C. Stimers,
"*Chief Engineer U. S. Navy.*

"R. W. McCleery,
"*Chief Engineer U. S. Navy.*

"Edward Faron,
"*Mechanical Engineer.*

"Rear-Admiral S. F. Dupont,
"*Commanding South Atlantic Blockading Squadron.*"

It is, however, proper to remark that over a month was consumed in repairing the damage to the "Montauk" created by this explosion.

The form of torpedo which was employed is uncertain; but it was evidently a small one, and exploded at a considerable distance below the floor of the ship, the depth of water at the point where the explosion took effect being nearly 7 fathoms.*

These disasters caused the Union officers to be more careful in their operations, and when entering channels under the enemy's control to institute searches more or less rigorous by dragging with grapnels, and sweeping the bottom with chains from small boats sent ahead under the protection of their guns.

So rapid was the progress of improvement in this mode of warfare, that, in their preparations to meet Admiral Dupont's attack upon Charleston, the rebels calculated more upon torpedoes as a means of defence, than upon the power and number of their batteries. General Beauregard, commanding the defences of Charleston, is asserted to have said that he "placed more reliance upon one torpedo, than upon five ten-inch columbiads."†

Refugees, deserters, and spies, all united in bearing testimony to the confidence of the rebels in their ability to destroy our iron-clad fleet by torpedoes alone, if it should venture within their lines of defence.

These reports and rumors, the disasters to the "Cairo" and "Montauk," and the great number of torpedoes everywhere found, caused the Navy Department, anxious for the success of the monitors, to apply to Mr. Ericsson for a design of a machine that would protect them from torpedoes, and at the same time enable them to free the channels of Charleston from the other obstructions known to exist, and believed to be a formidable barrier to their success.

---

* Admiral Dahlgren, in his report on the defences of Charleston (Sec. Navy's Report, 1864), states that the frame torpedo, Figs. 2 and 4, Plate IV., is probably the kind that was exploded under the "Montauk;" but, as these torpedoes were only used in connection with obstructions, and as the "Montauk" was a half mile below them at the time of the disaster, his conjecture is probably incorrect.

† Testimony of Captain M. M. Grey, rebel engineer in charge of submarine defences of Charleston. Rept. Sec. Navy, 1863, p. 286.

Mr. Ericsson accordingly prepared an apparatus which he believed would accomplish the object. It consisted of an immense torpedo, borne by a raft to be pushed ahead of the monitor, and exploded by coming into contact with any obstruction. (For description see p. 198.)

A great number of these machines were hastily built in New York, and immediately despatched to Charleston in charge of an officer who had experimented with them, and was acquainted with the mode of their application. They arrived off Charleston a few days previous to the attack of the 7th of April, and an attempt was made to attach the apparatus to the monitor "Weehawken." The novelty of the invention, a dread of its effects upon the vessels carrying it as well as upon friendly vessels in the event of collision, prevented its use, and the attack was finally delivered without it.

Admiral Dupont, than whom no braver man, more refined gentleman or truer patriot ever graced the profession of arms, while he had no excessive fear of torpedoes and never suffered them to interfere with his purposes, caused his iron-clads to be provided with "torpedo catchers" extemporized from spars, boarding nets, and grapnels rigged ahead of each vessel, hoping thus to explode the torpedoes, or prevent them from coming into contact with the vessel itself.

The attack of the iron-clads failed, as all the world knows, owing to the utter inadequacy of the means employed. Our vessels never penetrated the obstructions, and none suffered from the submarine defences of the enemy, although two of them the "New Ironsides" and "Weehawken" narrowly escaped their effects. The former was forced to anchor at the height of the battle, and swung immediately over an electric torpedo of enormous size, remaining in that position upwards of an hour. Captain Langden Cheves, a rebel artillery officer stationed in Fort Sumter, in a letter to a friend describing the attack, which was found on board the rebel iron-clad "Atlanta" captured soon after, thus refers to the circumstance:

"The "Ironsides" was for an hour directly over our big torpedo. Mr. ——, the operator, says that if he had had the placing of her, he could not have placed her better; but the confounded thing would not explode owing to some defect in the insulation of the wires."

A variety of testimony confirms this statement. The rebels for a time imputed treachery on the part of the operator, who was arrested and confined on this charge; but defective insulation was finally found to be the true cause of the failure.

Captain Grey, whose testimony has been before quoted, also asserts that he put down this torpedo a short time before Admiral Dupont's attack, and describes it as being a large boiler containing upwards of 2000 lbs. of powder, and anchored in the main ship channel abreast of Fort Wagner, where the wires were led, and the galvanic battery placed. Several others of this character were subsequently added to the submarine defences of Charleston, and the electric torpedo soon came into very general use, with disastrous results to our vessels.

In June, the iron-clad "Essex" discovered, in the Mississippi, near Port Hudson, a torpedo apparatus of great ingenuity, intended to be exploded by electricity, as well as by friction. The wires leading to it were severed, and the torpedo raised, placed upon the bank, and exploded by pulling upon one of the numerous wires which led from it, but which were entirely separate from the insulated electric wire, traced some distance into the woods.

By the exercise of great care and vigilance, our vessels managed to avoid the torpedoes of the enemy until the 22d of July, when the "Baron de Kalb," an iron-clad gunboat of great strength, was completely destroyed, by coming into contact with one in the Yazoo river. Admiral Porter, in his despatches to the Navy Department, conveys the best idea of this disaster, and we give such extracts as refer to the loss, as well as to the efforts made, under his direction, to recover the vessel and the valuable public property on board of her.

Under date 22d of July, 1863, after speaking of other operations, the Admiral continues:

" * * * Unfortunately, while the 'Baron de Kalb' was moving slowly along she run foul of a torpedo, which exploded and sunk her. There was no sign of anything of the kind to be seen. While she was going down, another exploded under her stern. The water is rising fast in the Yazoo, and we can do nothing more than get the guns out of her, and then get her into deep water, where she will be undisturbed until we are able to raise her.

"But for the blowing up of the 'Baron de Kalb,' it would have been a good move. We have generally obtained information of torpedoes from negroes and deserters, but heard nothing of this. Many of the crew were bruised by the concussion, which was severe, but no lives were lost. The officers and men lost everything. She went down in fifteen minutes. We must have her up again as soon as possible. We have much to contend with in these narrow rivers, and cannot guard against these hidden dangers while an enemy's flag floats. The usual lookout was kept for torpedoes, but this is some new invention of the enemy, which we will guard against hereafter. An attempt was made by the perpetrator, late Lieutenant Isaac N. Brown, to plant torpedoes once before, but the people of Yazoo City threatened to hang him if he did so. We felt sure they would not permit it on this occasion.

"While a rebel flag floats anywhere, the gunboats must follow it up. The officers and men risk their lives fearlessly on these occasions, and I hope the department will not take too seriously the accidents which happen to the vessels, when it is impossible to avoid them.

"I have the honor to be, very respectfully,

"Your obedient servant,

"David D. Porter,

"*Acting Rear-Admiral, Com'd'g Mississippi Squadron.*

"Hon. Gideon Welles,

"*Secretary of the Navy, Washington, D.C.*"

"U. S. MISSISSIPPI SQUADRON, FLAG-SHIP 'BLACK HAWK,'
"OFF VICKSBURG, *July* 22, 1863.

"SIR,—I had the honor to inform you of the blowing up of the 'Baron de Kalb' by a hidden torpedo, seventeen having been planted in the river, without wires attached to them. The water having risen two or three feet during the night, enabled all the vessels but the 'de Kalb,' to pass over them.

"I am not sure that we shall be able to raise the 'de Kalb,' as she sunk in twenty (20) feet of water, and we cannot yet ascertain the injuries, but every effort will be made. I ordered her guns, and every article that could be got, to be removed, and this duty was performed under the most difficult circumstances; every gun and carriage was saved undamaged; also everything else of value.

"Officers and men vied with each other in endeavoring to save the guns and stores; the work had all to be performed in fifteen to twenty feet of water, and the officers set the example in diving down to make fast to the gun-carriages; all the small arms were saved in the same way; also the paymaster's books and Government funds."

"MISSISSIPPI SQUADRON, FLAG-SHIP 'BLACK HAWK,'
"CAIRO, *August* 23, 1863.

"SIR,—In the last expedition I sent up the Yazoo to recover the 'Baron de Kalb,' it was ascertained that she was too much damaged to save her hull, two torpedoes having exploded under her, tearing her bow and stern all to pieces.

"Her guns and stores were saved (with the exception of her provisions), and part of her machinery taken off. The water was falling so rapidly that the gunboats were obliged to return precipitately from the river, to escape being kept up there the rest of the season.

"The iron, and all other portions of the hull, were removed to prevent it being of use to the enemy, in case he should return to those parts, which is not likely. I find that our visits to the Yazoo river cost the rebels more than I at first supposed.

"As the people of Yazoo City did not take the trouble to warn us of the existence of torpedoes after the enemy fled, which they had an opportunity of doing, three thousand bales of cotton were seized by General Herron, to pay for the gunboat that was lost through their treachery. The loss to the enemy in this expedition has been all the guns left on Yazoo river, eight hundred thousand dollars' worth of steamers, five hundred and fifty thousand dollars' worth of cotton, and as much more in other stores necessary for the maintenance of an army. The officers and men composing the naval part of this expedition have lost no reputation on account of the sinking of the 'de Kalb,' but have exhibited a perseverance and attention to duty worthy of the highest praise ; their labors in recovering their guns and stores will not be surpassed by any one on any other occasion.

"I have the honor to remain, very respectfully, your obedient servant,

"DAVID D. PORTER,

"*Acting Rear-Admiral, Com'd'g Miss. Squadron.*

"Hon. GIDEON WELLES,

"*Secretary of the Navy.*"

Commander Walke, commanding the "Baron de Kalb," at the time of her destruction, reports that the form of the torpedoes found in the immediate vicinity before and after the disaster, and which he, therefore, concludes were of a similar pattern to the one which destroyed his vessel, was that known to the rebels as "Singer's Torpedo." (See Fig. 2, Plate VI., and for description, p. 70.)

CHAPTER VII.

INJURY TO THE "BARNEY."—CAUSE OF FAILURE TO DESTROY HER.—ADOPTION OF THE TORPEDO SYSTEM BY THE UNITED STATES.—U. S. TORPEDOES IN ROANOKE RIVER.—LOSS OF THE "MAPLE LEAF."—RED RIVER EXPEDITION.—LOSS OF THE IRON-CLAD "EASTPORT."—GROWING IMPORTANCE OF THE SYSTEM.—PRECAUTIONS TAKEN BY ADMIRAL LEE IN ADVANCING UP JAMES RIVER.—LOSS OF THE "COMMODORE JONES," AND GREAT LOSS OF LIFE BY AN ELECTRIC TORPEDO.—CAPTURE OF OPERATORS AND BATTERIES.—RAISING ELECTRIC TORPEDOES.—EFFECT OF TORPEDOES.—GENERAL GRANT'S CAMPAIGN.

On the 8th of August, 1863, General Foster accompanied Captain Gansevoort, of the navy, in a reconnoissance of the enemy's position on the James river. They ascended the river to within a few miles of Drury's Bluff, in the gunboat "Com. Barney," accompanied by a few smaller vessels. On their return, while rapidly passing a point known as Cox's Wharf, an electric torpedo was exploded just astern of the "Barney," which careened the vessel violently, and threw an immense quantity of water on board, washing overboard twenty of her crew, several of whom were drowned. The vessel was for the time completely disabled, and was taken in tow by one of her consorts, and brought to a place of safety. The failure to destroy this vessel was owing, as the writer has since been informed by the operator of the battery on this occasion, to a defect in the battery itself, which failed to yield a sufficient current of electricity to explode the charge at the desired instant. This liability to failure of the Bunsen battery rendered it oftentimes uncertain; but the substitution of magneto-electric exploders made such accidents impossible.

Up to this period of the war, our naval forces were continually on the aggressive, and the defensive torpedo system had not been found necessary to our plans, or to the maintenance of our positions. Public despatches and the press were accustomed to treat of the subject with apparent detestation. Such expressions as "infernal machinations of the enemy;" "assassination in its worst form;" "unchristian mode of warfare," were familiar terms, employed to characterize the system.

The following correspondence shows, however, that with a change in our circumstances, high official sanction was not wanting to authorize the usage. It also serves as documentary evidence of the effect that the introduction of ships practically invulnerable to shot and shell has had upon naval warfare; and that the same reasons which induced the rebels to inaugurate the system of torpedo defence, also led the United States to its employment.

"NAVY DEPARTMENT, *September* 17, 1863.

"SIR,—I have the honor to present for your consideration a subject of great importance, connected with the maintaining possession of the sounds of North Carolina.

"Information received from time to time places it beyond doubt that the rebels are constructing, and have nearly completed, at Edwards' Ferry, near Weldon, on the Roanoke river, a ram and an iron-clad floating battery. It is represented that these vessels will be completed in the course of four or six weeks. It is further represented that an attack by land and water on Plymouth is contemplated.

"Our force of wooden vessels in the sounds, necessarily of light draught and lightly armed, will by no means be adequate to contend against the rebel ram and battery, should they succeed in getting down the Roanoke; and, in that event, our possession of the sounds would be jeoparded.

"It is impracticable for our vessels to ascend the Roanoke to any great distance, in consequence of the shallowness of the water, their exposed situation from the fire of sharpshooters, and the earthworks represented to be located at different points, particularly at Rainbow Bluff.

"Were our iron-clads, now completed, available for service in the sounds, they could not be sent there, as they draw too much water to cross the Bulkhead at Hatteras. Our light-draught ones will not be completed for some time to come.

"In view of all these facts, I deem it proper to suggest the importance of an effort on the part of the army to surprise and destroy the rebel ram and battery referred to, *or of obstructing the river by torpedoes* and piles or otherwise, so as to prevent their descent. Permit me to urge some measure of this sort. This department will be happy to co-operate, so far as it may be able, in adopting such steps as may seem practicable and adequate to secure us against threatening disaster.

"I am, very respectfully, etc.,

"GIDEON WELLES,
"*Secretary of the Navy.*

"Hon. E. M. STANTON,
"*Secretary of War.*"

"WAR DEPARTMENT,
"WASHINGTON CITY, *September* 19, 1863.

"SIR,—I have the honor to acknowledge the receipt of your letter of the 17th instant, in relation to the contemplated attempt of the rebels to take possession of the sounds of North Carolina, and to inform you that a copy of the same has been referred to Major-General Foster, with directions to take such action as may, in his judgment, be best suited to meet the emergency thus presented.

"Very respectfully, Sir, your obedient servant,

"EDWIN M. STANTON,
"*Secretary of War.*

"Hon. GIDEON WELLES,
"*Secretary of the Navy, Washington, D. C.*"

As a result of this correspondence, torpedoes were placed by the United States authorities at the mouth of the Roanoke river, where they remained until the close of the war. Their presence there became known to the enemy, and upon one occasion they succeeded in capturing the party detailed to explode them, and immediately attacked, with success, our wooden vessels stationed below, presenting the novel spectacle of eight powerfully armed and gallantly fought gunboats held at bay, and practically defeated, by one exceedingly crude specimen of a modern war ship.*

Except from the daring attacks upon our fleets by torpedo boats, no further casualties occurred from rebel torpedoes until the 1st of April, 1864, when the army transport "Maple Leaf" was totally destroyed by a floating torpedo in the St. John's river, Florida.

This immunity was due, partly to the great care and watchfulness of our officers, but mainly to the inactivity of our squadrons, which were sufficiently employed in guarding places already in our possession, and in blockading such of the enemy's ports as still remained to them.

The unfortunate Red River expedition was particularly disastrous to the naval force which accompanied the army. But for the energy, courage, and devotion of Admiral Porter, none of that flotilla would have been saved. By his orders and personal supervision of the advance, the vessels escaped the torpedoes which were laid in their path, and it was not until the disasters to the army compelled their return with less care and greater speed, that the "Eastport," a heavily armed and powerful iron-clad, coming into contact with a small floating torpedo, was so shattered by its explosion that she sunk, a harmless wreck, to the bottom of the river.

The story of the efforts to raise and save this vessel forms one of the most interesting episodes of the war, illustrative of the courage and perseverance of men when animated by the presence and personal energy of so able a commander as then wielded the naval arm on the Western waters.†

---

*One of the torpedoes, designed and constructed in Newbern for the defence of Roanoke river, was exploded by careless handling in the R. R. depot at that place, causing great havoc and destruction. They were formed from two casks, one placed inside the other, and were to be exploded by wires attached to friction primers—the wires being drawn by a concealed operator. Levers were also added, which, being touched by a vessel, would also explode them. Chloride of calcium was introduced between the barrels to absorb moisture.

† See report of Vice-Admiral Porter, in report of Secretary of the Navy, 1865, p. 524.

Upon the 4th of May following a joint expedition of the army and navy, under the command respectively of General Butler and Admiral Lee, proceeded up James river for the purpose of seizing City Point and Bermuda Hundred, and thence co-operating with the grand army under General Grant against Richmond.

The importance of the torpedo system, and the amount of respect which it then commanded from our naval officers, are best shown by the orders which Admiral Lee saw fit to communicate to his officers preparatory to entering into channels affording every opportunity for its practice.

After enumerating the vessels of the flotilla, the following instructions appear:

"All of these vessels will be fully prepared to drag for torpedoes themselves and with their boats, and to send boats to fire-rafts with grapnels, with which to tow the rafts clear of the vessel and on shore.

"Upon arriving at Harrison's bar, the 'General Putnam' and 'Stepping Stones' will go ahead and drag the bar carefully for torpedoes, taking care to keep one or two hundred yards apart, so that they do not explode the torpedoes under each other. As soon as a torpedo is discovered, the vessel making the discovery will at once signify it by hoisting the usual pennant, when every precaution will be taken by dragging with the boats and following slowly. After leaving Harrison's bar, the 'Stepping Stones,' 'General Putnam,' 'Delaware,' and 'Shawsheen' will together search the waters between that point and one mile above Bermuda Hundred for torpedoes—the 'Delaware' on the port side of the channel, the 'Shawsheen' on the starboard side, the 'General Putnam' and 'Stepping Stones' in mid-channel, in bow and quarter line as near as practicable. The iron-clads will not go up to their positions until this is done. The tugs attached to the iron-clads will act as tenders to them, under the squadron orders and instructions in regard to torpedo boats, etc. The 'Osceola' and 'Mackinaw' will take up positions from one-fourth to half a mile ahead of the iron-clads, in waters which they must previously drag for topedoes. The 'Commodore Jones' and 'Shokokon will take up a position off the mouth of Appomattox river, between City Point and Bermuda Hundred. The 'Eutaw,' 'Hunchback,' 'Commodore Morris' will take position below City Point to protect and cover the landing of troops, and be ready to render such assistance as may be necessary. The 'General Putnam' and 'Stepping Stones' will cover the boats of the 'Osceola' and 'Mackinaw' while dragging the river for torpedoes above Bermuda Hundred, which will be done as soon as those vessels have taken their position. The 'Delaware' and 'Shawsheen' will cover the boats of the 'Commodore Jones' and 'Shokokon,' which will, as soon as they have taken their position, proceed to drag the mouth of the Appomattox and examine the banks of that river for torpedoes."

A company of soldiers was applied for to scour the banks of the river for galvanic batteries and torpedo operators, under the protection of the guns of the advanced vessels; but so incredulous was General Butler as to the existence or effect of torpedoes that he denied the application and was inclined to ridicule the idea of taking any precautions against them. A detachment of sailors was therefore specially organized for this service, and after the landing of the army at Bermuda Hundred, it was busily engaged in the duty, confining its search, however, to the left bank of the river, which was held by the enemy, and upon which it was supposed the torpedo operators and their batteries would be concealed.

Notwithstanding the zeal and carefulness with which these duties were performed, on the 6th of May the "Commodore Jones" a large and heavily armed gunboat, was literally blown to fragments by an electric torpedo containing 2,000 lbs. of powder, placed by the rebels at a sharp bend of the river, called Deep Bottom. The channel there is from five to seven fathoms deep and about one hundred yards wide. (The accompanying sketch shows a plan of the locality, the position of the "Commodore Jones," the galvanic batteries and the fleet.)

FIG. 6.

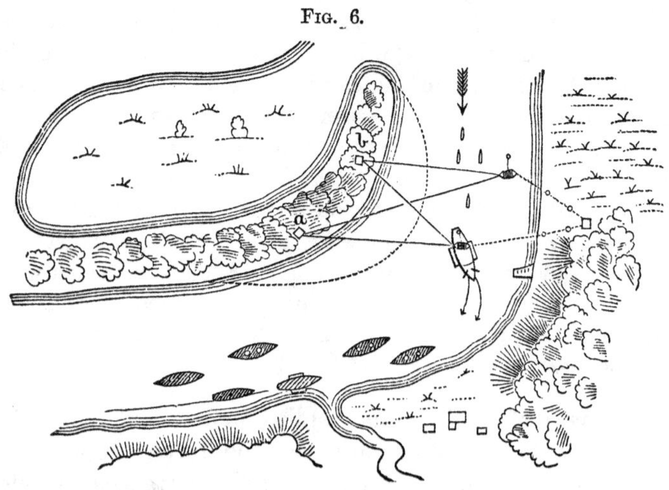

The details of this disaster are particularly interesting in the history of submarine warfare, it being the only instance where the large electric torpedoes were successfully employed; it also illustrates the vast power and annihilating effects of the explosion of such an immense quantity of gunpowder beneath a ship, and the uncertainty of dragging, and other expedients to discover or break the conducting wires when they are carefully laid.

The Confederates, duly advised by our slow and cautious advance, of the measures taken to render their devices unavailing, during the night previous to the arrival of our fleet at Deep Bottom, shifted the battery and wires to the right bank of the river, choosing for their location a narrow point covered with brush and undergrowth, and separated by overflow from the position of our army on that side of the stream.

At noon most of the fleet had reached Deep Bottom, and several had anchored to take coal, while the advance pushed slowly ahead following the shore detachment, searching the left bank. A negro here joined the squadron with the intelligence that torpedoes were placed in the deep water at the bend of the river. A signal was at once made to the advance to fall back and anchor, with the idea of instituting a more rigorous search in the place indicated by our colored ally.

The "Jones" was at this moment considerably in advance, and with heavy drags out astern, was slowly moving ahead. The small boats of the fleet were ahead of and around her, also engaged in dragging and sweeping the channel. The negro displayed great solicitude for this vessel, and repeatedly declared that she was very near the torpedoes. In obedience to the signal, the ill-fated craft commenced backing her engines, but had hardly gathered sternway, when suddenly, and without any apparent cause, she appeared to be lifted bodily, her wheels rapidly revolving in mid-air; persons declared they could see the green sedge of the banks beneath her keel. Then through her shot to a great height an immense fountain of foaming water, followed by a denser column thick with mud. She absolutely crumbled to pieces—dissolved as it were in mid-air, enveloped by the falling spray, mud, water, and smoke. When the turbulence excited by the explosion subsided, not a vestige of the huge hull remained in sight, except small fragments of her frame which came shooting to the surface.

Boats were instantly on the spot, and succeeded in rescuing the very few survivors of the crew, most of them terribly injured. The exact loss of life was never accurately ascertained, but sufficient data were made up from the survivors to put her loss in killed at forty officers and men. The wounded swelled the list of casualties to more than three-fourths of her complement. Nearly all on board at the time (quite a number being in the boats) were killed or wounded. One curious escape, however, is worthy of note. The engineer, who, deep in the body of the ship, was working the "starting bar" of the engine, backing it by hand, escaped without other injury than severe concussion; his only recollection was a chaotic end to his manipulations, and being dragged from the water into a boat.

Hardly had the spectators realized this sudden and overwhelming disaster to the "Jones" when three men were observed running towards the end of the point of land. One was instantly shot dead as he ran, the others disappeared amongst the bushes. A party landed at once, and pursued them to a pit, into which were led the conducting wires of another torpedo, where they were captured.

One was a master, and the other a private, in the "Confederate Naval Submarine Battery Service," and upon their persons were found articles of enlistment, showing the secret nature of their service, and the rules for its government.

Actuated by fear of personal consequences from their capture while engaged in such duty, these men pointed out the places where other torpedoes were located, so that eleven of these hidden monsters were discovered and raised in the course of the two following days. In each instance the electric batteries were first seized by the shore parties. These batteries invariably consisted of from nine to eighteen elements of Bunsen's battery, and the wires were usually so arranged, that the same torpedo could be fired from two points (*a*, *b*), one at the battery itself, and the other at some distance from it; the circuit being completed at the distant point by dipping the conducting wire into cups of mercury, connected by insulated wire with the battery. Two wires to each torpedo were used to complete the circuit; the submerged parts were insulated by two thicknesses of gutta-percha, and covered with spun yarn; they were also heavily weighted by sections of chain, lashed to them. Having removed the torpedoes from their path, the flotilla advanced to Chaffin's Bluff, when the disaster at Drury's Bluff caused the army to fall back to Bermuda Hundred, and the fleet to drop down to Dutch Gap, where they took position on the right flank of the army, and prepared to remain.

During the months of May and June great numbers of torpedoes were sent down upon the ships, with the current, and occasionally they were planted in the channel between Dutch Gap and City Point. The vessels were provided with "torpedo catchers," the channel was repeatedly searched, and, by great care, casualties were avoided.

To secure the position at Dutch Gap, obstructions to the enemy's approach were placed in "Trent's Reach," just above the fleet, and in connection with sunken vessels, booms and net work, large electric torpedoes were placed in the channel. An electrician was regularly attached to the squadron, specially charged with the care of the electric batteries. Most of the torpedoes previously taken from the rebels were here brought into our service, and thus, by the action of its officers, the U. S. Government was fully committed to this system of warfare.

In the mean time the army, under Gen. Grant, was slowly pushing its way towards its final resting-place on the James, and the Government was supplying that army by transports, sending them up the various rivers which intersected its line of march. These streams were obstructed by torpedoes, and the naval force on the Potomac was directed to clear the way for the transports. The following despatch accounts for the delay in this important service, and illustrates the effect which the torpedo system has upon the larger operations of war.

"UNITED STATES STEAMER 'ELLA,'
"NAVY YARD, WASHINGTON, *May* 26, 1864.

"SIR,—I have the honor to report to the department that the 'Yankee,' 'Fuchsia,' and 'Bell,' reached Fredericksburg on the 19th instant, since which time the Rappahannock river has been open for transports from its mouth.

"As the gunboats were compelled to ascend the river, by my instructions, with their torpedo fenders down, and to send flanking parties ashore, and boats ahead (to sweep for torpedoes) in the narrow and shallow parts of it, their progress was necessarily slow, but they had the satisfaction of reaching Fredericksburg without the loss of a man; the only injury sustained being the breaking of five buckets of the 'Yankee's' starboard wheel, by striking a rock.

"So impressed were the rebels with our operations on the 12th and 13th instant, as detailed in my report of the 16th inst. (No. 89), that, according to the statement of refugees, they immediately thereafter, to prevent their falling into our hands, either exploded or removed all the torpedoes which they had placed in the river above Bohler's Rocks.

"I am, Sir, very respectfully,

"Your obedient servant,

"FOXHALL A. PARKER,

"*Commander, Commanding Potomac Flotilla.*

"Hon. GIDEON WELLES,

"*Secretary of the Navy.*"

In all quarters where naval operations were projected, torpedoes were now recognized as not the least of the difficulties to be overcome.

In a despatch dated March 25th, 1864, Admiral Farragut, then before Mobile, thus refers to them :

"I am placing heavy iron cutters on the bows of my vessels, and shall also have torpedoes to place me on an equality with my enemy, if he comes outside. No doubt he will have the advantage of me inside, as they are planting them every day ; we can see them distinctly when at work.

"Torpedoes are not so agreeable when used on both sides ; therefore I have reluctantly brought myself to it,

"I have always deemed it unworthy of a chivalrous nation, but it does not do to give your enemy such a decided superiority over you.

"Very respectfully, your obedient servant,

"D. G. FARRAGUT,

"*Rear-Admiral Commanding W. G. B. Squadron.*

"Hon. GIDEON WELLES,

"*Secretary of the Navy, Washington, D. C.*"

CHAPTER VIII.

LOSS OF THE MONITOR "TECUMSEH."—REPORTS OF ADMIRAL FARRAGUT, CAPTAINS DRAYTON AND ALDEN.—THE "BROOKLYN" STOPPED IN BATTLE BY TORPEDOES.—LOSS OF THE "OTSEGO" AND "BAZELEY."—LOSS OF MONITOR "PATAPSCO."—NAVAL OPERATIONS AGAINST FORT FISHER AND WILMINGTON.—IMPRACTICABILITY OF "RUNNING THE BATTERIES."—ADMIRAL PORTER'S OPINIONS.—GENERAL BUTLER'S "POWDER BOAT."—TORPEDOES IN CAPE FEAR RIVER—LOSS OF THE "HARVEST MOON."—NAVAL PREPARATIONS IN MOBILE BAY.—LOSSES OF THE MONITORS "MILWAUKIE" AND "OSAGE," GUNBOATS "RODOLPH," "SCIOTA," "IDA," AND "ALTHEA."—SUMMARY OF LOSSES FROM DEFENSIVE TORPEDOES.

Following the loss of the "Commodore Jones," the next and perhaps the most terribly destructive casualty from torpedoes during the war, occurred in the attack upon the defences of Mobile Bay, by the fleet under Admiral Farragut. It resulted in the total destruction of the monitor "Tecumseh," Captain Craven, who, with seventy of his officers and crew, went down in that ill-fated vessel.

We select from the very full reports of that engagement, such extracts as refer to this disaster, or illustrate the influence of the torpedo system upon warlike enterprises.

Admiral Farragut, who, with the prejudices of a sailor, had often denounced iron-clads and torpedoes in a breath, yielded, as we have seen, to the necessities of the case, and prepared to use the latter if occasion offered; but he so far clung to his opinions as to prefer leading the attack in a wooden vessel.

The following extract is from his report of the battle:

"It was only at the urgent request of the captains and commanding officers that I yielded to the 'Brooklyn's' being the leading ship of the line, as she had four chase-guns and an ingenious arrangement for picking up torpedoes. * * * The 'Tecumseh' fired the first shot, and immediately the action became general.

"It was soon apparent there was some difficulty ahead. The 'Brooklyn,' for some cause which I did not then clearly understand, but which has since been explained by Captain Alden in his report, arrested the advance of the whole fleet, while, at the same time, the guns of the fort were playing with great effect upon that vessel and the 'Hartford.' A moment after I saw the 'Tecumseh,' struck by a torpedo, disappear almost instantaneously beneath the waves, carrying with her her gallant commander, and nearly all her crew! I determined at once, as I had originally intended, to take the lead; and after ordering the 'Metacomet' to send a boat to save, if possible, any of the perishing crew, I dashed ahead with the 'Hartford,' and the ships followed on, their officers believing that they were going to a noble death with their commander-in-chief.

"I steamed through between the buoys, where the torpedoes were supposed to have been sunk. These buoys had been previously examined by my flag-lieutenant, J. C. Watson, in several nightly reconnoissances. Though he had not been able to discover the sunken torpedoes, yet we had been assured by refugees, deserters, and others, of their existence; but, believing that, from their having been some time in the water, they were probably innocuous, I determined to take the chance of their explosion." * * * *

Fleet-Captain Percival Drayton, commanding the flagship "Hartford," reports:

"About thirty-five minutes past seven, I heard the cry that a monitor was sinking, and looking on the starboard bow, saw the turret of the 'Tecumseh' just disappearing under the water, *where an instant before* I had seen this noble vessel pushing on gallantly in a straight line to attack the enemy's ram 'Tennessee,' which had apparently moved out to give her an opportunity."

Captain Alden, commanding the "Brooklyn," whose movements were stated by the Admiral to have stopped the progress of the fleet, thus explains that point, from which it will be seen that the "Brooklyn" was stopped and backed after the fate of the "Tecumseh" had demonstrated the presence of torpedoes in the channel, and the danger to be apprehended from them, and not before, as would appear from the report of the Admiral:

"The starboard battery was opened on the fort as soon as the guns could be brought to bear. Our progress up the channel was slow, owing to our carrying, as directed, low steam, and the very deliberate movements of our iron-clads which occupied the channel close ahead of us. When we had arrived abreast of the fort, by a rapid and timely fire of grape their several batteries were almost entirely silenced.

"At this juncture I observed the ill-fated 'Tecumseh,' which was then about three hundred yards ahead of us, and on our starboard bow, careen violently over, and sink almost instantaneously. Sunk by a torpedo! Assassination in its worst form! A glorious though terrible end for our noble friends, the intrepid pioneers of that death-strewed path! Immortal fame is theirs! Peace to their manes! We were now somewhat inside of the fort, when shoal water was reported, and at the same time, as the smoke cleared up a little, a row of suspicious looking buoys was discovered directly under our bows. While we were in the act of backing to clear them, our gallant Admiral passed us and took the lead. Getting headway again as soon as possible, we pushed up the channel at full speed in his wake, when the rebel ram was discovered making for the flag-ship. At about 9 A. M. the 'Tennessee' was discovered standing for the fleet, and we, in company with the flag-ship and several other vessels, made toward him, firing solid shot from our bow-chasers. When within a short distance the 'Chickasaw' crossed our bows and prevented our ramming him. As soon as the ram was clear of the last-named vessel he made directly at us; put our helm a-port and made at him with full speed, but seeing our torpedo-catcher hanging under the bows, and thinking it was a real torpedo (as an officer belonging to her has since told me), he put his helm hard up and avoided us, giving some heavy shots in passing."

The following "General Order," promulgated through the fleet, shows the estimate placed upon the torpedo defences of Mobile by the Admiral and his followers:

"UNITED STATES FLAG-SHIP 'HARTFORD,'
"MOBILE BAY, *August* 6, 1864.

"(General Order No. 12.)

"The Admiral returns thanks to the officers and crews of the vessels of the fleet for their gallant conduct during the fight of yesterday.

"It has never been his good fortune to see men do their duty with more courage and cheerfulness; for, although they knew that the enemy was prepared with all devilish means for our destruction, and though they witnessed the almost instantaneous annihilation of our gallant companions in the 'Tecumseh' by a torpedo, and the slaughter of their friends, messmates, and gun-mates on our decks, still there were no evidences of hesitation in following their commander-in-chief through the line of torpedoes and obstructions, of which we knew nothing, except from the exaggerations of the enemy, who had given out 'that we should all be blown up as certainly as we attempted to enter.'

"For this noble and implicit confidence in their leader he heartily thanks them.

"D. G. FARRAGUT,
"*Rear Admiral, Commanding W. G. B. Squadron.*"

Two officers only were saved from the "Tecumseh." Their report of the circumstances attending the disaster is exceedingly meagre, but it completes the official story of her loss:

"*Joint Report of Acting Masters C. F. Langley and G. Cottrell.*

"UNITED STATES SHIP 'POTOMAC,'
"PENSACOLA, *August* 6, 1864.

"SIR,—Believing that we are the only surviving officers of the United States monitor "Tecumseh," we feel it our duty to report the circumstances attending her loss, and of the safety of a boat's crew.

"When nearly abreast of Fort Morgan, and about one hundred and fifty yards from the beach, a row of buoys were discovered stretching from the shore, a distance from one to two hundred yards. It being reported to Captain Craven, he immediately gave the vessel full speed, and attempted to pass between two of them. When in their range a torpedo was exploded directly under the turret, blowing a large hole through the bottom of the vessel, through which the water rushed in with great rapidity.

"Finding that the vessel was sinking, the order was given to leave our quarters, and from that moment every one used the utmost exertions to clear himself from the wreck.

"After being carried down by the vessel several times, we were picked up in a drowning condition by one of our boats." * * *

Captain Craven was not ignorant of the use and effect of torpedoes. The "Tecumseh," under his command, had been in the advance up the James river, and he had witnessed but a few yards distant the utter annihilation of the "Commodore Jones." The writer had then the pleasure of his intimate personal acquaintance, and believes that he but expresses the opinion of all his brother officers in saying that he was a perfect naval commander—cool and courageous, resolute and active in every enterprise—learned in his profession, gentlemanly in word and thought, and enthusiastic for the cause in which he was fighting.

Previous to his detachment from the James river squadron and orders to the Gulf, he had immediate charge of the obstructions and torpedoes at Dutch Gap. He deemed the system of great importance in the art of war, and anticipated the gravest results from its use. Though devoid of personal fear, he dreaded the effect of submarine explosions upon iron-clads and monitors particularly, whose want of buoyancy would cause them to sink too rapidly to enable their occupants to escape. These ideas he frequently expressed. How little influence such feelings had upon his conduct is shown by the gallant manner in which he met his death.*

* I cannot refrain from adding to this history of torpedo warfare that anecdote of Craven, which illuminates the story of this catastrophe :

He was inside the turret when the ship was struck by the torpedo. Of course it is impossible to conceive the scene within that pent-up iron-cased craft. Men are selfish on such occasions as a rule, and then it was "save himself who can!" Capt. Craven and the pilot both rushed to the ladder leading to the top of the turret, whence only possible safety could be found. Both could not go, and Craven drew aside and, pointing up, said : "*After you,*

After the surrender of the forts guarding the harbor, great numbers of torpedoes of the forms shown in Pl. VI., Figs. 1 and 2, were removed from the various channels and anchorages, and it was supposed that it was one of these cheap contrivances which destroyed the "Tecumseh." The writer has been informed, however, by an officer specially employed in the rebel torpedo service, that it was a large electric torpedo fired from Fort Gaines.

In removing the torpedoes, five men were killed and eleven seriously wounded by the explosion of one carelessly handled.

On the 9th of December following, a small fleet of wooden vessels attempted to ascend the Roanoke river, N. C., to a point called Rainbow Bluff. Fully warned of the fact that the river was at many places obstructed with torpedoes, the vessels proceeded with great caution. Every expedient was resorted to by which their presence could be detected or their explosion be rendered harmless. Nevertheless, the "Otsego," a large "double-ender," encountered a buoyant torpedo, and was totally destroyed by its explosion. Several of her crew were killed; but as the water was shallow, and the accompanying vessels free to assist their comrades, most of them were rescued.

A small gunboat, named the "Bazeley," proceeded promptly to the assistance of the "Otsego;" but as she was in the act of running alongside, a torpedo exploded beneath her, and blew her to fragments. So crippled was the force by the loss of these vessels that the expedition was abandoned.

These losses to our fleets were speedily followed by a very terrible disaster to the monitor "Patapsco," Lieut.-Commander Quackenbush, in Charleston outer harbor, on the night of the 15th of January, 1865.

The vessel on this occasion was performing picket duty between Forts Sumter and Moultrie when she struck a floating or barrel torpedo, and instantly sunk in five and one-

---

Sir!" The pilot dashed up the ladder and was saved, while Craven saw the last of daylight through that narrow aperture, and went to his death crowned with an act of as true heroism as ever lit up the dark history of war. The story is related by the pilot.

half fathoms of water. Nearly every soul below, to the number of sixty-two officers and men, went down in her.

Admiral Dahlgren gives a long and circumstantial account of this catastrophe, from which the following extracts are taken:

"When near Sumter, Lieutenant-Commander Quackenbush steamed down once more, and for the last time. While approaching the 'Lehigh' buoy there was a shock—a sound of explosion—a cloud of smoke on the port side, and in less than half a minute the 'Patapsco's' deck was under the surface.

"Lieutenant-Commander Quackenbush and his first lieutenant were standing on the top of the turret looking to the course of the vessel, for she had grounded once already on the shoal near the 'Lehigh' buoy, when standing down the first time. They saw and heard only what is stated above.

"The captain gave the order to start the pumps and lower the boats, but scarcely a whole minute was allowed for the least effort.

"Five officers and thirty-eight men were saved; sixty-two officers and men are missing. The survivors were those who happened to be on deck, and two men from the windlass-room; three from the berth-deck; one from the turret-chamber; and nearly all those who were in the fire-room. Their names are annexed.

"From such accounts as I can gather in so short a time as has elapsed, it would seem that the explosion occurred on the port side, under the ward-room, blowing it up, so as to drive up the table and three officers who were sitting about it. The spar-deck was not blown through, but the look-out on the port side, and some ten feet from the edge of the deck, was thrown up suddenly, and fell back with such force as to be nearly senseless. His rifle exploded, and he was aware that the ball passed near him.

"A man in the windlass-room saw a flash and heard a sound like that of a shell near him. The lamp was extinguished; he heard the water coming in, and escaped up the hatch on deck.

"It appears, also, that there was no disrupture of the vessel at the berth-deck, nor further aft; that no water came in there, save at the hatches, as the 'Patapsco' settled in the sea; and that her bow went down first, throwing the stern high up for an instant, so that a man standing there had to grasp at something to keep upright.

"It is believed that the berth-deck ladder was dislodged by the shock, and in the panic could not be replaced; hence no men there were saved, except those who rushed aft into the fire-room.

"The 'Lehigh' had got under way when the 'Patapsco' passed, and followed her movements in drifting and steaming, but did not go so far up, and retained her position assigned as a support.

"She anchored near the 'Lehigh' buoy about a quarter of eight o'clock, and some twenty or twenty-five minutes later heard an unusual, but not very loud report; saw a cloud of smoke; lost sight of the 'Patapsco,' which previously had been dimly visible through the obscurity of the night. Then heard men's voices, as if from the water, and fearing something wrong, sent her boats to the 'Patapsco,' and weighed anchor. The disaster soon became known.

"The top of the 'Patapsco's' smoke-pipe is seen above the water, but as yet there has not been leisure to determine the precise position relatively to other objects. It is stated at six to eight hundred yards from Sumter, and below it.

"The 'Patapsco' had her torpedo fenders and netting stretched around her. Three boats with drags had preceded her, searching to some depth the water they had passed over, while steam-tugs and several boats were in different positions on the bow, beam, and quarter."

The greatest care that human foresight could exercise was used to prevent the catastrophe. Torpedoes had never before been found in that precise locality, but our officers had learned to expect them at any point accessible to the enemy. Subsequent investigation showed that the rebels having ascertained the custom of our vessels to patrol the waters between Sumter and Moultrie under cover of darkness, had placed during the night previous to this disaster sixteen barrel torpedoes about the "Lehigh" buoy, one of which caused this serious disaster.

The "Patapsco," with her ghastly cargo, the battle-scarred veteran of many a fight, in which her armor successfully resisted the power of shot and shell to destroy her, still buried in the shifting sands of Charleston bar, bears terrible testimony to the vast power of this new engine of war.

Closely following this catastrophe came the naval operations against Wilmington. The channels of approach to the city, from Forts Fisher and Caswell up to the wharves of the city, were carefully guarded by torpedoes. Any attempt to force the passage by the forts would have been utterly useless, and must have proved disastrous to the vessels attempting it. So narrow and tortuous is the channel commanded by Fort Fisher, that, at any time, it is difficult for the lightest-draft vessels; and had the leading vessel of an attacking fleet been destroyed or sunk, she would have constituted an impassable barrier to the advance of the others. After the fort had been reduced, and the torpedoes had been removed, and after the channel had been sounded and carefully buoyed, nearly all the gunboats of lightest draft got badly aground in entering the river, and remained so during a whole tide. Admiral Porter says in his report:

> "We were 48 hours getting gunboats of lightest batteries over the first bar, and they had to anchor under the guns of the heaviest fort. Three days were consumed in getting the gunboats over the Rips, commanded by twenty 10-inch guns, and not a gunboat would have been left, had they attempted to run the batteries."

His intimate knowledge of the locality, and the facilities afforded by the nature of the channels for the advantageous use of torpedoes, caused the Admiral to foresee the impracticability of such an attempt, although "running batteries" had become such a popular idea with our people. The events connected with the capture of Fort Fisher form one of the most glorious pages of our naval history. The result fully vindicated the judgment of Admiral Porter, and still further established his reputation as the ablest naval commander of the age.

But one circumstance of the attack needs mention here—the explosion of the powder-boat, by which it was intended to demolish the fort or paralyze the garrison previous to an assault.

This idea, conceived in the fertile brain of General Butler, and suggested by him to Admiral Porter with great enthusiasm and confidence, was carried out by the latter with his usual energy, thereby showing his readiness to try any experiment which gave a promise of results, although he had little faith in its fulfilling the General's sanguine expectations.

An old steamer, laden with 180 tons of gunpowder, fuzed in various parts of its mass, so as to be ignited at the same instant, was taken by bold and experienced officers within a short distance of the fort, where it was exploded without injury to any one. To this failure of his scheme to insure an easy victory has been attributed the premature decision of the General that Fort Fisher was impracticable to assault, and his hasty withdrawal from the vicinity, leaving the work to the Admiral and his more resolute coadjutor, General Terry, who promptly appeared on the scene and performed his part of the plan, which, despite General Butler's defection, the Admiral had never for a moment abandoned.

The torpedoes found in Cape Fear river were of two kinds—the large electric torpedoes being part of the permanent defences, and the "barrel torpedoes" which were used as occasion required. In huge mounds of earth connected with Forts Fisher, Caswell, and Anderson were arranged, with much system, the batteries by which the torpedoes were to be exploded. Many of these were the usual arrangement of Bunsen; but here, for the first time during the war, was found the magneto-electric battery, referred to before as Wheatstone's Magnetic "Exploder." (Plate XV., Figs. 1, 2, and 3.)

Fort Anderson, situated half way between Fort Fisher and Wilmington, being in due time reduced, and the torpedoes in front of it removed, or rendered harmless by the seizure of the electric machines employed to explode them, the fleet anchored just below the forts and obstructions which constituted the last defences of Wilmington.

On the night of the 20th of February great numbers of barrel torpedoes, fitted with the chemical fuze before described (Plate V., Fig. 1), were sent down upon the fleet, necessarily crowded together in the narrow channel. Admiral Porter estimates the number at two hundred. Warned by the picket boats scouting in advance, the boats of the squadron were speedily manned, and for several hours were busily engaged in guiding these machines clear of the vessels, and sinking them by musketry. A cutter from the "Shawmut" was blown to pieces in this dangerous duty, and four were killed and wounded. One effected a lodgment under the paddle-box of the "Osceola," where it exploded, tearing the wood-work into fragments.

The next morning two large fish-nets were spread across the river to catch these troublesome visitors.

The next casualty referred to is that to the "Harvest Moon;" the circumstances attending the destruction of this vessel are best related by Admiral Dahlgren himself, whose report is here inserted.

Report of Rear-Admiral John A. Dahlgren.

"FLAG-STEAMER 'NIPSIC,'
"GEORGETOWN ROADS, *March* 1, 1865.

"SIR,—My latest despatches, Numbers 82 and 83, had been closed, and not hearing anything of General Sherman at this place, I was on my way to Charleston, but was interrupted for the time by the loss of my flag-ship, which was sunk by the explosion of a torpedo. This took place at 7.45 A. M. to-day, and the best information I now have is from my own personal observation. What others may have noticed will be elicited by the court of inquiry which I shall order.

"The "Harvest Moon" had been lying near Georgetown until yesterday afternoon, when I dropped down to Battery White, two or three miles below, intending to look at the work and leave the next day. Accordingly, this morning early the "Harvest Moon" weighed anchor and steamed down the bay. She had not proceeded far when the explosion took place. It was nearly eight o'clock, and I was waiting breakfast in the cabin, when instantly a loud noise and shock occurred, and the bulkhead separating the cabin from the ward-room was shattered and driven in towards me, and a variety of articles lying about me were dispersed in different directions. My first impression was that the boiler had burst, as a report had been made by the engineer the evening before that it needed repair badly. The smell of gunpowder quickly followed, and gave the idea that the magazine had exploded. There was naturally some little confusion, for it was evident that the vessel was sinking, and she was not long in reaching the bottom. As the whole incident was the work of a moment, very little more can be said than just related. But one life was lost, owing to the singularly fortunate fact that the action of the torpedo occurred in the open space between the gangways and between the ladder to the upper deck and the ward-room, which is an open passage-way occupied by no one, and where few linger save for a moment. Had it occurred further aft or forward, the consequences would have been fatal to many. A large breach is said to have been made in the deck just between the main hatch and the ward-room bulkhead. It had been reported to me that the channel had been swept, but so much has been said in ridicule of torpedoes that very little precautions are deemed necessary, and, if resorted to, are probably taken with less care than if due weight were attached to the existence of these mischievous things.

"I have the honor to be, very respectfully,

"Your obedient servant,

"J. A. Dahlgren,

"*Rear-Admiral, Com'd'g S. A. B. Squadron.*

"Hon. Gideon Welles,

"*Secretary of the Navy.*"

The war was now drawing to a close, but a terrible record of the efficiency of the torpedo system of defence was to be added to its history by the events in Mobile Bay, where our fleet was pushing forward to add its weight to the crushing forces everywhere brought to bear upon the yielding Confederacy.

Admiral Thatcher, who had relieved Admiral Farragut in the command of the Gulf Squadron, in reporting the serious losses in his command from the torpedoes, remarks :

"Before sending the monitors over the shallow bar into Blakely river, I had it thoroughly dragged for torpedoes, and many were removed. We continued to drag until no more could be found, and it was believed that we could successfully advance upon the forts; but the results proved the impossibility of doing so without endangering the loss of all our light-draft vessels. These hidden instruments of destruction abound everywhere in these shallow waters."

Within the space of two weeks five gunboats, two of them heavy double-turreted monitors, were totally destroyed by coming into contact with buoyant torpedoes. A launch was also blown to fragments, and the greater part of its crew killed or wounded in endeavoring to clear the channels.

We append the reports of the several commanding officers of these vessels, which form the most complete record of the details of these disasters.

Report of Lieutenant Commander James H. Gillis.

"United States Steamer 'Genesee,'
Mobile Bay, *March* 30, 1865.

"Sir,—I take the earliest opportunity to make a report of the sinking of the United States steamer 'Milwaukie,' under my command, on the afternoon of the 28th instant. I had proceeded up the Blakely river, in company with the United States steamer 'Winnebago,' to within about one and a-half mile of the lower fort, on the left bank of the river, for the purpose of shelling a rebel transport, supposed to be carrying supplies to the fort; had succeeded in causing the steamer to retreat up the river, and was dropping with the current to resume my former position, keeping the bows of the vessel headed up stream; my object in so doing being to avoid, in turning, the accident which caused the sinking of the 'Milwaukie.' I had returned within about two hundred yards of the United States iron-clad 'Kickapoo,' then lying at anchor, and supposed the danger from torpedoes was past, as I was where our boats had been sweeping, and also exactly in the same place where the United States iron-clad 'Winnebago' had turned not ten minutes before, when I felt a shock, and saw at once that a torpedo had exploded on the port side of the vessel, abaft the after turret, and, as near as I could determine at the time, about forty feet from the stern. My first object, after realizing the impossibility of saving the vessel, was to save the crew, and I am happy to be able to state that this was done without the loss of a single person. There was naturally some confusion at first, the hatches being closed, and but three being provided with levers to open them with from below, and those who were not on deck being dependent on those who were, for other means of egress; but a single command served to restore order, and all came on deck in a quiet, orderly manner. The stern of the vessel sank in about three minutes, as near as I can judge; but the forward compartments did not fill for nearly an hour afterwards, giving the crew an opportunity of saving most of their effects. I saw every man off the vessel, sending them to the 'Kickapoo,' Lieutenant Commander Jones, for instructions, and then proceeded to the flag-ship, reporting to you in person, and obtaining your permission to proceed to Pensacola, for the purpose of procuring such appliances as would be necessary in raising the 'Milwaukie.' I am happy to be able to add, that I have obtained the services of two experienced divers, and also a steam pump, and there is every prospect of my retaining my old command until I have the pleasure of seeing her guns once more used against those who are, no doubt, now exulting over her supposed loss.

"I have the honor to be, very respectfully,

"Your obedient servant,

"J. H. Gillis,

"*Lieutenant-Commander, U. S. N.*

"Acting Rear-Admiral H. K. Thatcher,

"*Commanding W. G. Squadron, Mobile Bay, Ala.*"

All efforts to raise the "Milwaukie" were unavailing, as her hull was found to be completely shattered by the explosion.

Report of Lieutenant-Commander William M. Gamble.

"Mobile Bay, *March* 29, 1865.

"Sir,—I have the honor to submit the following report of the circumstances attending the loss of the United States iron-clad 'Osage,' under my command.

"About two P.M., this instant, being at anchor inside of Blakely bar, in company with iron-clads 'Kickapoo,' 'Winnebago,' and 'Chickasaw,' and gunboat 'Octorara,' with a strong breeze from the eastward, I deemed it necessary to move my anchorage to avoid colliding with the United States steamer 'Winnebago,' which vessel had dragged close alongside. I weighed anchor, and had moved off to a safe distance ahead and on her starboard bow, when I stopped and ordered hands ready to let go the anchor in two (2) fathoms water, the last sounding given after I had pulled the bell to stop. Almost immediately after stopping, I ordered three (3) bells rung to back, and moved forward from the pilot-house, intending to step on the turret to order the anchor let go, but had not taken more than three steps from my position at the forward door of the pilot-house when a torpedo exploded under the bow, and the vessel immediately commenced sinking. I ordered the executive officer, Acting-Master G. W. Garrison, to take as many men below as necessary, and search for wounded or killed, and to send all the rest of the crew on the hurricane-deck, except two hands at each boat to haul them alongside.

"My orders were executed promptly, and, although the ship filled and settled rapidly, two killed and the five wounded below were passed up. Three others were wounded on deck. The names of the killed and wounded I will furnish you as soon as I can ascertain them. The wounded were conveyed to the nearest ship for medical attendance. It was impossible to save but few articles belonging to the ship, as she almost immediately filled. As the position to which I moved the 'Osage' had been thoroughly dragged by boats, I am of the opinion that the torpedo by which she was sunk was submerged and drifting. I respectfully request that a board of officers may be ordered to investigate the circumstances attending the loss of the 'Osage.'

"I am, Sir, very respectfully, your obedient servant,

"WILLIAM M. GAMBLE,

"*Lieutenant-Commander U. S. N.*

"Acting Rear-Admiral H. K. THATCHER,

"*Commanding W. G. Squadron.*"

Report of Acting Master N. M. Dyer.

"UNITED STATES STEAMER 'RODOLPH,'
BLAKELY RIVER, ALA., *April* 2, 1865.

"SIR,—It becomes my duty to make you the following report relative to the sinking of this vessel yesterday by the explosion of a torpedo. Having received orders to report on board the 'Metacomet' at 10 A. M., I had left the ship for that purpose, leaving my vessel at anchor a short distance inside the bar in charge of my executive officer, Acting Ensign J. F. Thomson. From him I have obtained the following information, which embraces all the facts connected with this unfortunate affair up to the time of my arrival on board: At 1 P. M., in obedience to signal from flag-ship, weighed anchor, and passed within hail, receiving orders to take a barge alongside, containing my apparatus for raising the 'Milwaukie,' and proceeded with it inside the bar. Crossed the bar, and stood up toward the 'Milwaukie' at 2.40 P. M. When directly between the 'Chickasaw' and 'Winnebago,' exploded a torpedo under our starboard bow, from the effect of which the ship rapidly sank in twelve feet of water. I arrived on board at 3.20 P. M., and found the wounded properly cared for by the promptness with which boats were sent to our assistance from the vessels in the vicinity. The torpedo exploded under our starboard bow, about 30 feet abaft a line drawn at right angles with our stem, coming through the gun-deck, at the break of the platform on which our Parrott guns were mounted, and from the effects of the explosion that can be seen, I should judge there was a hole through her bow at least 10 feet in diameter. * * * * I regret to report a loss of 4 killed and 11 wounded.

"Very respectfully, your ob't serv't,

"N. M. DYER,
"*Acting Master Commanding.*

"A. R. Admiral H. K. THATCHER,
"*Commanding Gulf Squadron.*"

Report of Acting Vol. Lieut. J. W. Maguire.

"UNITED STATES STEAMER 'SCIOTA,'
"OFF MOBILE, ALA., *April* 14, 1865.

"ADMIRAL,—I have the painful duty to respectfully report the sinking of the United States steamer 'Sciota,' under my command, by a rebel torpedo, and the loss of four men and wounding of six others. In obedience to orders from Fleet-Captain E. Simpson, I had finished coaling the barge from the brig 'American Union,' and had delivered to the 'Itasca,' 'Sebago,' and 'Genesee' the working parties belonging to the aforesaid vessels, and was proceeding towards the eastern shore on an east-southeast course for the purpose of delivering ten men of the working party to the United States steamer 'Elk,' when I ran against a torpedo, which was below the surface of the water, exploding it, causing the vessel to sink immediately nearly decks to the water. The explosion was terrible, breaking the beams of the spar-deck, tearing open the water-ways, ripping off starboard fore channels, and breaking fore topmast. I have examined the decks and water-ways immediately over the place where the explosion took place, and, in my opinion, the damage is not so extensive as to prevent raising her. I have also questioned those of the crew who were on the berth-deck at the time of the explosion, and their evidence in regard to the effect upon the berth-deck by the explosion leads me to think that it struck the vessel below the line of the berth-deck, and under and abreast of the fore rigging at the first bow cant or round of the bow. Since the sinking of the vessel I have recovered three of the bodies of the missing men. I must thank the Captain of the 'Cowslip' for his prompt assistance in removing the wounded from this vessel.

"I have the honor to be, respectfully, your obt. servt.,

"J. W. MAGUIRE, U. S. N.,
" *Volunteer Lieut., Commanding.*"

Report of Acting Ensign F. Ellms.

"MOBILE BAY, *April* 15, 1865.

"SIR,—On the morning of April 13, 1865, the United States steamer 'Ida,' under my command, proceeded from the flag-ship 'Stockdale' under orders to report to Lieut.-Commander John Irwin, and place the steamer under his orders. After reaching the 'Cincinnati,' and reporting, I was ordered to proceed to the United States steamer 'Genesee,' laying about two miles below the obstructions; when about two-thirds of the way down the steamer struck a torpedo on her starboard side, crushing in her timbers, bursting her boilers, and tearing up her decks; she filled in a few moments in ten feet of water, where she now lies, directly in mid-channel. Every possible assistance was rendered by the vessels in sight to save life and property. The guns have been taken off, and a portion of the engine has been removed.

"Respectfully your obedient servant,

"F. ELLMS,

"*Acting Ensign.*"

"HOSPITAL ROSS, MOBILE, *April* 19, 1865.

"SIR,—I have the honor to report the loss of the United States steamer 'Althea.' On the 12th ultimo I was ordered by Captain Low to drag the channel with a chain attached to spars laid across the stern. Pilot J. Denton was ordered on board to instruct me where to go. I proceeded to drag, and when abreast of battery Huger, the chain getting afoul of an old wreck, I tried to pull it out and failed, and, as it was found impossible to clear the chain, I ordered it to be slipped. After this was done I attempted to return to the 'Octorara,' but the vessel ran afoul of a torpedo, which exploded near the after part of the pilot-house, a little to the starboard; the vessel sunk immediately in 10 or 12 feet of water, and I regret to state that two men were killed, two others badly wounded, and that I am badly injured in the left leg and foot.

"I am, Sir, very respectfully,

"F. A. G. BACON,

"*Acting Ensign, late Com'd'g U. S. Steamer 'Althea.'*

"*Acting Rear-Admiral* H. K. THATCHER,

"*Com'd'g West Gulf Squadron, Mobile, Alabama.*"

The naval operations of the war closed with the surrender of Mobile. It remains but to sum up the casualties resulting from the system of torpedo defence.

Seven monitors, and eleven wooden vessels of war were totally destroyed by submerged torpedoes while actively engaged against the enemy's ports. Several other vessels, iron-clads and wooden, were temporarily disabled, and, during the same operations, not a vessel of any kind was lost, and but few materially damaged by the heaviest artillery yet employed in actual warfare. At the same time we must bear in mind that two years of the war had passed before the rebels made systematic use of the torpedo, and that during these two years the navy was most actively and successfully engaged in waters affording every opportunity for its advantageous employment.

No one now doubts that our naval superiority would have been in some degree neutralized, had this system of defence been practised in its improved form at the commencement of the war.

There is no doubt as to its efficacy. We have been taught, and other nations have learned through our experience, how terribly destructive it can be made. No one can foresee the improvements that will hereafter be made in its application, now that the attention of engineers is steadily directed to its development; but we feel satisfied in asserting that, as the testimony now stands, the present system of harbor defence bids fair to be revolutionized by the introduction and general use of this new engine of war.

CHAPTER IX.

OFFENSIVE TORPEDOES.—THE "ATLANTA."—FORMS OF REBEL OFFNSIVE TORPEDOES.—FUZES.—ATTACK UPON THE "NEW IRONSIDES."—PRECAUTIONS TAKEN AGAINST SUCH ATTACKS.—DESTRUCTION OF "HOUSATONIC."—ATTACK ON "WABASH" AND "MEMPHIS."—ATTACK ON FRIGATE "MINNESOTA," EXTENT OF INJURY.—EFFORTS OF THE UNITED STATES TO USE TORPEDOES OFFENSIVELY.—EFFECTS OF TORPEDO BOATS ON THE JAMES RIVER.—U. S. OFFICERS OBSTRUCT THE RIVER.—CORRESPONDENCE BETWEEN ADMIRAL LEE AND GENERAL BUTLER.—GENERAL GRANT'S OPINION OF TORPEDO BOATS.—WOOD AND LAY'S TORPEDO BOATS.—DESCRIPTION OF THEIR APPARATUS.—DESTRUCTION OF REBEL IRON-CLAD "ALBEMARLE."

Having traced the history and noted the results of the defensive torpedo system from the commencement of the Rebellion to its close, let us go back to the first appearance of vessels carrying torpedoes as part of their offensive armament, and note the results flowing from this method of attack.

We have seen how this idea, born of Bushnell's derided efforts, impressed itself upon Fulton's mind, and have noted the opposition, ridicule, want of encouragement, and censure the scheme encountered in turn, from the Governments of France, England and the United States.

The failure of his experiments, and the adverse opinions of the highest naval authorities of the times, caused him to abandon the subject for other more promising enterprises. He was in the position of many other inventive geniuses, before and since, who, carried away with a new idea, claim much more for it than the world is prepared to admit, and, failing to demonstrate on the instant to the fullest extent of their anticipations, the usefulness and practicability of their invention, bring the whole matter into general discredit.

It will be remembered that several of the United States Commissioners were gravely impressed with the importance of Fulton's plans, and in their reports, while acknowledging the failures of the experiments they were called upon to witness, predicted for the system a future success. It is probable that these reports, and Fulton's ardent espousal of the torpedo system, even under the cloud of repeated failures, induced the Confederate authorities, urged by their necessities, to give the system a trial. Satisfied of its usefulness by experiments, they seized upon it without a moment's hesitation or delay.

The capture of the iron-clad "Atlanta," armed with a formidable torpedo projecting from her ram-like bow, afforded the first practical proof of their having adopted the system of what may be termed offensive torpedoes, and already was it found to be developed to an immense capacity for harm. No one who saw the "Atlanta" but was at once impressed with the serious nature of the business.

The offensive torpedoes employed by the rebels during the war were of various forms and sizes. They were usually made of stout copper, although barrels were occasionally used, and contained from 50 lbs. to 150 lbs. of fine powder, according to the size of the vessel to which they were attached.

Plate X., Fig. 1, shows a "Ram Torpedo," used on the rebel iron-clads at Richmond and Charleston during the latter period of the war. The iron braces are intended to support the weight of the torpedo, particularly when lifting it out of the water. Five chemical or sensitive fuzes project from the upper half of the hemispherical surface. The shape indicated by the figure is given to it, in order that the centre of the charge may be as near the object as possible when exploded. The case is filled with powder through one of the fuze holes. Plate X., Figs. 2 and 3, are also ram torpedoes. No. 2 shows the form of one taken from the rebel iron-clad "Charleston." It is formed from a strong cask, and fitted with seven sensitive fuzes. Fig. 3 is a soda-water tank, which were at first used for torpedoes very extensively. They were supported by iron straps, as shown in the figure, and inclined upwards, with the idea that so presented they could be more advantageously used against the overhanging sides of monitors. Fig. 4, Plate X., is the form of torpedo used with the small torpedo boats, or "Davids;" they are of copper, and contain from 50 lbs. to 70 lbs. of powder.

All the offensive torpedoes, as well as most of the defensive torpedoes of the rebels, were exploded by means of contact fuzes, of the forms shown in Plate V.

Fig. 1 is an excellent arrangement, by which a plunger passes through a metallic screw-cap and rests upon a cap of soft annealed copper soldered to the edge of the metal stock; the conical head of the primer, filled with Gen. Rains' detonate, rests just below the end of the plunger, and receives the impact of a blow upon it. The fuze is screwed firmly into the shell of the torpedo. The fuze was principally used when the torpedo was formed from barrels.

The form of fuze shown by Fig. 2 has already been described.

Fig. 3 is a form used very generally, and was known as Capt. Lee's sensitive fuze, although its action and detonating material was the same as that employed in other and better fuzes.

Fig. 4 is the form of fuze which later in the war was used for offensive torpedoes, to the exclusion of all others. In this fuze, contact of the primer is secured by sliding up the interior cylinder *a*, which carries the primer until it is pressed lightly against the copper covering cap; the cylinder is second in position by turning the set screw shown at *b*. The safety cap *c*, which is placed over, but does not touch, the thin copper cap, and protects it from accident, is a brass cover sufficiently thick not to be indented by any blow that it could possibly receive in service. The whole is screwed into a bushing, which has been previously brazed firmly into the torpedo shell. A leather or gum washer (*d*) is placed under the head to make the joint tight.

The torpedoes were usually fixed to the end of a spar from twenty to thirty feet in length; the other extremity being attached to the vessel carrying it by a goose-neck, fitted to a socket bolted to the vessel's bow near the water line.

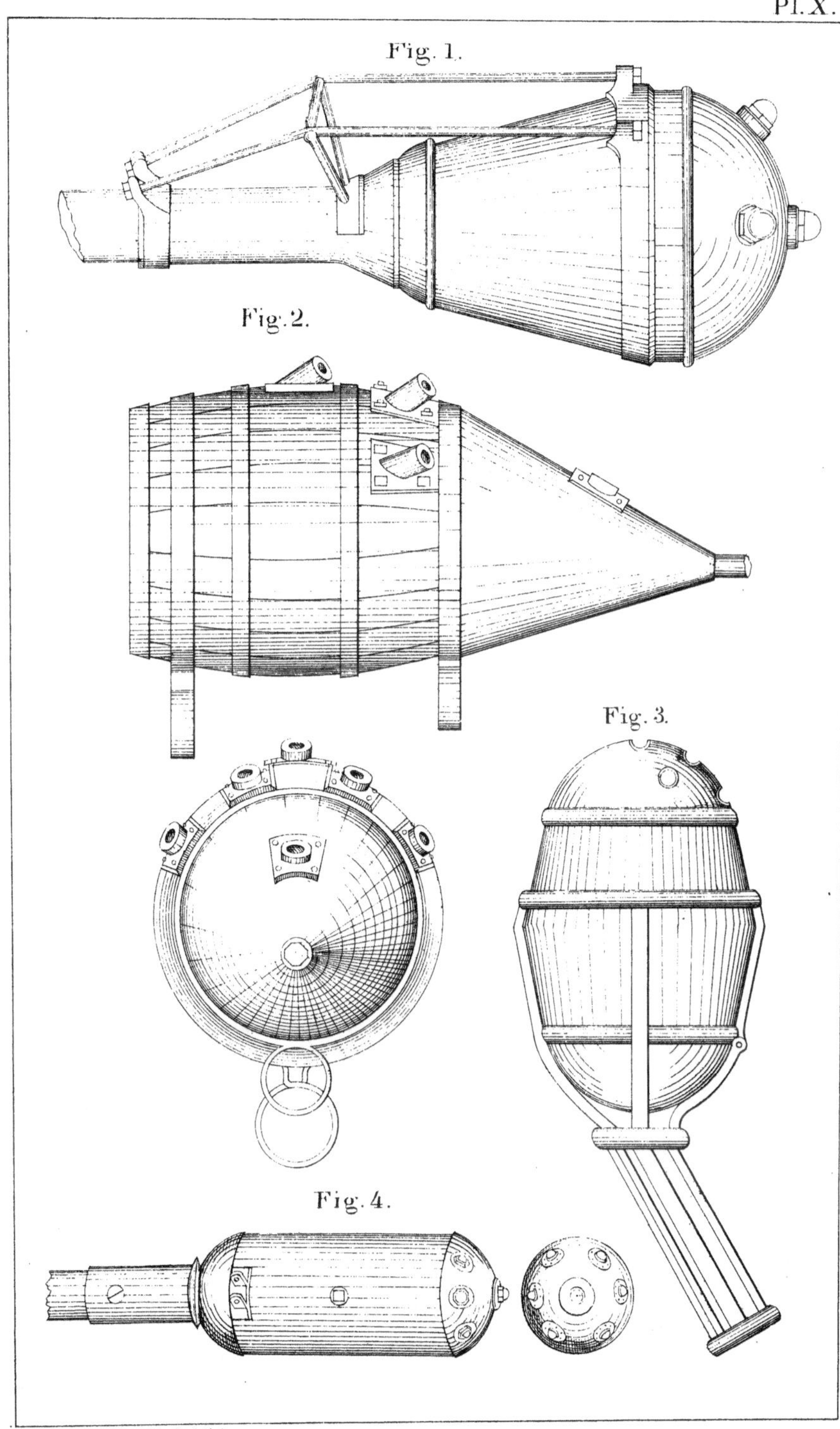

D. VAN NOSTRAND, Publisher.

Guys from the spar to the sides of the vessel kept the spar in its position when submerged, and it was lowered and raised by tricing lines and tackles. Weights were found necessary to secure the rapid submergence of the torpedo when lowered into the water.

Every description of vessel in the rebel service was armed with a torpedo, in addition to their regular armaments, with the intention of using them in action; but it soon became known to the Union authorities that torpedo boats were being constructed specially designed to attack our fleets under cover of darkness, and our vessels, warned of the project, were generally prepared to receive them.

The first attempt to use the torpedo boat was that upon the "Ironsides," off Charleston, on the night of the 5th of October, 1863. The circumstances of this affair are interesting, in view of the novelty of this application of torpedoes to actual warfare, and may be thus briefly summed up.

At about 9 o'clock a small object was descried by the sentinels, approaching the ship from seaward; being taken for a boat, it was hailed in the usual manner. A rifle-shot from the now rapidly approaching craft was the only reply, and the officer of the deck fell mortally wounded. At the same instant, a tremendous explosion alongside shook the huge hull of the "Ironsides" to its centre—an immense column of water deluged her decks, and for a moment there was considerable confusion and alarm, during which the torpedo boat drifted out of sight.

Boats were sent in pursuit, but nothing could be seen of their daring assailant. Two men were, however, discovered floating by the aid of life-preservers—one of them was the Captain of the torpedo boat. He stated that the explosion filled his craft nearly full of water, and, thinking she was sinking, he abandoned her. She had left Charleston that evening soon after dark, and steamed down outside the fleet, when the vessel was turned around and steered directly for the "Ironsides." Four men constituted her crew, and her torpedo contained sixty pounds of powder.

The subsequent history of this vessel is, that, deserted by all but one of her crew, she drifted for an hour helplessly in the tide without motive power. Her engineer, after being in the water for some time, found himself near her, and succeeded in getting on board, lighting her fires anew, and navigating her safely back to Charleston. Here she remained until the close of the war, occasionally venturing out to attack our fleet.

Upon the occupation of Charleston she was found there with eight others similarly constructed, and was brought to the Naval Academy, where she is preserved as one of the relics of the war. These vessels were built of boiler iron, and were of the shape known as "cigar shape." They presented but a very small target above the surface, but were usually clumsy and dangerous craft in a seaway. Under full steam they could attain a speed of seven knots per hour.

The name "David" was given to the first of this form of craft, likening her to the David of Holy Writ, who, with a sling, slew Goliah. This name, like that of the "Monitor," became familiar to our people, and was used as a generic title for all such craft.

Investigation showed that the injuries to the "Ironsides," although severe, were not sufficient to cause her withdrawal from the service.

The failure to destroy the "Ironsides" caused a temporary cessation of these attacks, although it made such an impression upon the minds of those exposed to similar attempts that extraordinary precautions were adopted.

Lookouts were doubled, chain-cables made ready for slipping, and high steam carried at night, so that the ship could move at speed upon the instant. Commanders of vessels on the "inside" blockade were directed to employ their boats at night in rowing guard around their ships. Steam tugs were attached to each squadron in great numbers, and detailed to the duty of guarding the frigates and iron-clads, by steaming slowly around them, in readiness to run down any suspicious-looking object observed in their vicinity. When at all practicable, booms, nets, and other devices were used as additional protections.

The position of our fleet before Charleston afforded peculiar facilities for this species of attack. A large force of iron-clads and transports were collected within a narrow space inside the outer bar, while a number of wooden ships of war, frigates, sloops, and gunboats maintained the blockade of the northern channels still used by blockade runners.

Considerable anxiety was felt for the safety of the monitors of this fleet, as they were the particular objects of dread to the enemy, and essential to the preservation of the situation ; at the same time they were exceedingly open to attack by torpedo boats, and were, therefore, protected by every device that ingenuity could suggest.

Notwithstanding all these precautions, and contrary to Admiral Dahlgren's belief,* the "Housatonic," a heavily armed steam sloop-of-war, then lying on the outside blockade of Charleston Harbor, was attacked and utterly destroyed by a "David" on the 17th of February, 1864. (See Frontispiece.)

---

* Flag-Steamer "Philadelphia,"
Off Morris Island, *January* 15, 1864.

Sir,—The Navy Department has received information that the rebels have a plan to blow up this fleet, and considers it of sufficient importance to inform me thereof.

I can hardly think that the design would extend beyond the iron-clads that constitute the inner blockade, for the outer vessels are distant and difficult of access ; still it would be unwise to omit any proper precautions, and I therefore advise that you will take such measures as may suffice to defeat any attempt of the kind.

I enclose for your information the directions prescribed to the iron-clads. You can use these, or whatever else may seem more adaptable to the purpose.

Let this be circulated among the commanders of the vessels outside for their guidance.

Respectfully, your obedient servant,
J. A. Dahlgren,
Rear-Admiral, Commanding S. A. B. Squadron.

Captain Joseph F. Green,
Commanding United States Steamer "Canandaigua,"
Senior Officer present, off Charleston Bar.

The Captain of the "Housatonic" was severely wounded, and the report of the affair was made by the executive officer, who gives us the principal features in the document hereto annexed:

"UNITED STATES STEAMER 'CANANDAIGUA,'
"OFF CHARLESTON, S. C., *February* 18, 1864.

"SIR,—I have the honor to make the following report of the sinking of the United States steamer 'Housatonic' by a rebel torpedo off Charleston, S. C., on the evening of the 17th instant.

"About 8.45 P. M., the officer of the deck, Acting Master J. K. Crosby, discovered something in the water about one hundred yards from and moving towards the ship. It had the appearance of a plank moving in the water. It came directly toward the ship; the time from when it was first seen till it was close alongside, being about two minutes. During this time the chain was slipped, engine backed, and all hands called to quarters. The torpedo struck the ship forward of the mizzen-mast on the starboard side, in a line with the magazine. Having the after pivot gun pivoted to port, we were unable to bring a gun to bear upon her. About one minute after she was close alongside, the explosion took place, the ship sinking stern first, and heeling to port as she sank. Most of the crew saved themselves by going into the rigging, while a boat was despatched to the 'Canandaigua.' This vessel came gallantly to our assistance, and succeeded in rescuing all but the following officers and men, viz.:

"Ensign E. C. Hazeltine, Captain's Clerk C. O. Muzzey, Quartermaster John Williams, landsman Thomas Parker, second-class fireman John Walsh.

"The above officers and men are missing, and are supposed to have been drowned.

"Captain Pickering was seriously bruised by the explosion, and is at present unable to make a report of the disaster.

"Very respectfully, your obedient servant,

"F. J. HIGGINSON,
"*Lieutenant.*

"Rear-Admiral JOHN A. DAHLGREN,
"*Commanding S. A. B. Squadron.*"

Admiral Dahlgren in reporting to the department this, the first successful application of the torpedo boat to purposes of war, thus comments upon its importance and influence as an engine of war:

"The department will necessarily perceive the consequences likely to result from this event; the whole line of our blockade will be infested with these cheap, convenient, and formidable defences, and we must guard every point.

* * * * * *

"I have attached more importance to the use of torpedoes than others have done, and believe them to constitute the most formidable of the difficulties in the way to Charleston. Their effect on the 'Ironsides' in October, and now on the 'Housatonic,' sustains me in this idea.

"The department will perceive, from the printed injunctions issued, that I have been solicitous for some time in regard to these mischievous devices; though it may not be aware of the personal attention which I have also given to the security of the iron-clads. I naturally feel disappointed that the rebels should have been able to achieve a single success, mingled with no little concern, lest, in spite of every precaution, they may occasionally give us trouble. But it will create no dismay nor relax any effort; on the contrary, the usual inquiry will be ordered, though the whole story is no doubt fully known.

"I desire to suggest to the department the policy of offering a large reward of prize money for the capture or destruction of a "David"—I should say not less than $20,000 or $30,000 for each; they are worth more than that to us.

"I have the honor to be, very respectfully, your obedient servant,

JOHN A. DAHLGREN,

"*Rear-Admiral, Commanding S. A. B. Squadron.*

"Hon. GIDEON WELLES,

"*Secretary of the Navy, Washington, D. C.*"

It is important, in order to complete the history of this affair, to add that the "David" which destroyed the "Housatonic," never returned to port, but was supposed to have been submerged by the disturbed water caused by the explosion, or carried down with her huge antagonist. The following rebel document, captured after the fall of Charleston, explains the rebels' ideas on this point:

"Office Submarine Defences,
"Charleston, S. C., *April* 29, 1864.

"General,—In answer to a communication of yours, received through headquarters, relative to Lieutenant Dixon and crew, I beg leave to state that I was not informed as to the service in which Lieutenant Dixon was engaged, or under what orders he was acting. I am informed that he requested Commander Tucker to furnish him some men, which he did. Their names are as follows, viz.: Arnold Becker, C. Simpkins, James A. Wicks, F. Collins, and —— Ridgeway, all of the navy, and Captain J. F. Carlson, of Captain Wagoner's company of artillery.

"The United States sloop-of-war was attacked and destroyed on the night of the 17th February. Since that time no information has been received of either the boat or crew. I am of the opinion that, the torpedoes being placed at the bow of the boat, she went into the hole made in the 'Housatonic' by explosion of torpedoes, and did not have power sufficient to back out, consequently sunk with her.

"I have the honor to be, General, very respectfully, your obedient servant,

"M. M. Gray,
"*Captain in charge Torpedoes.*

"Major-General Dabney H. Maury,
"*Mobile, Ala.*"

Confederate General Maury, in his report of the defences of Mobile, gives the following account of the torpedo boat which sunk the "Housatonic:"

* * * "It was built of boiler iron, about 35 feet long, and was manned by a crew of nine men, eight of whom worked the propeller by hand; the ninth steered the boat and regulated her movements below the surface of the water; she could be submerged at pleasure to any desired depth, or could be propelled on the surface. In smooth, still water she could be

exactly controlled, and her speed was about four knots. It was intended that she should approach any vessel lying at anchor, pass under her keel, and drag a floating torpedo which would explode on striking the side or bottom of the ship attacked. She could remain submerged for half an hour without inconvenience to her crew. Soon after her arrival at Charleston, Lieutenant Paine, of the Confederate navy, with eight others, volunteered to attack the Federal fleet with her. While preparing for their expedition, the swell of a passing steamer caused the boat to sink suddenly, and all hands, except Lieutenant Paine, who at the moment was standing in the open hatchway, perished. She was soon raised, and again made ready for service. Lieutenant Paine again volunteered to command her. While lying near Fort Sumter, she capsized, and again sunk in deep water, drowning all hands except her commander and two others. Being again raised and prepared for action, Mr. Aunley, one of her constructors, made an experimental cruise in her in Cooper river. While submerged at great depth, from some unknown cause, she became unmanageable, and remained for many days on the bottom of the river with her crew of nine dead men. A fourth time was the boat raised, and Lieutenant Dixon, of Mobile, of the 21st Volunteers, with eight others, went out of Charleston harbor in her, and attacked and sunk the federal steamer 'Housatonic.' Her mission at last accomplished, she disappeared forever with her crew. Nothing is known of their fate, but it is believed they went down with their enemy."

Notwithstanding the fate of the "David," the rebels continued to improve upon the torpedo boat, and, as the following report shows, again attempted to use it:

"UNITED STATES STEAMER 'MEMPHIS,'
"NORTH EDISTO RIVER, S. C., *March* 6, 1864.

"SIR,—I have the honor to report that an attempt has been made by the rebels to blow up this ship, but am happy to state did not succeed.

"At 1 A. M. a torpedo-boat was discovered about fifty yards distant, approaching us rapidly on the port quarter from up river. We immediately beat to quarters and slipped the chain;

in an instant the torpedo was under our port quarter, and we could not bring a gun to bear on her. The watch being armed at the time, we were enabled to concentrate a rapid fire with muskets, revolvers, and pistols down upon her, and into what looked like a hatchway, nearly in the centre ; the rapid firing seemed to stop her progress, and dropping about twelve feet astern, in an instant she darted ahead again, and at the same time we rang to go ahead, and our propeller, I think, must have caught and broke some of her gear, as she appeared to be disabled and drifted up river ; in a few moments they showed a light, at which we fired a 12-pound rifle shot ; she then disappeared, and an armed boat was immediately despatched to search for and capture her if possible, but returned without success. This torpedo boat was about twenty-five feet long, painted lead color, and in appearance was like a ship's boat in the water, bottom up.

"I am, Sir, very respectfully, your obedient servant,

"R. O. Patterson,
"*Acting Master, Commanding.*

"Captain S. C. Rowan,
"*Commanding S. A. B. Squadron.*"

Admiral Rowan formed an opinion, gathered from facts elicited from the officers of the "Memphis," that the failure to destroy the vessel was probably owing to the breaking of the torpedo spar by the propeller of the steamer.

Following the attempt upon the "Memphis," on the 9th of April a more determined and successful attack with one of these pigmies was made upon the steam frigate "Minnesota," flag-ship of the North Atlantic Blockading Squadron, then lying off Newport News, at the mouth of the James river, surrounded by a large fleet of iron-clads, gunboats, and transports.

Here, as at Charleston, preparations had been made in anticipation of such attacks. Tugs were particularly relied upon to protect the larger vessels, and one was specially detailed to guard the "Minnesota"—a protection which, as will be seen, failed to be of any service.

The following are the official reports of this affair:

"UNITED STATES SHIP 'MINNESOTA,'
"OFF NEWPORT NEWS, VA., *April* 9, 1864.

"SIR,—I have to report that last night about 2 o'clock, while riding to the ebb tide, a dark object was discovered slowly passing the ship, about two hundred yards distant. It was thought to be a boat, and hailed; to the hail was answered 'Roanoke.' By this time it was directly abeam, seemingly without any power of locomotion. The officer of the deck promptly gave orders to the tug astern to go and examine it, and repeated his orders several times before getting any reply, and, while endeavoring to have this order executed, the object, a 'David,' approached the ship just abaft the port main chains and exploded a torpedo under her, the 'David' making off in the direction of the Nansemond river. Several muskets and a round shot were fired at it, and every effort made to send in pursuit, but the tug 'Poppy' had failed to keep the required look-out, and also had allowed her steam to go down, which was not discovered until the 'David' had disappeared. Vessels were sent in search, but failed to find her.

"I submit the accompanying report of Acting Ensign Birtwistle, officer of the deck at the time specified. It is difficult to say how far the ship may be damaged, although she manifests no leak. The shock was quite severe, and I should be glad to have a survey to ascertain the extent of injury sustained.

"I am, very respectfully, your obedient servant,

"J. H. UPSHUR,
"*Lieut.-Commander, Com'd'g U. S. Steamer 'Minnesota.'*

"*Acting Rear-Admiral* S. P. LEE,
"*Commanding North Atlantic Blockading Squadron.*

"UNITED STATES STEAMER 'MINNESOTA,'
"OFF NEWPORT NEWS, VA., *April* 9, 1864.

"SIR,—At 1.45 this morning, while in charge of the deck, the quartermaster directed my attention to a boat adrift, a little forward of the port beam, and about one hundred and fifty yards distant, and while passing to the port side of the bridge the sentry at the gangway hailed her; she answered, 'Roanoke.' I then hailed her, and could not make out her reply. I went down off the bridge and hailed her from the quarter; she answered, 'Roanoke.' I told him not to come alongside; he answered, 'aye, aye.' I hailed the tug 'Poppy' three times, and told him to see what that boat was. He answered, 'aye, aye.'

"I thought the boat was nearing us, and could not see any oars. I sent a messenger to call you, sir, and ordered the boat to keep off, or I would fire into him. I repeated the order, but discovered she was nearing us fast. I then ordered the 'Poppy' twice to run that boat down. I then saw the glimmer of a light. The quartermaster said he could hear her puff. I jumped to a convenient gun; called for help to train it. The sentries on the gangways and forward fired three shots at her; but before I could fire the gun she was inside of range. I jumped back from the gun, and the explosion followed. I then met you at the cabin hatch, and in answer to your inquiry, said it was a torpedo. Men were rushing on deck, the drum beat to quarters, and I went forward and fired a shell from a nine-inch gun in my division. After the explosion, I thought sure the 'Poppy' would capture her, or I would have remained at the quarter-deck guns. The rest, sir, you saw.

"I am, Sir, very respectfully,

"JAMES BIRTWISTLE,

"*Acting Ensign.*

"Lieutenant Commander J. H. UPSHUR,

"*Commanding United States steamer 'Minnesota.'*"

The effect of this explosion furnishes interesting data in regard to submarine warfare, and we therefore add the report of a Board of Survey appointed to ascertain the injuries to the "Minnesota":

"UNITED STATES IRON-CLAD 'ROANOKE.'

"NEWPORT NEWS, VA., *April* 12, 1864.

"ADMIRAL,—In obedience to your order of April 9, we have held a strict and careful survey to ascertain the amount of injury or damage sustained by the explosion of a torpedo under the port side of the United States steamer 'Minnesota,' as far as we can ascertain.

"DESCRIPTION OF INJURY.

"*Port after shell-room.*—First and third futtocks of two frames badly sprung. The diagonal straps sprung off. The deck sprung, nine planks being sprung off from the beams about three-fourths of an inch. The linings of the bulkhead sprung badly. Amidship bulkhead started inboard about six inches.

"*Spirit-room.*—Forward frame broken; planking sprung; second frame badly sprung; bilge-streak broken and sprung off; third frame sprung; planking sprung outboard from timbers about one inch; two (2) buts of second bilge-streak sprung up; decks started up; one deck plank broken over the spirit-room.

"The centre of the injury appears to be about six feet below the surface of the water. The shelving of the port magazine started; port steerage bulkhead broken; one ladder broken and all the rest unshipped; nine deck planks of port steerage broken; in the port after magazine the shelving has been shattered; two butts on the gun-deck started upon the port side at No. 13 gun; seventeen planks from the water-way; two axletrees on gun-deck broken, and one on spar-deck broken of nine-inch gun-carriages; two lower half-ports on spar-deck and two lower half-ports on gun-deck broken; preventive plate for main channel, next to after one, sprung out about half an inch; one of the bolts of the crane for spare spars, in the main chains, started one inch. The paymaster's store-rooms in the cockpit on the port side show the power of concussion, all the shelves being broken and disarranged. Carefully examined the outside of the ship abreast of the place of injury, and were unable to find any of the copper torn off, or any inequalities on the bottom of the ship. The bulkhead of the shaft-alley, abreast of the shell-room, started inboard about six inches for a distance of fifteen feet on the port side.

"The binnacle on the quarter-deck forward of the mizzen-mast unshipped from its pedestal on the bridge and thrown three feet towards port side.

"DAMAGE DONE IN THE ORDNANCE DEPARTMENT.

"Number of shell-boxes destroyed,		9-inch	....	78
" " bags	"	9 "	....	32
" canister broken	"	11 "	....	5
" sabots and straps	"	9 "	....	110

"Three 9-inch gun-carriages are disabled, the fore axletree of one being broken in two places, the others badly sprung. Two elevating screws that were attached to the guns on the above carriages were rendered useless by being bent; also the elevating screw of the 11-inch pivot by the same cause. The following equipments are broken and rendered useless: three (3) 9-inch sponges, two (2) 9-inch rammers, two (2) ordinary handspikes, one (1) roller handspike; also four (4) tompions and two (2) reinforce sight aprons missing from 9-inch guns on port side.

"Very respectfully, your obedient servants,

"GUERT GANSEVOORT,
"*Captain.*

"JOSEPH FYFFE,
"*Lieutenant Commanding U. S. S. Commodore Morris.*

"J. W. STIMSON,
"*Carpenter.*"

Besides the damages above enumerated, a great quantity of stores in the paymaster's department were utterly destroyed, the contents of boxes, barrels, and bales being inextricably mixed together.

The following despatch, captured a few weeks later in a telegraph station on the James, furnishes an important item in addition to the data already supplied—*i. e.*, the amount of powder contained in the case of this torpedo:

"Hon. S. R. MALLORY,
"*Secretary of Navy,*
"*Navy Dept., Richmond, Va.:*

"Passed through the Federal fleet off Newport News, and exploded fifty-three (53) pounds of powder against the side of the flagship 'Minnesota,' at 2 A. M., 9th inst. She has not sunk, and I have no means yet of telling the injury done. My boat and party escaped without loss under the fire of her heavy guns and musketry, and that of a gunboat lying to her stern.

"HUNTER DAVIDSON.

"*April* 11, 1864."

The boat employed on this occasion differed materially from the "Davids" of Charleston, it being simply a steam launch, with machinery and helmsman protected from musketry by boiler iron.

Upon the 19th of April an attempt was made upon the steam frigate "Wabash" on the outside blockade off Charleston, which was avoided by the early discovery of the approaching "David." The frigate slipped her cable and moved ahead at full speed, directing the fire of her broadside and a fusilade of musketry in the supposed direction of her diminutive assailant. The darkness, the small size of the target, and the confusion of the moment prevented any accuracy of aim, and the "David" returned in safety to Charleston. A curious and novel spectacle—a mighty frigate with her tremendous armament and crew of seven hundred men absolutely put to flight by four men in a little boat of less than a ton burden, whose only armament was a few pounds of powder extended on a spar ahead of her!

These attacks coming in rapid succession, the growing importance of the system aroused the U. S. authorities, and they prepared to imitate the devices of the enemy.

In the sounds of North Carolina the officers charged with holding those waters with a wooden fleet against the rebel iron-clad "Albemarle," which had already won a victory at Plymouth, fitted a torpedo to a clumsy gunboat, the "Miami"—the same vessel of which a foreign officer once remarked that he "had noticed our vessels with two bows, but this one appeared to have two sterns." In the furious engagement which soon ensued an attempt was made to use this vessel against the "Albemarle," but the captain of the "Miami" failed to strike his more active antagonist.

The arming of the tugs and smaller gunboats lying in the James river, at Dutch Gap, with torpedoes, has already been alluded to. These arrangements were, however, but temporary expedients, to counterpoise as far as possible similar, but more perfect, devices of the enemy. We have seen that the uncertainty as to the results of using torpedoes in a naval combat, caused the army and naval commanders to obstruct the river with electric torpedoes and sunken vessels. General Grant was pushing for the south side of the James; the necessity for holding our position there, ready to receive his army, was equalled by that of the enemy to prevent, if possible, such a transfer of our forces. They had above us a powerful iron-clad and torpedo fleet, as yet inactive. Every indication pointed to the probability of a determined effort on their part to break our hold upon the James, and by controlling the river, prevent Grant from crossing. To do this they relied almost entirely upon their torpedo devices. Barges were filled with combustible matter and armed with torpedoes; fire rafts loaded with turpentine were prepared, with the intention of sending them down upon the fleet at night, and following them with a score of torpedo boats and iron-clads.

General Butler urged upon Admiral Lee the necessity of obstructions, in a correspondence which illustrates the respect which the torpedo boat system of attack commanded, and the influence which it was supposed to have upon the greatest military operations.

Admiral Lee remarks, in reply to the suggestion of the obstructions by General Butler:

"I am unwilling to do anything which can be construed as implying an admission of superiority of resources on the part of the enemy."

To this General Butler replies, under date of June 2d:

"I am aware of the delicacy naval gentlemen feel in depending upon anything but their ships in a contest with the enemy, and if it was a contest with the enemy's ships alone, I certainly would not advise the obstructions even at the great risk of losing the river. But in a contest against such unchristian modes of warfare as fire-rafts and torpedo boats, I think all questions of delicacy should be waived by the paramount consideration of protection for the lives of the men and the safety of the very valuable vessels of the squadron."

To this the Admiral replies on the next day:

"In reply to that part of your communication of yesterday, which I have the honor to acknowledge, which refers to the lives of the men and the safety of the very valuable vessels under my command, as being the primary reason for obstructing the river, I would wish to be understood as regarding the loss of life and material as incidental to the contest which would occur should the enemy make an attack on us, whatever the result should be. The first consideration with me is, the necessity heretofore represented by you to me, of holding this river beyond a peradventure, for the great military purposes of General Grant and yourself. In consulting my own desires, I would do everything to induce, and nothing to prevent, the enemy from trying to assert their strength in a purely naval contest, which, in my opinion, would give us a naval victory. The only contingency of such a battle is the unknown effect of the novel instruments of war—torpedo vessels—which are to be employed by them, and which, as the attacking party, give them, perhaps, an advantage which might possibly balance our certain superiority in all other fighting material.

"I have the honor to be, General,

"Very respectfully yours,

"S. P. LEE.

"*Acting Rear-Admiral, Commanding N. A. B. Squadron.*

"Major-General B. F. BUTLER,

"*Com'd'g Department Virginia and North Carolina.*"

General Butler asserting that the "military necessity of holding the river was overwhelming," and General Grant also agreeing that the enemy's use of torpedo boats made the situation uncertain, Admiral Lee consented; the obstructions were placed, and the rebels awoke to find that their opportunity had passed for proving the power of their torpedo boats and rams.

The Navy Department in the meantime turned its attention to the subject, and invited proposals from ingenious mechanics and inventors for plans of torpedo boats, and torpedoes to use with them. Many were offered, but those of Chief Engineer W. W. Wood, and Engineer Lay were adopted, and the construction of the boats and torpedoes commenced during the spring of 1864.

Messrs. Wood's and Lay's plans embraced two kinds of vessels—one an ordinary steam launch, armed with the torpedo—the other, an iron-clad vessel of the monitor species, with a torpedo arrangement, to be operated by steam; both of which were adopted.

Plate XI. represents the torpedo, boat, and apparatus. The torpedo consists of a copper cylindrical case, through the centre of which is a hollow tube, at the bottom of which is fixed a large cone for a fulminate cap; at the end is inserted a ball of iron, the size of eleven inch grape, which is held at this point by a pin, passing through a "stuffing box." An inclined partition divides the interior into a magazine and air chamber; the torpedo is thus made a few pounds specifically lighter than water. The disposition of the charge causes it to take a position in the water with the air chamber uppermost, and the trigger line attached to the pin, to lead, so as to give a direct pull from the boat, as shown in the plate. It is claimed that the air chamber also gives *direction* to the force of the explosion. The torpedo shell is filled with powder, through an opening on the upper side of the shell, and the cone is capped through an opening and tube on its under side. The inventor claims that the effect of the air chamber is to increase *the force* of the explosion, (vide p. 196.) By reference to the drawings the following description of the manner of operating the torpedo will be understood:—A spar rests in supports and guides alongside the gunwale of the boat, the forward guides moving on pivots. At its forward end, or the head of the torpedo bar, is a "scoop," arranged to receive the torpedo-shell when it is desired to be ready for action. When placed, the bight of a rope previously fastened to one side of the "scoop," is passed around the score, in the rear of the shell, and the rope is then passed over a sheave on the opposite side of the scoop, and the end made fast to a cleat on the bow of the boat, allowing slack line a few feet shorter than the operating bar. The shell is then set well back into the scoop, and secured in that position by a pin passing through a lug on the shell, which projects through an opening in the scoop. To the pin which confines the ball is attached a line, the end of which is held in the hands of the operator. A single whip,

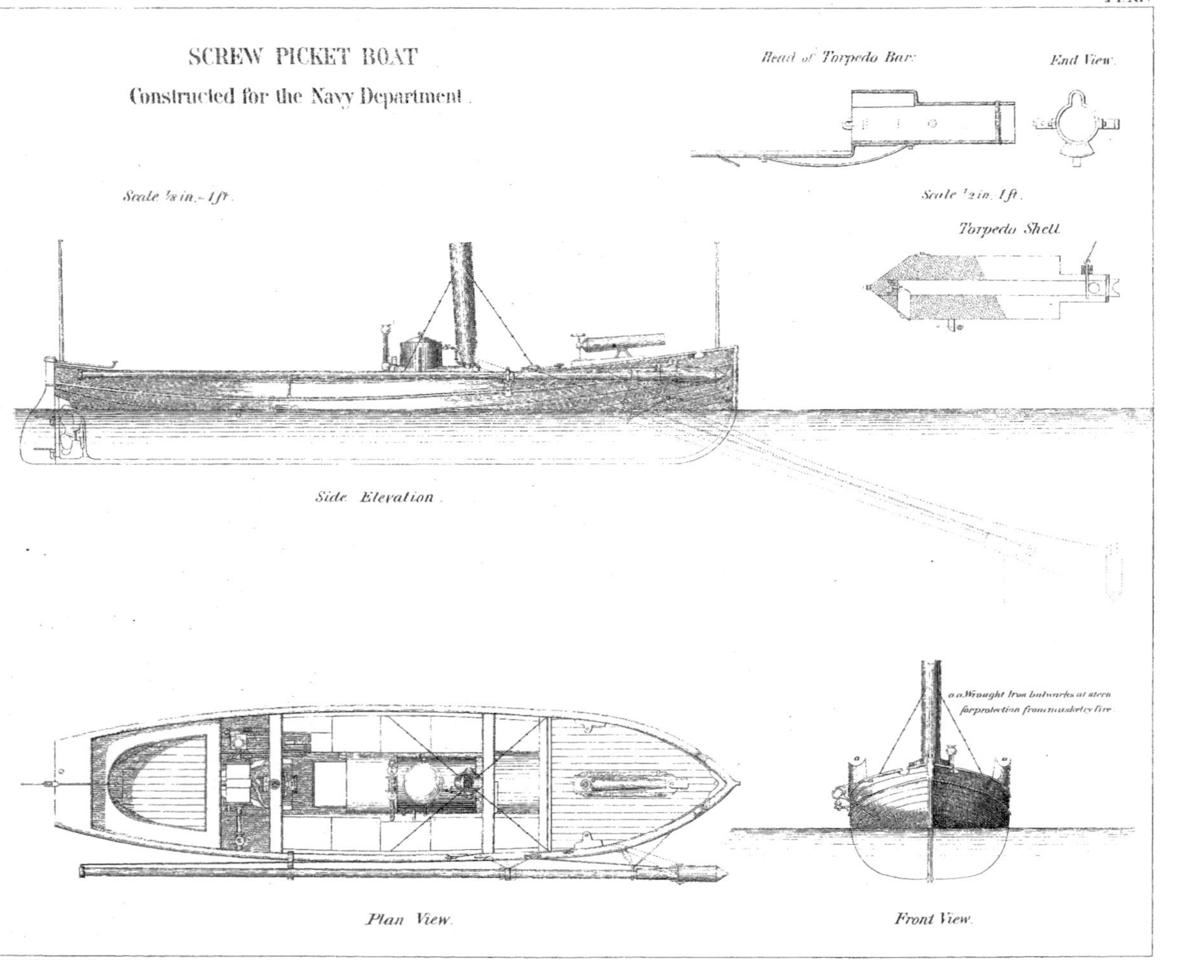

D. VAN NOSTRAND, Publisher.

attached to the after end of the bar, is manned by the crew, and when at the proper distance from the vessel attacked, is hauled upon vigorously, and the bar extended in advance of the boat and submerged at the same time. When at its full length, the pin, which has kept the shell in position, is withdrawn, and the sudden tightening of the rope passed around the score of the shell throws it clear of the bar, when it assumes the position shown by the dotted lines of the side elevation. The operator then pulls upon the trigger line, the weight falls and the charge is exploded.

A number of steam launches, originally designed for picket service, were fitted with this apparatus, and were supplied to each squadron. They had good speed, were easily handled, and against an enemy offering opportunities for their employment they would have been very formidable. For armament, these boats carried a twelve-pounder boat howitzer on the bow, and a force of from twelve to fifteen men.

The advantages claimed for this torpedo arrangement are: 1st, that any steam launch or boat could be used as a torpedo boat; 2d, the torpedo is fired at a distance from the boat, and can be projected beyond the reach of the spar—therefore *contact* is unnecessary; 3d, several torpedoes can be successively used, as the *spar* remains uninjured by the explosion; 4th, the torpedo can be exploded at a greater depth than would be given by the length of the spar.

It was with this seemingly complicated apparatus that Lieut. Cushing accomplished the destruction of the rebel iron-clad "Albemarle," which had become the "terror of the sounds," and threatened to drive our vessels before it. In two hard-fought battles she had been victorious, and it became a matter of necessity that she should be conquered or destroyed. Lieut. Cushing, volunteering for the enterprise, was given command of a steam launch fitted with the apparatus described. How well he accomplished his task we leave him to tell, and add the well-deserved complimentary letter addressed to him by the Secretary of the Navy.

Report of Lieutenant W. B. Cushing.

"ALBEMARLE-SOUND, N. C., *October* 30, 1864.

"SIR: I have the honor to report that the rebel iron-clad 'Albemarle' is at the bottom of the Roanoke river.

"On the night of the 27th, having prepared my steam launch, I proceeded up toward Plymouth, with thirteen officers and men, partly volunteers from the squadron. The distance from the mouth of the river to the ram is about eight miles, the stream averaging in width some two hundred yards, and lined with the enemy's pickets. A mile below the town was the wreck of the 'Southfield,' surrounded by some schooners, and it was understood that a gun was mounted there to command the bend. I therefore took one of the 'Shamrock's' cutters in tow, with orders to cast off and board at the point if we were hailed.

"Our boat suceeded in passing the picket, and even the 'Southfield,' within twenty yards, without discovery, and we were not hailed until by the look-outs on the ram. The cutter was then cast off and ordered below, while we made for our enemy under a full head of steam.

"The rebels sprung their rattles, rang the bell, and commenced firing, at the same time repeating their hail, and seeming much confused.

"The light of a fire ashore showed me the iron-clad, made fast to the wharf, with a pen of logs around her about thirty feet from her side.

"Passing her closely, we made a complete circle, so as to strike her fairly, and went into her, bows on. By this time the enemy's fire was very severe, but a dose of canister, at short range, served to moderate their zeal and disturb their aim. Paymaster Swan, of the 'Otsego,' was wounded near me, but how many more I know not. Three bullets struck my clothing, and the air seemed full of them.

"In a moment we had struck the logs, just abreast of the quarter-port, breasting them in some feet, and our bows resting on them. The torpedo boom was then lowered, and, by a vigorous pull, I succeeded in diving the torpedo under the overhang, and exploded it at the same time that the 'Albemarle's' gun was fired. A shot seemed to go crashing through my boat, and a dense mass of water rushed in from the torpedo, filling the launch and completely disabling her.

"The enemy then continued his fire at fifteen feet range, and demanded our surrender, which I twice refused, ordering the men to save themselves, and removing my own coat and shoes. Springing into the river, I swam, with others, into the middle of the stream, the rebels failing to hit us.

"The most of our party were captured, some drowned, and only one escaped besides myself, and he in a different direction. Acting Master's Mate Woodman, of the 'Commodore Hull,' I met in the water half a mile below the town, and assisted him as best I could, but failed to get him ashore.

"Completely exhausted, I managed to reach the shore, but was too weak to crawl out of the water until just at day-light, when I managed to creep into the swamp, close to the fort. While hiding a few feet from the path, two of the 'Albemarle's' officers passed, and I judged from their conversation that the ship was destroyed.

"Some hours' travelling in the swamp served to bring me out well below the town, when I sent a negro in to gain information, and found that the ram was truly sunk.

"Proceeding through another swamp, I came to a creek and captured a skiff belonging to a picket of the enemy, and with this, by eleven o'clock the next night, had made my way out to the 'Valley City.'

"Acting Master's Mate William L. Howorth, of the 'Monticello,' showed, as usual, conspicuous bravery. He is the same officer who has been with me twice in Wilmington harbor. I trust he may be promoted when exchanged, as well as Acting Third Assistant Engineer Stolesbury, who, being for the first time under fire, handled his engine promptly and with coolness. All the officers and men behaved in the most gallant manner. I will furnish their names to the department as soon as they can be procured.

"The cutter of the 'Shamrock' boarded the 'Southfield,' but found no gun. Four prisoners were taken there.

"The ram is now completely submerged, and the enemy have sunk three schooners in the river to obstruct the passage of our ships.

"I desire to call the attention of the Admiral and Department to the spirit manifested by the sailors on the ships in these sounds. But few men were wanted, but all hands were eager to go into the action, many offering their chosen shipmates a month's pay to resign in their favor.

"I am, Sir, very respectfully, your obedient servant,

"W. B. Cushing,

"*Lieutenant United States Navy.*

"The name of the man who escaped is William Hoftman, seaman on the 'Chickopee.' He did his duty well, and deserves a medal of honor.

"Respectfully,

"W. B. Cushing. U. S. N.

"Rear-Admiral D. D. Porter,

"*Commanding N. A. Blockading Squadron.*"

"Navy Department, *November* 9, 1864.

"Sir,—Your report of October 30 has been received, announcing the destruction of the rebel iron-clad steamer 'Albermarle,' on the night of the 27th ultimo, at Plymouth, North Carolina.

"When last summer the department selected you for this important and perilous undertaking, and sent you to Rear-Admiral Gregory at New York to make the necessary preparations, it left the details to yourself to perfect. To you and your brave comrades, therefore, belongs the exclusive credit which attaches to this daring achievement. The destruction of so formidable a vessel, which had resisted the combined attack of a number of our steamers, is an important event touching our future naval and military operations. The judgment as well as the daring courage displayed would do honor to any officer, and redounds to the credit of one of twenty-one years of age.

"On four previous occasions the department has had the gratification of expressing its approbation of your conduct in the face of the enemy, and in each instance there was manifested by you the same heroic daring and innate love of perilous adventure; a mind determined to succeed, and not to be deterred by any apprehensions of defeat.

"The department has presented your name to the President for a vote of thanks, that you may be promoted one grade, and your comrades also shall receive recognition.

"It gives me pleasure to recall the assurance you gave me at the commencement of your active professional career, that you would prove yourself worthy of the confidence reposed in you, and of the service to which you were appointed. I trust you may be preserved through further trials ; and it is for yourself to determine whether, after entering upon so auspicious a career, you shall, by careful study and self-discipline, be prepared for a wider sphere of usefulness on the call of your country.

"Very respectfully, etc.,

"GIDEON WELLES,
"*Secretary of Navy.*

"Lieutenant W. B. CUSHING, U. S. N."

CHAPTER X.

DISCUSSION OF THE OFFENSIVE TORPEDO SYSTEM.—THE CASES OF THE "HOUSATONIC" AND "ALBERMARLE."—RESULTS SHOW THAT THE PRACTICE OF THE SYSTEM IS NOT NECESSARILY HAZARDOUS.—MORAL EFFECT OF A TORPEDO ATTACK.—VALUE OF THE SYSTEM TO THE WEAKER NATIONS.—IMPERFECTIONS OF BOATS USED DURING THE WAR EASILY REMEDIED.—SUBMARINE BOATS.—HISTORY OF SUBMARINE OPERATIONS. —DESCRIPTION OF A U. S. PLUNGING-BOAT.—SURFACE TORPEDO BOATS. —THEIR REQUIREMENTS.—DESCRIPTION OF THE "SPUYTEN-DUYVIL." —IMPROVEMENTS TO BE MADE.—WATER-TIGHT COMPARTMENTS.—THE "23 LIGHT-DRAFT MONITORS."

The question so aptly put by Fulton—"*Whether there be within the genius and inventive faculties of man, the power to place a torpedo beneath a ship in defiance of her powers of resistance,*" has been answered most decidedly by the events of the rebellion.

The attacks upon the "Ironsides" and "Minnesota," the destruction of the "Housatonic" and the "Albermarle," considered in the light of great practical experiments, not only prove the vast power of the system, but establish the fact that a torpedo *can* be placed and exploded to the injury or destruction of a ship, under circumstances offering the least conceivable advantages for its successful employment.

A review of these events will be found interesting and instructive, foreshadowing as they do a revolution in the art of naval warfare of which no one can confidently predict the end.

The cases of the "Housatonic" and the "Albermarle" are each surrounded by circumstances peculiarly illustrative of the adaptation of the system to naval warfare, and will be looked upon as the most important, inasmuch as they were the only instances where the attack resulted in the destruction of the vessel. In the former, a powerful, heavily-armed, steam sloop-of-war, at anchor off a blockaded port, prepared at all points for immediate service, forewarned of the nature of the attack that was to be made upon her, and guarded with extreme vigilance, is suddenly alarmed by the appearance, close at hand, of a small floating object which approaches out of the darkness. In a moment, before an effort can be made to resist or avoid what appears but "a plank floating upon the water," the huge hull is struck a deadly blow and sent swiftly to the bottom of the sea.

In the other instance, the "Albermarle," an iron-clad, which by the invincibility of her armor had withstood the united powers of a large and well-appointed fleet of wooden vessels in two hard-fought combats—which had driven our forces from important footholds in the enemy's country, gained by many a battle; which had endangered the supremacy of our arms in a wide region where it had never before been questioned—this type of the modern war-ship, lying in apparent security moored to a wharf, separated from her enemies by many miles of a tortuous river-course, protected by booms of logs, and guarded by a large and vigilant force against any effort to destroy her, is struck as by lightning and rendered harmless for ever.

The "Housatonic" was a wooden steamer, virtually at sea, the "Albemarle" an iron-clad far within the lines of the enemy's defences; both were instantly destroyed—the former by a torpedo driven against her sides by a plunging torpedo boat, the latter by an ordinary steam launch provided with an apparatus which exploded a torpedo at a considerable distance from the assailant. The plunging boat went down with her victim, and her bold crew perished; the launch also sank, but most of her crew escaped with their lives. Both attacks were delivered suddenly under cover of darkness, and neither torpedo boat suffered any damage from its enemy. Lieut. Cushing was found to have been mistaken in attributing the sinking of his craft to the shot which "seemed to go crashing through her sides," for when Plymouth was retaken, the launch was raised uninjured and restored to the service. In his impetuosity and daring he pushed her with full steam power against the "Albemarle," and the descending column of water thrown up by the explosion filled and sunk her.*

The fact that both these torpedo boats of different forms were lost in the two instances where their attacks were successful, argues little against the system illustrated by their performances. Their destruction was not necessarily involved in their antagonists', but is plainly attributable to easily remedied faults of construction in the boats themselves. Indeed, with the dire record of disasters attending the experimental trips of the rebel plunging boat, it is a matter of great surprise that she should have been sent upon such an enterprise, or that any one could have been found willing to go in her.

The principal objection urged against this species of torpedo warfare, is its extremely hazardous character, and there have been many who have pointed to these instances as proof of the assertion that desperation only can instigate such attempts, and that success is only to be obtained with the certain destruction of the attacking party. That such a result is very far from being certain, even with the most imperfectly constructed torpedo boats, is clearly shown by the escape uninjured of both the craft which successfully exploded their torpedoes against the sides of the "Minnesota" and "Ironsides." In the former case, it will be remembered that the safety of the "David" can scarcely be said to have been endangered by her exploit. In no single instance of the many recorded did a torpedo boat, shielded by the darkness, and protected by her diminutive size, ever suffer any damage from the "powers of resistance" of her selected antagonist.

The peculiar courage which the practice of the system has called for is the same that is required

* This launch at the end of the war was sent to the Naval Academy, where she was fitted up very elegantly by Vice-Admiral Porter as a steam yacht. Here she developed a wonderful speed, steaming easily 10 knots per hour, and, when pushed, 12 knots. Her rig was that of full-rigged brig, and with her crew of neatly-dressed boys, presented a beautiful representation of a miniature gunboat. Upon a trial trip, after a few alterations by the engineer who had rearranged her machinery, her boiler exploded, killing Mr. Hoyt, the engineer, and four men.

to put to practical test any new and extraordinary engine of destruction. Let the practicability of the system be proved by successes, its defects remedied by experience in failures, and, above all, let its use become familiar to a brave people, and no more desperation will be necessary to its application than is needed to go into any battle, where life is held cheap in the service of a good cause. To lead a forlorn hope, to board an enemy's ship, to storm a battery, and, with deference we say it, to go to sea in a monitor, require the common attributes of true manliness. The annals of war show thousands of instances which have involved more real danger to the actors than can possibly be incurred by delivering a swift attack upon a vessel of war, however large and powerful, in a *properly constructed torpedo boat*, while the chances of successful results are greater than in ordinary battles, however carefully planned and bravely fought.*

It will have been noticed that all these attacks upon our vessels were made by a single torpedo boat, which selected her antagonist from a large fleet, each vessel of which was equally open to attack. What results would have come from a systematic and simultaneous attack by a large number of these cheap contrivances can only be estimated by the alarm and destruction caused by one. It is fair to presume that the effect would be in direct proportion to the number of torpedo boats employed.

At the time of the attempt to blow up the "Ironsides" and

---

* A writer in an article in the February number of the *United Service Magazine* for 1868, upon submarine apparatus, thus refers to torpedo boats: "There is another way in which a torpedo may be applied, but only under circumstances which might be guarded by extreme vigilance, and *which would be almost certain death to the operator.* It was twice tried during the American war—once with success, on the other occasion it was a failure as regarded the attempt to blow up the vessel, and the bold sailor who made it was hoisted with his own petard. The danger of the boat on board of which the operator is stationed being swamped, may be obviated by one built for the special purpose. In the experiments made at Chatham lately, though large columns of water were forced into the air, the launch from which the experiments were made was not injured by the explosion, nor was any water worth mentioning taken in." This extract is a fair example of the accuracy of English writers upon the subject of the torpedo operations of the rebellion.

"Minnesota," those vessels were surrounded by great numbers of vessels of all classes—monitors, frigates, gunboats and transports—necessarily crowded together within a very limited space. To have opened a heavy and promiscuous fire upon so small an object, but dimly seen for an instant, however carefully and deliberately directed, would have been more disastrous to friendly vessels than to the enemy, who could only be reached by some chance shot.

But it is impossible to convey an idea of the bewilderment that occurs in the best-disciplined ship upon such an occasion. One must have been an actual witness, to appreciate it. Suffice to say that it is sufficient to render cool aim and effective fire absolutely impossible, and that it lasts long enough to permit the operators to withdraw into the darkness whence they emerged. Its suddenness and an undefined terror of its annihilating effects when the attack is delivered, creates a moral impression upon the assailed which adds to its effectiveness, and diminishes the chances of successful resistance.

The case of the "Housatonic" points to an application of the offensive torpedo system, particularly important to a Government which, like that of the United States, is opposed to the maintenance of large standing fleets—that is, its use to prevent or break up a blockade, by destroying or driving the blockading force from the immediate vicinity of a port. To render it effective, boats must be built specially designed for the purpose, and men must be trained and accustomed to their employment, as artillerists and other soldiers are drilled to the use of their weapons against the day when they will be called upon to use them.

The torpedo boats brought into actual service during the war were but imperfect machines, ill adapted to the service to which they were put. Who can doubt but that as great improvements will hereafter be made in them as have marked the progress of invention in other engines of war? The ordnance and small-arms of to-day bear no more resemblance to those with which the battles of the last century were fought, than do the turreted monitors to the vessels which composed the fleets of Nelson and Collingwood; and it is but reasonable to suppose that the torpedo boat which will figure in the next naval war will be equally incomparable to that of Bushnell or Fulton, or the contrivances in use during the rebellion.

Two distinct forms of torpedo boats naturally suggest themselves in considering this species of warfare: a submarine boat, which shall be navigable above or beneath the surface with entire safety to her crew, and a vessel which, moving only upon the surface, will answer the conditions imposed by the nature of the service to which it is devoted.

There seems no insurmountable objection in the way of the construction of a submarine boat; the principal difficulty has been one that ought to be remedied by the application of our increased knowledge of mechanics and chemistry, since the period when it was first conceived—that is, to regulate or purify the supply of air, so as to enable the operators of the boat to remain a considerable time beneath the surface. The general use of torpedoes, offensive and defensive, seems to lead to the introduction and use of such a boat, and it cannot be long before the inventive genius of man will supply the demand made upon it.

Submarine operations commenced by the invention and successful use of the "diving-bell," in the 16th century; but the earliest project for submarine navigation of which there is any record appears to be that of Cornelius Debbrel, who, during the reign of James I., constructed a boat to carry twelve rowers, besides passengers. He is also stated to have discovered a liquid which had the property of restoring air when it became impure by breathing. He died before his plans were perfected, and his secret died with him. Later, a man named Day constructed a diving-boat, but on his second trial-trip below the surface, he remained there, and was never heard of afterwards. Neither of these inventors contemplated using his machine as an engine of war, or had any idea of the effect of submarine explosions. About the same time with these experiments, another contrivance was invented by an Englishman, and is thus described in the *Philosophia Britannica:*

"It consisted of thick, strong leather, which contained half a hogshead of air, so prepared that none could escape, and constructed in such a manner that it exactly fitted the arms and legs, and had a glass placed in the fore part of it. When he put on this apparatus, he could not only walk on the ground at the bottom of the sea, but also enter the cabin of a sunken ship, and convey goods out of it at pleasure. The inventor is said to have carried on this business for forty years, and to have grown rich by it."

Neither of these inventions were generally known or understood even during the time of their existence. Bushnell certainly knew nothing of them, so that his submarine boat may justly be considered an entirely original conception. Fulton borrowed his ideas from Bushnell, but it does not appear that he greatly improved upon the original boat, or upon the torpedoes.

Since Fulton's experiments at Brest, and up to the period of the rebellion, submarine operations have been conducted, for wrecking and engineering purposes, in diving-bells and various forms of submarine armor, in which the diver is supplied with fresh air by air-pumps; but until the boat which destroyed the "Housatonic" was constructed, no attempt appears to have been made to produce a vessel to be propelled beneath the surface; and from her history we may take it for granted that she was, for all practical purposes, a failure.

The Government of the United States also constructed a plunging torpedo boat at an early period of the late war. Its inventor was a Frenchman, to whom the Government paid the sum of $10,000 for his machine, and entered into an agreement with him by which he was to operate the vessel against the enemy, under the command of an officer selected by the Navy Department. For every successful enterprise in which he and his boat should be engaged, he was to receive an additional sum of $5,000.

This boat was built under his superintendence, at the Washington Navy Yard, and an officer applied for and received orders to take charge of her, with the express design of using her to blow up the rebel iron-clad "Merrimac" at Norfolk.

Upon reporting for his novel command, this officer found the boat apparently completed; but the inventor, having received the $10,000, had decamped, taking with him the knowledge necessary to the operation of the principal part of his so-called invention, which was an apparatus by which the air contained in the boat was to be restored after it became impure by breathing.

This boat was built of boiler iron, treble riveted, in form like a cigar, thirty-five feet long, and six feet in diameter. She was to be sunk by admitting water into a water-tight compartment which extended along her length, and raised by expelling the water by means of two forcing-pumps. The weight of sixteen men was required to sink her when the compartment was full. The boat was propelled above and below the surface by sixteen oars, eight on each side, each constructed on the principle of the webbed foot of a waterfowl, being formed of two pieces, opening and closing like a book, hung at their junction to a rod, which was connected with a crank designed to be worked backward and forward by manual labor. It was found upon trial that a speed of only two-and-a-half knots could be attained on the surface by this machinery, worked by a full crew of sixteen men.

A row of thick glass "dead-lights" admitted light to the interior, where were two machines intended to purify and restore the air. One was a chemical apparatus to manufacture oxygen, and the other consisted of a vessel containing lime, with a bellows attachment by which the air was to be forced through it.*

Owing to the disappearance of the inventor, who alone pretended to understand its operation, this apparatus was never tested; in fact, it was considered that he had imposed

* It has been suggested that a number of jets or sprays of water admitted into the interior of a submarine boat, will tend to restore the purity of the air; but it does not appear that any reliable experiments have ever been made to test the value of this suggestion.

upon the officials at the Navy Department, and that the "invention" was worthless. Nothing was ever accomplished with this boat beyond making a few experimental trips to the bottom of the river. She was subsequently fitted with a propeller, and dispatched in tow of a steamer to Port Royal, but was lost in a gale off Cape Hatteras.*

Whatever difficulties may exist in regard to making a submarine boat effective for placing and exploding a torpedo beneath a ship, there can be none in constructing a surface boat which will answer the purpose, and be free from the defects discovered in those used during the war.

The first question is, what are the requirements of such a vessel? 1st, It should be swift, easily managed, and capable of being turned rapidly in obedience to its helm. 2d, It should be practically invulnerable, and should expose as small a surface to view as possible. 3d, Its machinery should be noiseless, and be capable of discharging any number of torpedoes in succession, in any direction from itself. 4th, It should be completely covered, so as to render swamping impossible. 5th, Its torpedo arrangement should be such that contact of the vessel or of the torpedo with the ship attacked would be unnecessary. 6th, It should be devoted solely to torpedo warfare.

The nearest approach to a complete torpedo boat is the craft designed and built by Engineers Wm. W. W. Wood and John L. Lay, U. S. Navy, yclept the "Spuyten Duyvil." Unfortunately, she was not completed until the time for testing her powers in actual service had passed; but there is no doubt that she is the most formidable engine of destruction for naval warfare now afloat of which the public have any knowledge.

A drawing of this ingenious and remarkable vessel is given in Plate XIV., where an elevation and plan of the bow is shown.

---

* My informant states that he heard indirectly that it was part of the absconding Frenchman's design to emerge from the boat in a submarine armor when the boat was beneath a ship, and having attached a torpedo to her bottom, return to his position, leaving the torpedo to be exploded by its own machinery.

By reference to the drawings, the following general description will be understood:

Length aft of stern-post to forward edge of gate-frame	73′ 11″
Length over all	84′ 2″
Breadth moulded	19′ 0″
" extreme	20′ 8″
Depth of hold	9′ 11″
Draft when launched, with 10 tons torpedo machinery and 2½ tons motive engine on board	4′ 0″
Draft when equipped	7′ 5½″
" going into action (sinking-tanks full)	9′ 1″
Displacement	206.9 tons
Thickness of armor plating on sides	5″
" " " on deck	3″
" " " on pilot-house	5″

In the bow is an opening communicating with an air and water-tight box or chamber, which is opened and closed by a sliding sluice-valve, worked by a shaft geared to a rack on the back of the valve. The valve and gearing is contained in a water-tight casing, communicating with the interior of the chamber, and the end of the vertical shaft projects through the top of the casing, and is furnished with a ratchet-wheel, the teeth of which are adapted to a pawl. On drawing back this pawl from the wheel, the sluice-valve falls by its own gravity, and closes the box water-tight. The water thus confined in the chamber is discharged by one of the large centrifugal pumps used in supplying the sinking chambers when in action. It can be accomplished in three seconds.

The torpedo is held in a *casing* secured to the end of the *operating bar*, which is rigged out by means of a chain fastened to its inner end, and passing around a *barrel shaft* turned by steam power; the operating bar is rigged in by a chain fastened to its outer end, and passing around a barrel shaft in the interior of the water-tight chamber. The two barrel shafts are so geared and connected that they revolve in opposite directions at the same time, both being driven by the same engine, placed in a suitable position in the hold of the vessel. Both chains are guided, and the turns prevented from overriding on the barrel shafts by blocks traversing on guiding bars arranged in front of each. The operating bar is made of malleable iron, is square, with the corners removed; it passes through a spherical stuffing-box, so placed in rear of the water-tight chamber, and fastened to it, as to form a universal water-tight joint; the bar also passes through a *sleeve*, fitted with friction rollers on the inside, the sleeve being so hung in a frame that it can be moved vertically and laterally by means of an independent engine suitably placed and connected. This sleeve and stuffing-box are intended to guide the operating bar as it goes out; by the former the desired inclination is given to the bar, and if it is desired to project the bar laterally, the sleeve is made to traverse along a cross-head to the proper position.

The operating bar is hollow, and within it is a rod, the rear of which projects a given distance beyond the rear of the bar, in which the rod can be moved longitudinally to a limited extent, a suitable packing being so secured to the rod as to prevent the water from passing through the interior of the bar. The internal rod passes through and into the casing for holding the torpedo; at this end of the rod are hinged two levers, forming together jaws for grasping the head of the torpedo shell; both levers are acted on by springs which close the jaws; the straight arms of the levers project through slots on opposits sides of the casing, both slots terminating in front in bevelled ends. The torpedo is placed in the casing; lugs on the torpedo shell, which slide along grooves formed in the casing, prevent it from turning; the open jaws receive the head of the torpedo, which being pushed back into the casing together with the rod and its jaws, the latter, owing to the springs, close on the projection of the torpedo and hold it fast at the end of the operating bar.

The torpedo, as seen in Pl. XI., has two chambers, separated from each other by a yielding wad or diaphragm, the larger chamber containing the explosive material, the other being an air space to direct and concentrate the force of the explosion.

A tubular chamber is contained within the shell, and at one end of this chamber a spherical weight is confined by a pin, which can be withdrawn, thereby permitting the weight to fall on a cap charged with detonate, and placed on a nipple at the end of the tubular chamber, this release of the weight taking place after the torpedo has been submerged and discharged clear of the operating bar, and when it occupies a vertical position in the water. One end of a cord is attached to the releasing pin, and is coiled in a chamber formed on the under side of the casing, the opposite end of the cord being attached to any part of that chamber.

OPERATION. The torpedo casing being within the water-tight box, the sluice valve down, and the box freed from water, a plate on the top of the box is removed, and the torpedo is placed in the casing, and pushed back into it so that the jaws of the internal rod close upon the projection at its base; the releasing cord is attached as described. The covering plate is then adjusted, and the apparatus is ready for action.

As the vessel approaches the enemy the sinking tanks are filled, so as to submerge her further into the water, and thus present as small a target to the enemy's fire as possible. Having determined the angle at which it is desirable to submerge the torpedo, the sleeve, operating bar, and parts connected therewith are elevated—the bar turning on a centre coinciding with the centre of the spherical stuffing box, which forms a perfectly water-tight ball and socket joint.

The vertical position of the operating bar having been thus determined, its proper lateral position should next be decided, for it may become necessary to project the torpedo laterally from the vessel; this is done by causing the sleeve to traverse athwart ships by devices for the purpose, which carries the operating bar to the desired position. The vessel is now brought close to the enemy, stopped, and the propeller reversed; the driving machinery is now started, the barrel shafts revolve, rigging out the operating bar. When it is fully extended, the action of the drums is simultaneously reversed without reversing the engine, and the operating bar is quickly withdrawn into the vessel. Immediately that bar begins to move back, the rear end of the internal rod comes into contact with a plate, which arrests its progress, while the bar continues to move rearward. The consequence of this arrest of the rod is the pushing of the torpedo from the casing, and by the levers of the jaws striking the bevelled ends of the slats in the casing, the jaws are opened and the submerged torpedo released.

The plate by which the internal road is arrested, is removed by a projection on the operating bar, as the latter continues to move backwards. In the meantime the submerged torpedo, owing to its buoyancy, rises and comes into contact with the vessel against which it is destined to be exploded. Owing to the backward movement of the operating bar, the cord attached to the releasing pin is gradually withdrawn from the chamber; this cord is of such a length that when the operating bar is in the act of completing its backward movement, the cord is pulled, the pin withdrawn, and the weight permitted to fall on the detonating cap placed on the nipple at the bottom of the tubular chamber. The disharge consequently takes place, and this at a time when the operating rod has been moved to a safe position, away from the torpedo, and within the box or chamber. The operating bar having reached the limit of the backward movement, the motion of the driving engine is arrested preparatory to adjusting another torpedo in the place previously occupied by that discharged.

The "Spuyten Duyvil" may be considered by many as lacking that simplicity of arrangement necessary to perfect operation under the extraordinary circumstances attending a torpedo attack; but it is due to the merits of the invention to remark, that, when handled with coolness and deliberation, no practical difficulties have been found to exist in the working of her apparatus, and in all the experiments made with her, it has proved entirely effective. It is easy to suggest difficulties which may arise when she comes to be used to blow up an enemy's ship, but there are few which could not be obviated by that skilful management which results from constant practice.*

The inventors claim to have made most important improvements upon their first invention, by which the operation is greatly simplified, and rendered much more certain in its effects, without the slightest risk of the vessel's being "hoisted by her own petard"—the danger of which appears to be the chief objection to the "Spuyten Duyvil," whose forward motion must have ceased before the operating bar can safely be extended, and the torpedo exploded.

These improvements consist in so constructing the torpedo boat and torpedo machinery, that a number of torpedoes are projected at the same instant to a considerable distance from the broadside of the vessel as it passes the enemy's ship, and this without arresting the speed or changing the course of the torpedo boat for an instant.

The torpedo is still further improved, so that it can be fired by electricity as well as by the mechanical device already explained.

During the present month (April, 1868) experiments made with this new apparatus and torpedo have fully demonstrated its practicability; the torpedo having been projected in a straight line beneath the surface the required distance, carrying with it considerable weight, and with the same accuracy that attends the firing of a gun.

It is designed to equip a practically invulnerable vessel of high speed with this apparatus, and it is confidently asserted that eight or ten torpedoes can be projected simultaneously

---

* The "Spuyten Duyvil" was attached to the James River squadron during the early part of 1865, where she wss employed as a picket launch until the fall of Richmond. She then had the honor of conveying President Lincoln to Richmond on the memorable occasion of his first visit to that city. Subsequently she was engaged in removing the Union and rebel obstructions by blowing them up with her torpedoes.

from her broadside to any given depth, which will explode with all reasonable certainty along a line of over 100 ft. of the length of an enemy's ship.

The iron-clads constructed by Mr. Reed for the British navy are provided with water-tight compartments, and it has been claimed by English writers that these vessels cannot be sunk by a torpedo, or, at least, time would be given to repair any damage that might be caused by the explosion of one beneath them.*

Whatever may be the value of Mr. Reed's system of construction, it is not likely that it would save a vessel from sinking if a single torpedo were successfully exploded beneath the ship, and that nothing short of dock yard repairs, supposing them available, would be of any use in stopping such a leak as would result from the explosion. But it is certain that, if plans now contemplated are successfully introduced into practice, no system of water-tight compartments would save a vessel from destruction when successfully assailed, *i. e.* when two or more torpedoes are successively exploded beneath the ship.

There is still another form of torpedo boat which may be said to have been forced into the United States service during the last stages of the rebellion, which merits but a passing description. The utter failure of the notorious twenty-three light-draft iron-clads to support the weights they were designed to carry, left them upon the hands of the Navy Department, so much useless material. To make them available for any warlike purpose, the idea was conceived of converting them into torpedo boats, and was so far carried out that a number of them were fitted with the apparatus designed for the picket launches previously described. Their low rate of speed rendered them in a great measure valueless, although in other respects they were well suited to the purpose.

---

* *U. S. Magazine*, Feb., 1868, p. 218.

CHAPTER XI.

ELECTRIC TORPEDOES.—NECESSARY PARTS OF APPARATUS.—AUSTRIAN SYSTEM.—COLONEL SCHOLL'S FUZE.—PLATINA FUZE.—STATHAM'S FUZE. —COLONEL VERDU'S ELECTRO-MAGNETIC INDUCTION MACHINE.—RHEOTOME.—M. SAVARE'S IMPROVEMENT.—WHEATSTONE'S MAGNETO-ELECTRIC EXPLODER.—BEARDSLEE'S EXPLODER AND FUZE.—ABEL'S FUZE.—RUSSIAN FUZE.—GUYOT'S FUZE.—ENGLISH EXPERIMENTS WITH MAGNETO-ELECTRICITY AND MAGNET FUZES.—WEST POINT EXPERIMENTS WITH BEARDSLEE'S APPARATUS.—ELECTRIC TORPEDOES PART OF PERMANENT DEFENCES. —BUOYANT TORPEDOES.—METHODS OF REMOVING THEM.—ILLUMINATION OF HARBORS.—SUBMARINE GUNS.—GENERAL DISCUSSION OF THE DEFENSIVE SYSTEM.

Military and naval engineers seem to have agreed that the most useful form of defensive torpedo is that which is exploded by an electric battery, and their attention has recently been particularly directed towards perfecting the apparatus by which its explosion may be controlled. It is also admitted that the general employment of the electric torpedo will greatly modify the system of harbor defence as now practised, while, in connection with far less costly works, naval enterprises against seaports will be rendered much more hazardous undertakings than they have ever yet been considered.

The principal argument in favor of the electric over any other form of defensive torpedo is that it is harmless, except when it is desired to bring its power into action; and that its explosion is not left to chance or accident, but is controlled by the intelligent will of an operator.

The application of electricity to produce explosions of gunpowder is, as we have seen, of comparatively recent date. It was suggested to Fulton during his time, but discarded by him as impracticable. In 1839, General Paisley is stated to have employed "galvanic firing to submarine charges on the wreck of the 'Royal George,' at Spithead,"* and we have

* Ency. Brit., vol. iv., p. 757.

noted, in a previous part of this work, how earnestly Colonel Colt labored to bring it into public favor.

The Russians were, however, the first nation who regularly and systematically introduced electric torpedoes as a portion of their harbor defences. They used voltaic batteries of great power, but proof of their effectiveness is altogether wanting.

The principal parts of a complete electrical apparatus necessary to ignite gunpowder, are three in number, viz.:

1. The electro prime mover, or apparatus by which the electricity is generated.

2. A metallic conductor, insulated by gutta-percha, or other non-conducting substance.

3. Fuzes or mine primers, which by their inflammation produce that of gunpowder.

We propose to describe briefly the several forms of these parts which have been used in mining operations.

For some time previous to the year 1851, Austrian engineers were accustomed to ignite blasting charges in their stone quarries by electricity, generated with plates of glass, and collected in Leyden jars, using but one conducting wire connected with the electrical apparatus, the other being in contact with the earth, near the opening of the mine. An uninsulated fine brass wire, suspended by poles, like an ordinary telegraph wire, was employed as a conductor.

The fuze, or mine primer, was an invention of an Austrian engineer, Colonel Scholl. Plate XII., Fig. 1, shows it in full size. It is terminated by a hollow wooden cone that is thrust into the powder by means of a wooden rod, grooved at the sides for the wires; within the cone is a quantity of gun-cotton; the base is closed by a cork stopper, split at the end to receive the wedge-shaped end of the rod, to which it is tied with twine; the grooves for the conductor are filled with pitch, and the ends of the wires are brought close to each other, within the mass of gun-cotton, so that the electric

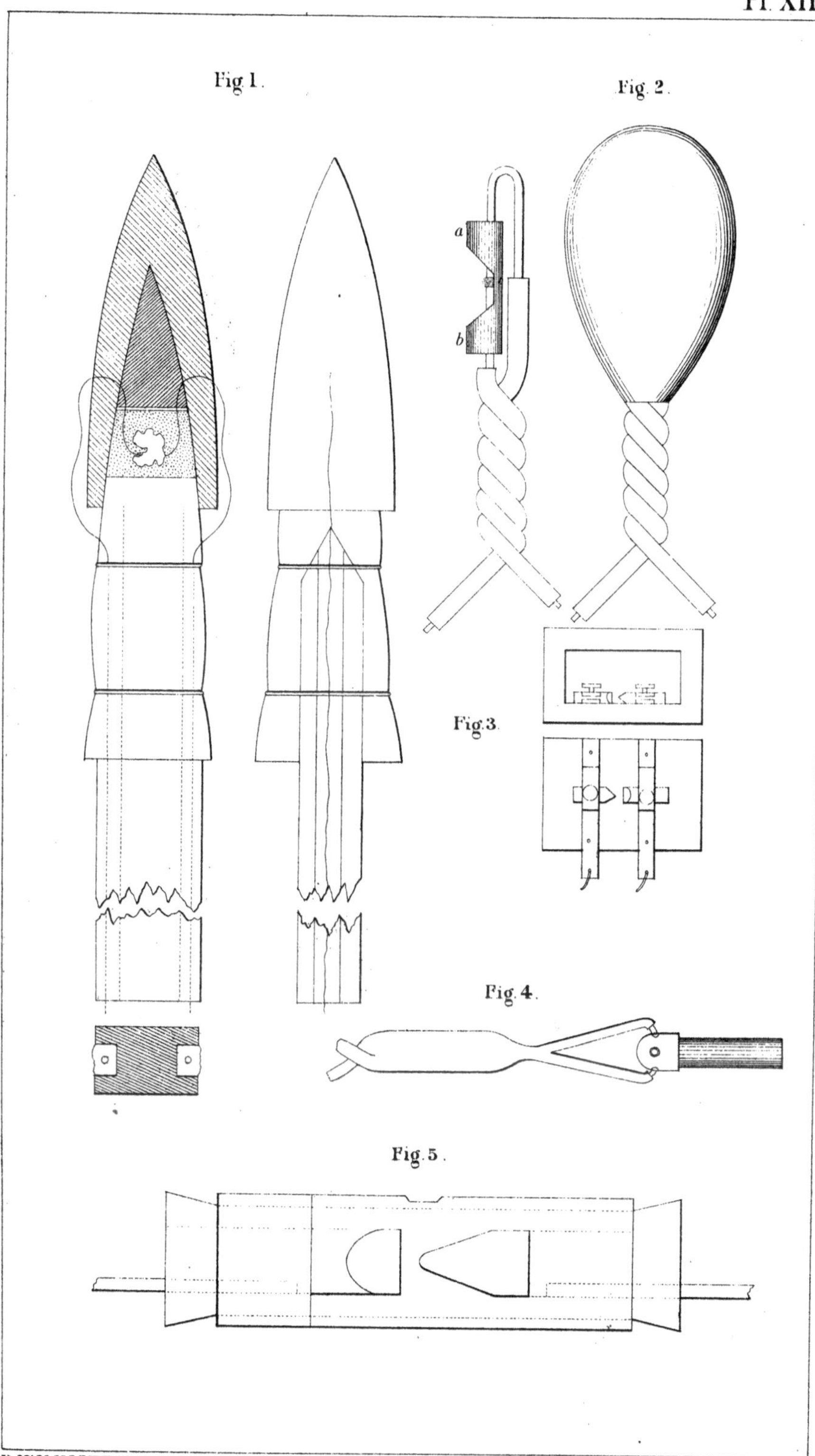

D. VAN NOSTRAND, Publisher.

spark, as it passes from one to the other, explodes it, and thus ignites the charge.* With this exceedingly simple apparatus, hundreds of charges have been fired without failure, at distances from the operators of over a mile. By using a properly insulated wire there seems to be no reason why it cannot be made equally efficient for the explosion of torpedoes.

Voltaic piles of a single liquid, as those of Wollaston or Munk, or more frequently piles with a constant current, as those of Daniel or Bunsen, have generally been used to explode gunpowder, until within a very short period.

The conductor invariably employed consists of red copper wire, a little less then one-tenth of an inch in diameter, covered with two layers of gutta-percha, the total diameter being about thirty-five hundredths of an inch. In this state it has the necessary flexibility to enable it to be coiled up and reduced to a small compass for transportation, and will remain intact for a long time under water. The conducting wires of electric torpedoes intended for the permanent defence of a harbor, may be additionally protected in the same manner as submarine telegraph cables.

The fuzes that have been employed with the voltaic piles form a most important part of the apparatus. They are of different forms, but are all based on the principle that if in a metallic conductor that communicates by its extremities with two poles of a pile, a break is made, and certain moderate conductors only are interposed, the ignition of this interposed substance at the instant the electrical circuit is closed will be sufficient to inflame gunpowder. Very fine platina wire was at first used to connect the ends of the conductor. Its effectiveness is greatly increased by surrounding the platina wire with fulminate of mercury—a substance highly sensitive to electrical action. Such an arrangement was originally adopted by the rebels (see Plate IX., Fig. 2), and used by them with effect.

When a copper wire has been covered for some time with vulcanized gutta-percha, the interior of the tube, on with-

---

* Delafield's Art of War in Europe.

drawing the wire, remains covered with a thin layer of sulphide of copper, which is a moderately good conductor of electricity. If a section of the tube thus formed be interposed between the ends of the conducting wires, and a current of sufficient intensity be caused to circulate through the wire, it will leave the wire at the break, and pass through the sulphide of copper; but here sufficient resistance will be set up to ignite the sulphide, and, if it is in contact with gunpowder, will explode it. Statham's fuze is constructed on this principle, but it is very uncertain in its action without fulminate of mercury as a priming substance. This is kneaded up with gum-water, and a small fragment of the paste placed between the metallic extremities of the conductor, is then dusted with mealed powder and allowed to dry. Plate XII., Fig. 2, shows Statham's fuze improved.

"The gutta-percha tube, *ab*, being prepared and cut as shown, the extremities of copper wires, considerably smaller than the conducting wire, and insulated by a thin layer of gutta-percha, are uncovered and scraped, and then inserted into the tube, allowing an interval of .15 of an inch. The wires are then bent as shown in the figure, and the priming inserted between the terminals. The whole is covered with a bag of gutta-percha filled with fine powder."

Abel, a distinguished English electrician, has discovered a priming substance which is said greatly to exceed in sensitiveness any other composition. It is prepared by reducing separately to the finest state of division 10 parts of subphosphide of copper, 45 parts of subsulphide of copper, and 15 parts of chlorate of potassa, and rubbing them well together in a mortar, with the addition of sufficient alcohol to thoroughly moisten the mass. The mixture is then carefully dried, and may be safely kept in close vessels until required for use.*

All the immense mines employed by the allies to blow up the Russian fortifications and docks at Sebastopol were fired

* Noad's Text-Book of Electricity, p. 314.

by direct currents from voltaic batteries and the platina or Statham's fuze. Much difficulty was experienced in securing proper explosions, and occasional disasters occurred. It is stated that the English engineer officers did not consider the process employed by them as reliable for military purposes.

It is known that a temperature of 500° Fahr. is necessary to heat platina wire to incandescence, so that to ignite powder by this means at considerable distances we should require a voltaic battery of great power, not only from the number but from the surface of the elements, for intensity and quantity are both necessary in the electric current.* Apart from the employment of powerful batteries, and often the use of two conducting wires, difficulties were constantly met with. The process gave uncertain results, especially over considerable distances, and finally it was not capable of producing the simultaneous explosion of a number of separate charges—a most important desideratum, as may be readily conceived, in the application of torpedoes to harbor defence.

Colonel Verdu, a Spanish engineer, has invented an apparatus, which, with Statham's fuze charged with fulminate of mercury, has effected the simultaneous explosion of five mines in a circuit. It consists in the application of what are termed in physics *currents of induction.* The voltaic pile is reduced to a single element of Bunsen's carbon battery, used to excite a Ruhmkorff coil, which thus becomes a multiplier of the current of induction. It substitutes for the direct and continuous current of the pile, often too feeble in its effects to produce the desired result, an inducted current,

* The length of the platina wire, which connects the terminals of a conductor, should be four-tenths of an inch, and its diameter four-thousandths of an inch; these dimensions have been found to give the best results. With it a single element of Bunsen's battery will ignite mealed powder through 155 yds. of No. 31 copper wire; collodion and mealed powder, 230 yds. By adding to this mixture dry chlorate of potassa the distance is increased to 230 yds. If fulminate of mercury is substituted for the mealed powder it can be ignited through a circuit of 285 yds. By passing the platina wire through a groove cut in the head of an ordinary friction match, and covering the wire with collodion, a very good fuze for voltaic electricity is obtained. It has been ignited at a distance of 395 yds.—*Mem. d'un Officier du Genie*, No. 17.

producing interrupted sparks, extremely energetic, and calculated, under most circumstances and at considerable distances, to attain the proposed end.*

Fig. 7.

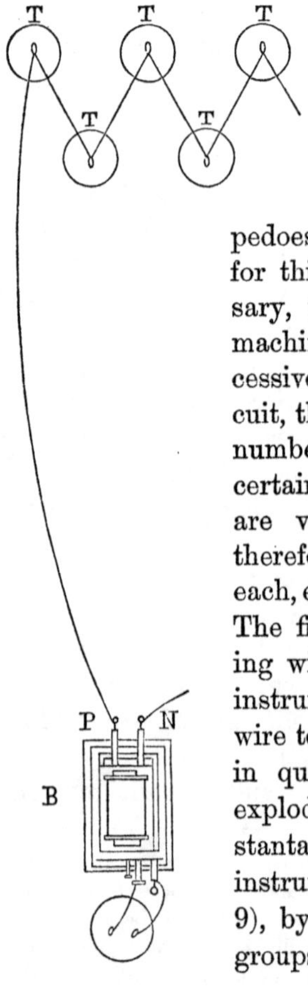

Fig. 7 shows Colonel Verdu's method of exploding a group of five torpedoes simultaneously. T T are the torpedoes, B the battery and coil, P the positive, N the negative pole.

Fig. 8 shows his arrangement for exploding twenty-five torpedoes practically at the same instant; for this five conducting wires are necessary, for, the discharge from the coil machine becomes so enfeebled by successive interruptions in the metallic circuit, that it will not be certain to ignite a number of charges in one circuit beyond certain limits, which with Statham's fuze are very narrow. The torpedoes are, therefore, arranged in groups of five each, each group to form a special circuit. The five extremities of the five conducting wires are brought together near the instrument, and then by making each wire touch the pole of the coil apparatus, in quick succession, the torpedoes are exploded with a rapidity practically instantaneous. Colonel Verdu suggests an instrument called a "Rheotome" (Fig. 9), by which simultaneous explosions of groups can be effected.

* For a full description of this electro-magnetic induction machine, see Delafield's Art of War in Europe.

Fig. 8.

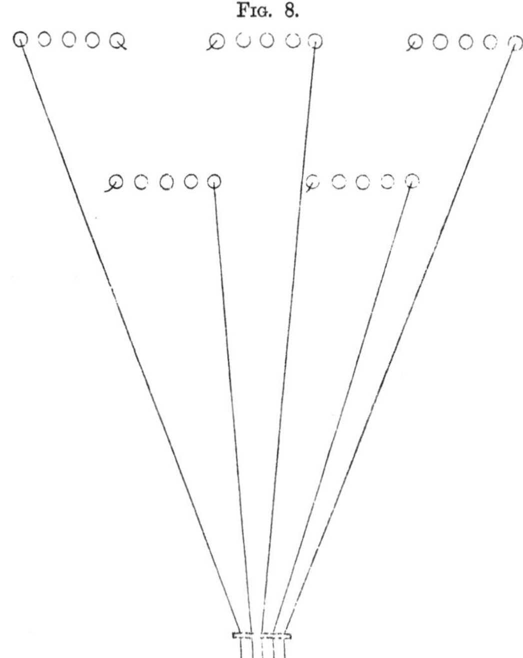

Fig. 9.

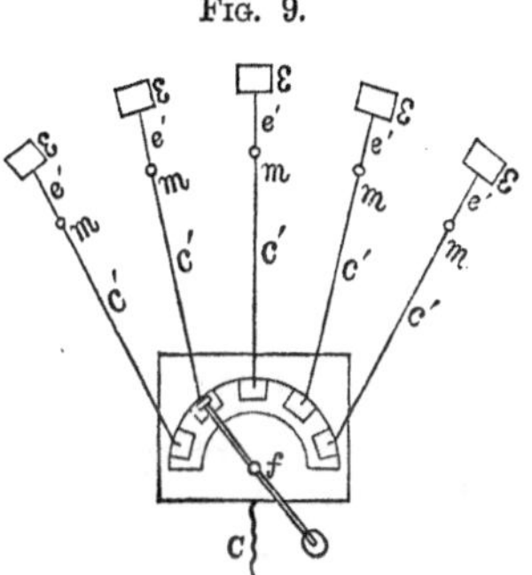

c represents a wire connecting one pole of the coil with a metallic index, *f*, which, by means of an insulated handle, may be made to describe a semicircle as rapidly as desired. Binding screws are provided to receive the separate wires, *c'*, leading to the groups, *m;* they are insulated from each other by glass or ebonite. The index, as it passsss each screw, presses upon metallic plates connected with them, thus bringing the torpedoes into connection with the coil machine. The wires *(e')* and plates *(e)* connect the groups and coil with the earth.

If the fuzes are so constructed that their explosion destroys the continuity of the terminals of the wire, the conducting wires to the torpedoes can be connected directly with a main wire leading to the pole of the coil. Those branches and fuzes which happen to offer the best facilities to the passage of the current will explode first, and the further passage of the current in their direction is prevented, and the remaining fuzes and torpedoes in their turn will be exploded. This arrangement is shown in Fig. 10; it was suggested by M. Savare, and successfully tried in France in 1854, with a view to its application to military mines and blasting operations.

Fig. 10.

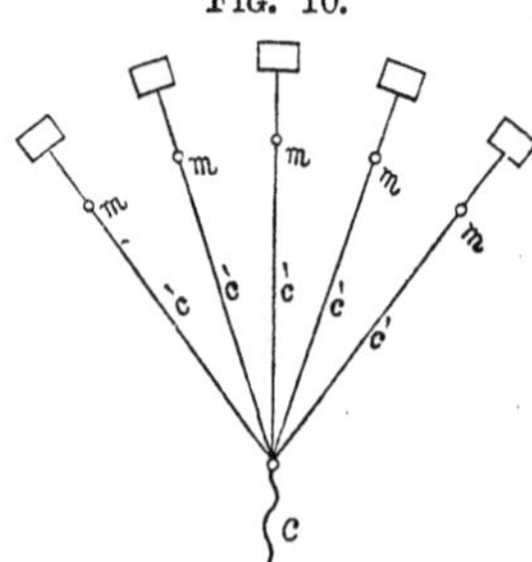

Colonel Verdu's arrangement is the best and most certain method of exploding torpedoes or mines in which the voltaic pile is used as a prime mover; but, like all other adaptations of voltaic electricity, this machine is subject to considerable irregularity, and liable to injury from a variety of causes.

The vast importance of the torpedo system of warfare, so strikingly illustrated by its efficacy during the rebellion, has directed the attention of the most prominent electricians of all countries to the subject of exploding gunpowder by electricity.

The result has been the introduction of magneto-electric machines, which have entirely superseded the voltaic piles and induction machines, like that of Colonel Verdu. Several forms of these instruments have been patented in this and in other countries, two of which are selected for description. Both are so simple in their construction, compact in their form, certain to effect their object, and so little liable to derangement and injury, that nothing seems to be wanting in either of them. Advantages are claimed by the designers of these two instruments for their inventions, but both embody the same principles, and may be considered equally effective.

Wheatstone's magnetic "exploder" is the invention of the English electrician, whose name it bears. It was imported

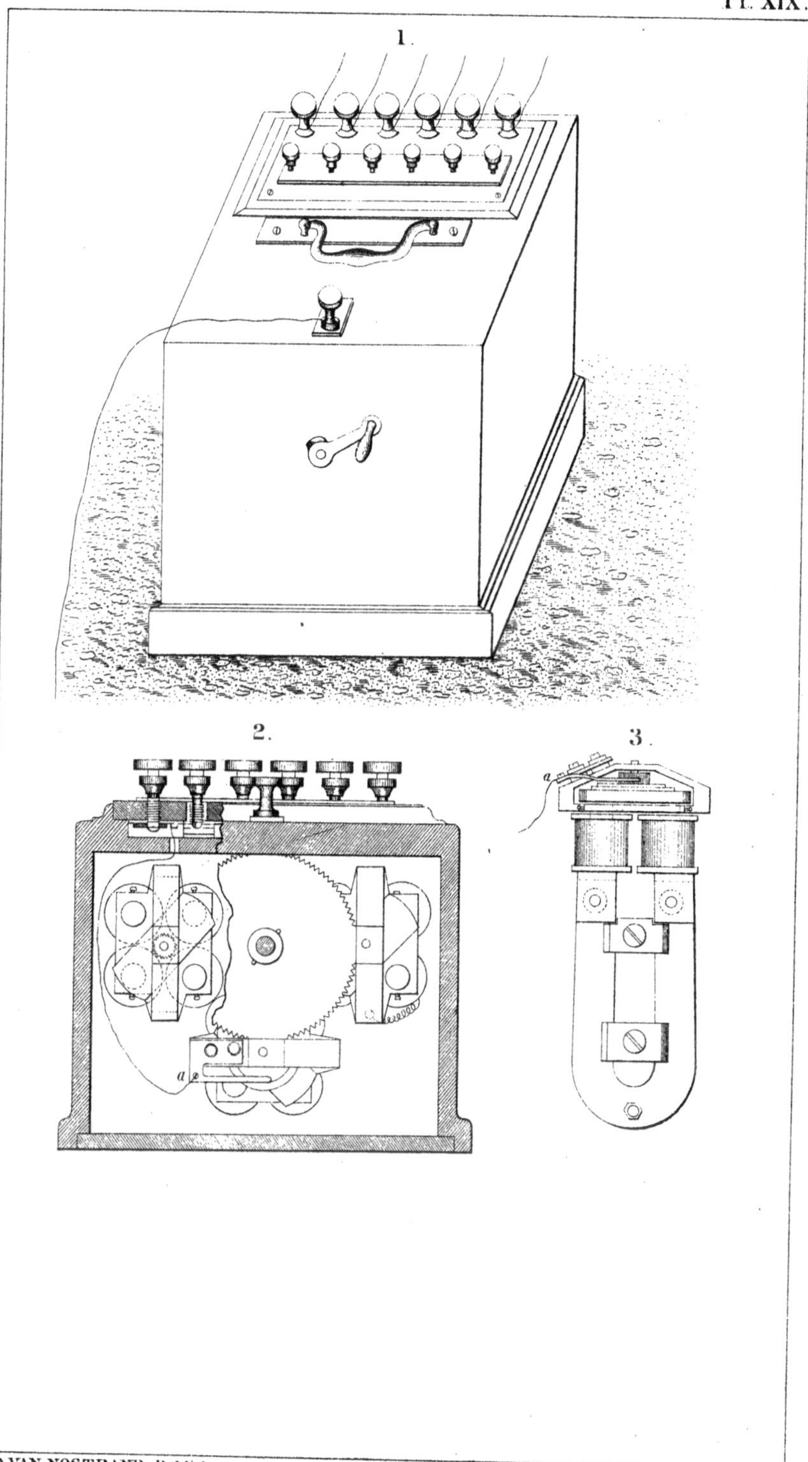

D. VAN NOSTRAND, Publisher.

by the rebels during the summer of 1864, and subsequently employed by them, in connection with Abel's "magnet fuze," hereafter described, to explode the torpedoes placed after its introduction.

Plate XV., Figs. 1, 2, 3, are sketches drawn to a scale of 3''=1ft. of this ingenious instrument. The drawings are made from one captured at Fort Anderson, Cape Fear river.

"Fig. 1 is a representation of the machine ready for service. Fig. 2 shows the arrangement of the magnets and machinery for obtaining multiplied motion. Fig. 3 is an elevation of the magnet from which the current is taken to the conducting wires leading to torpedoes."

The following description shows its action and effects:

"Three compound horse-shoe magnets, of seven bars each, 5½'' long, ⅞'' wide, 1¾'' thick, are placed horizontally; to each pole of each magnet are fixed two soft iron bars, surrounded by coils of insulated wire (there being twelve coils, four to each magnet). The coils of all the magnets are united together so as to form, with the external wires and the earth, so many single circuits. An axis carries three soft iron armatures in succession before each of the coils. All the magnets simultaneously charge the wire, and produce the effect of a single magnet of more than six times the dimensions of one of them; so that, when aided by a multiplying motion communicated by the toothed disc and pinion on the axis of the armatures, a very rapid succession of powerful currents is produced. The coils being stationary and the armatures alone in motion, the circuit is never broken during the action of the instrument. A key-board of ebonite is let into the top of the box, with six binding screws for conducting-wires, in metallic connection with six ebony-headed keys or circuit-closers; a metallic plate beneath the ends of these keys is connected by an insulated wire to the coils at *a*, where there is an arm pressing firmly upon a disc on the top of the armature, and revolving with it, so arranged as to break the circuit when the opposite wave of electricity is induced. The machinery being in motion, the operator, by pressing upon the keys, closes the circuit to the corresponding wires."

This apparatus is contained in an elegant mahogany box, forming a cube of about eight inches. It can easily be carried or moved about by one man. Its exploding power, when compared with any voltaic battery, is extraordinary, it being claimed for it that twenty-five charges in divided circuits can be fired with such rapidity that the effect upon the ear is as one explosion.

Another form of a magneto-electric machine for exploding mines is shown in Plate XV., Figs. 1 and 2. It is the invention of Mr. G. W. Beardslee, of New York, and differs from the Wheatstone exploder only in the machinery by which the multiplied motion is obtained, and the arrangement of the magnets, by which the inventor claims that a current of less intensity, but of greater quantity, is induced than is obtained by the Wheatstone instrument.

"It consists of a star-shaped compound magnet of ten points or poles, composed of a number of cast-iron plates placed together, each of 15 inches in diameter, the whole forming a compound plate 1 inch in thickness. The positive and negative poles alternate, and the whole is made to revolve rapidly by multiplying motion on an axis passing through its centre. The spaces between the points are filled with wood. The magnet is placed horizontally and above a soft iron ring upon which are ten cylinders of soft iron so arranged that they will all be covered at the same time by the poles of the magnet. These cylinders are each covered with 440 yards of silk-covered copper-wire coiled tightly upon them. The ends of the coils are joined together so that a continuous current can pass around any number of 'spools' desired, and can be arranged in sets according as more or less intensity of current is desired. To obtain quantity, the coils are separated into independent groups, each group throwing its current simultaneously into a common conductor, producing a single current.

"The lower surface of the points or poles are placed close to the upper ends of the coils, and by revolving the magnet rapidly by means of a crank, geared so that one revolution produces two of the magnet, the polarities of the soft iron cylinders are reversed, and a current induced running in opposite directions. The coils are $1\frac{1}{8}$ inches long, and 1 inch in diameter.

"The whole is secured in a cast-iron frame, and confined in a box 18 inches long, 13 inches deep, and 17 inches wide, as shown in Fig. 1. Binding screws for the conducting wires connect with the ends of the coils, and an index with an insulated handle closes the break in the circuit.

"Machines in which the magnets have more and less numbers of points, have been constructed on the same general principle."

The fuzes used with the magneto-electric machines are of great importance in securing certain explosions. Two forms seem to have given the best results.

That invented by Mr. Abel, and used in connection with Wheatstone's Exploder, called Abel's magnet fuze, has given the greatest satisfaction in England and France, and, all things considered, is as reliable as any that has been tried. Noad in his work on electricity thus describes it. See Plate IX., Fig. 3; also Plate XII., Fig. 4, which shows the fuze as prepared for service.

"In a boxwood head (*a*), there are three perforations, one through the centre, the others on each side and perpendicular to it. In the centre one is placed a gutta-percha tube containing two separated copper wires, $\frac{1}{16}$ of an inch apart, allowing the two ends to protrude from the head, bared of the gutta-percha covering; these ends are pressed into grooves in the boxwood head and passed into the side perforations, where they are secured by copper tubes driven tight into the holes. The circuit wires are then entered into these tubes, and the connection thus completed with the interior double wire. The lower end of the latter protrudes below the head $\frac{3}{4}$ of an inch, and is cut so as to make a clean sectional surface, the ends of the wire being carefully kept apart. This end is covered with a cap of tin foil containing about a grain of Abel's priming material (see p. 164), which is compressed slightly by the end of the double covered wire. The fuze is enclosed in a paper or tin case containing fine powder, which case is secured to the boxwood head, and the bottom closed with a plug of plaster."

Mr. Beardslee has patented a fuze, or, as he calls it, "cartridge," which if not as sensitive as Abel's, is remarkable for its efficiency, simplicity, and for the results that have been obtained with it. See Plate XV., Fig. 3, for sketches of this fuze, full size. Twin wires separately insulated are made to unite with two copper plugs of conical form ($\frac{5}{8}$ of an inch sprigs), driven obliquely into a cylinder of hard dry wood (*a*), and as nearly in contact as possible and yet preserve insulation; the larger ends are even with the end of the cylinder. By means of a file a groove is made across them, and the circuit is completed by plumbago; a line drawn by a soft lead pencil through the groove answers the purpose. The points of juncture of the wires and the plugs are covered with a mass of beeswax, and the whole is enclosed in a paper case, leaving space for a small charge of rifle powder at the base. The fuze is then coated with gum-lac.

The fuze that was employed by the Russians for their electric torpedoes is shown in Plate XII., Fig. 3. It consists of two cylinders of charcoal, bevelled at the end and placed in the same line on the bottom of a small box, in such a manner that the bevelled edges are about two-hundredths of an inch apart, and perpendicular to each other. Strips of copper hold the charcoal, by means of set screws, and the conducting wires are attached. India-rubber is placed in the bottom of the box, upon which the copper strips rest, and the box is filled with powder. The sensitiveness of this fuze is further increased by the addition of an inflammable coating of sulphide of antimony. Captain Guyot, who suggested the above addition, improved upon this arrangement of the fuze, by employing a glass tube instead of a wooden box (Fig. 5), the ends of the tube being stopped with cork, which contains the charcoal cylinders and the end of the circuit wires. The tube is then filled with fine powder, through the opening *(a,)* and the whole is enclosed in a cartridge of powder.

This fuze is stated to be less sensitive than Statham's or Abel's, but it is sufficiently certain, and has the advantage of requiring no detonating composition.*

Two other fuzes have been experimented with abroad,

* No. 17, Memorial de l' Officier du Genie.

with unsatisfactory results; one invented by M. Savare, previously alluded to, and another by Lieut. Mereau; both having for their object, to obtain simultaneous explosions, by preventing the ends of the conducting wires from coming into contact with the ground, or water, at the time of the explosion, which would complete the circuit and prevent the current from igniting other fuzes.

Having noticed the principal apparatus heretofore employed to explode mines and torpedoes, it remains to give the results of such experiments as have been made with the different machines and fuzes. The first of which we have satisfactory accounts, are related in the "Professional Papers of the Royal Engineers," and were conducted by a Royal Commission, at Chatham, England. The following extracts are taken from their report:

"1. The explosion of a single charge of powder by means of the phosphide of copper (Abel's) fuze, and a magneto-electric apparatus of the smallest size, is absolutely certain.

"2. Abel's fuze is as safe and permanent as any arrangement employed in the service for the ignition of powder by friction or percussion.

"3. By the employment of Wheatstone's magnetic exploder, the ignition at one time of fuzes varying in number from two to twenty-five, is certain, provided they be arranged in branches of divided circuits. To attain this result it is only necessary to use a single wire, insulated by a coating of gutta-percha or rubber, and simple metallic connections of the apparatus and the charge with the earth.

"4. The explosion of from 12 to 25 charges may be thus effected at a distance of at least 600 yards from the apparatus, with a rapidity practically simultaneous. This refers to charges on land.

"5. The number of submarine charges which can with certainty be exploded with the exploder, is more limited—from two to ten may be exploded with certainty, particularly if the charges are imbedded in sand or mud. [Note.—These reports are founded upon experiments made with a Wheatstone instrument, subsequently improved, as shown in our sketch, Plate XIX., by the addition of the key-board holding separate wires to each charge or group ; this arrangement is the invention of Count du Moncel, and applied in the year 1863, by Wheatstone, to his machine.] By the employment of separate wires leading from the instrument to each charge, or adopting Count Moncel's rheotomic arrangement, there is little doubt but that the same results would be obtained in submarine operations as in those on land.

"6. The most important precautions necessary to secure success in the use of the magnet are—proper insulation of all the circuit wires, and thorough protection of all connections of wires from moisture.

"7. The system of firing charges by magneto-electricity possesses important advantages over the application of the voltaic battery in the following particulars :

"*a.* The magnetic exploder is at any time ready for immediate employment ; it is easily transported by hand * * * ; it is not liable to injury or derangement, provided the most ordinary care be applied to its preservation and transport. It may be employed for many years without suffering any important diminution of its power. Its arrangements being purely mechanical, any ordinary workman can repair any injury it may sustain.

"*b.* The magnet fuze is more certain than any fuze arrangement applied with the voltaic batteries. It may be kept in any climate, and will bear rough handling without chance of injury.

"*c.* The implements and materials required for carrying on operations with the magnet are few, inexpensive, and readily procurable. They occupy but little space, and require no more care than ordinary artisans' tools.

"*d.* All the operations necessary in the employment of the magnet are of the simplest possible character, and can be performed by a person of the most ordinary intelligence.

"It can be confidently asserted that the general certainty of the magneto-electric apparatus is decidedly greater than that of voltaic batteries. * * * * *

"The reporters are strongly of the opinion that the instrument which will (in special cases) furnish results far surpassing in magnitude those attained by the most powerful voltaic batteries hitherto applied, is the hydro-electric apparatus of Armstrong, which they feel convinced may be so arranged in its details as to admit of ready application, with confidence, in the most extensive mining operations. A considerable number of experiments would, however, still be required before its adoption in such instances could be recommended. [NOTE.—This refers to the experiments with Sir William Armstrong's hydro-electric machine, capable of producing electricity in enormous quantities by effluent steam. See Noad's Text-Book, p. 29.] For all operations of a general character, however, it is considered that the results obtained up to the present time have satisfactorily proved that the system of exploding charges by a magneto-electric current is, in point of simplicity and certainty, superior to any other which has hitherto received application, and that no impediment whatever exists to its being at once adopted into military practice."

The results of experiments in this country with Beardslee's machine and fuze have been equally satisfactory, and in some particulars still more extraordinary. Although his machine was patented in 1859, its application to the explosion of torpedoes did not occur to him until later, the patent being principally for telegraphic purposes. His first experiment with his fuze was in February, 1863, when, in presence of the President and many officers of note, he, with his field telegraph instrument, exploded a number of "fougasses" a few hundred yards from the instrument. Under orders from the Navy Department, in February, 1864, he used his apparatus in removing the piling obstructions in Elizabeth river, using torpedoes consisting of india-rubber bags, containing 200 pounds of powder, proving the efficiency of his machine and fuze to ignite submarine charges.

In January, 1865, a series of experiments were instituted

at West Point by General Delafield, who appointed a board of officers to witness and report upon the efficiency of Mr. Beardslee's plans for exploding torpedoes at great distances and depths.*

The following is a brief resumé of the experiments there conducted. The machine usually employed was the one already described, viz., a ten point radial magnet, although magnets having but six points were occasionally employed with some of the minor experiments. The conductor was composed of seven strands No. 23 tinned iron wire, insulated by a covering of india-rubber. But one conducting wire was used, the water completing the circuit :

"1. An iron tank containing 50 lbs. of powder was exploded at the word of command, in twenty-eight feet of water, through five miles of wire laid on the ice, which was very solid and thick. The explosion made an opening 30 feet in diameter, and covered the ice with mud over a space 100 feet in diameter.

"2. A 13-inch shell was exploded in 120 feet of water, over the same length of wire. This produced no fracture of the ice, although the concussion was plainly felt.

"3. Twenty 8-inch shells were placed on the ice, about 8 feet apart, along an insulated wire, connected with the machine by about three-quarters of a mile of wire. At the word, 17 of the shells were exploded at the same moment."

In April the experiments were continued with the following results :

"1. Sixty 8-inch shells were arranged in three sets of 20 each, as shown in Plate XV., Fig. 6, the shells in each set being 8 feet apart. The usual ground connection was supplied by a common copper wire. Fig. 6 shows the arrangement of shells and connections with machine. All the ground wires of the cartridges, in each set, were connected with one ground wire, making three ground wires leading to the machine ; the insulated wires were arranged in the same manner. The ground wires

* This Board consisted of Professor W. H. C. Bartlett, Major G. H. Mendall, and Capt. G. T. Balch, U. S. A.

were fastened to one of the poles of the instrument, while the three insulated wires were brought together near the opposite pole, to which was attached a short piece of wire, its end bared for a half an inch, of the insulating substance, so that it could be drawn rapidly across the three ends of the circuit wires of the groups, in order to make the explosions practically simultaneous. At first only 17 of the shells in the first set exploded, owing to the faulty arrangement of the circuit wires, which caused the current to pass from one wire of the cartridges to the other. This being prevented by a new arrangement, 14 in the first set, 19 in the second, and 17 in the third were exploded simultaneously.

"2. Three torpedoes, containing 60 lbs., were placed about 150 feet apart respectively, in 4, 5, and 50 feet of water, and exploded upon the same circuit, and with one wire. The one in 4 feet exploded instantly, succeeded immediately by the one in 5 feet ; and after the lapse of a minute, the motion of the magnets being arrested, the effects of the explosion of the third were visible, it throwing up a mass of mud and water six or eight feet over the spot where it had been sunk."

The report of the Board was highly favorable to Mr. Beardslee's system. Such failures as occurred, were, in their opinion, due to faulty connections rather than to defect in principle.

The War and Navy Departments, in the mean time, purchased a number of Beardslee's machines, and substituted them for the voltaic batteries previously in use. In March, Mr. Beardslee was put in charge of all the U. S. torpedoes in the James river, previously mentioned as having been placed at the obstructions near Dutch Gap, and personally instructed the officers and men employed to operate them. No opportunity, however, occurred for using them, and the close of the war, in April, put an end to further practical advancement in this new species of warfare. In October, 1865, Mr. Beardslee conducted a series of experiments in England, by authority of the British Admiralty, and our own Government instituted similar proceedings at about the same time, which will be referred to under the head of Theories of Explosions.*

Mr. Beardslee has patented an invention for coupling conducting wires, called a "Union," which has been successfully used, and deserves mention :

Plate XV., Fig. 4. The two strands of wire which it is desired to connect, pass through two discs of metal (*a a*), placed face to face, and of hard rubber (*b b*), in a gutta-percha tube (*d*). The wires of each strand are separated radially, and spread out on the face of each disc ; between each disc and the top and bottom of the tube, is placed a tube of vulcanized rubber (*b b*), and a metal washer (*c*). The tube is closed by a water-tight screw plug of gutta-percha (*e*). For connections under water, the whole should be covered with pitch, if it is to remain submerged for any length of time.

Plate XV., Fig. 5, shows a form of electric torpedo proposed by Mr. Beardslee, and the method of exploding it, by arranging two or more fuzes in the mass of powder, which, by their simultaneous explosion, cause the more complete combustion of the charge, and thereby an increased effect. The cylindrical case is made of galvanized iron, the top and bottom being of cast-iron. The conducting insulated wire passes through the rubber "union" at *B*, and is secured at the bottom of the case at *D;* the end which now becomes the ground wire is separated at a proper interval, and passes out through a brass "union" at *C*, where it may be fastened to the head of the shell. Two or more of the cartridges, or fuzes, are then secured to the conducting wire and ground, as shown in the figure. The charge is contained within an interior chamber, surrounded by an air-chamber (*A A*).

* The following additional experiments made by Mr. Beardslee with his apparatus, are interesting :

Powder has been fired over the telegraph circuit, between Washington and New York, a distance of 200 miles, with a ten-point magnet and the Beardslee fuze. With both wires brought to the poles of the magnet, the "cartridge" or fuze is readily ignited, although a section of several feet of the rubber insulator is removed, and the bared portions placed in water. The secondary conductor, plumbago, is so intensely ignited by the electrical current, as to set fire to the wooden end of the fuze.

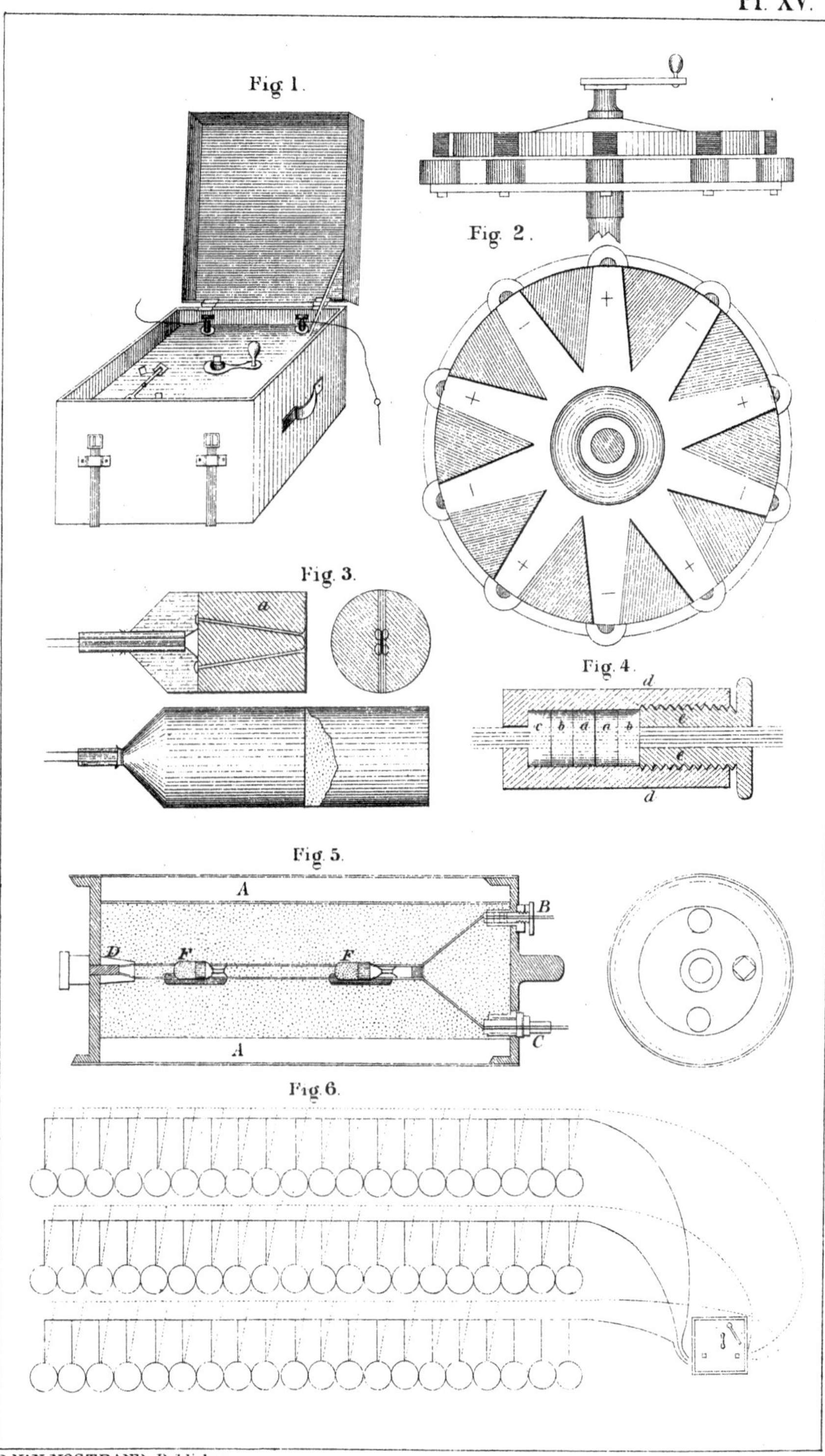

D. VAN NOSTRAND, Publisher.

In dealing with the subject of defensive torpedoes, we have thus far confined our attention to electric torpedoes, which, as they must be connected with the permanent fortifications, may be considered as belonging to that system, and naturally fall to the charge and direction of the army engineer, rather than to that of the naval officer.

The use of floating submerged torpedoes, however, is so intimately connected with the safe navigation of the channels through which ships of war assisting in the defence of a harbor must at all times be able to pass, that they should evidently be under the direction of the naval force, as part of the floating defences. Useful as they are in the defence of a harbor, they are exceedingly dangerous to the parties employing them; and unless their positions are accurately known, so as to be avoided, a port may be as effectually closed to our own vessels as to those of an enemy. The loss of the "Schultz" in the James, and the "Marion" and "Ettiwan" at Charleston, are cases in point. The rebels followed the practice of leaving narrow and crooked channels open for the passage of transports, gun-boats, and blockade-runners, and the immunity of their vessels is mainly due to the intimate knowledge of the naval officers of the situation of these defences, they having sole charge of this branch of torpedo operations.*

Fulton's idea of attaching machinery to submerged floating torpedoes, by which they are released from their moorings after a stated interval, and rise to the surface, although never perfected by him, seems practicable, and, if carried out successfully, would add much to the efficiency of the system. The form of the floating submerged torpedo is altogether unimportant; a great variety of shapes and a multiplicity of arrangements for exploding them were proposed by both sides during the war. The rebels were peculiarly prolific

* The value of buoyant torpedoes to a blockading force, as can readily be understood, is very great. They can be placed in channels at night; and, as the object of a blockade is to close the harbor to *all vessels*, the principal objection to their use becomes an advantage. The mere fact that they were in use, would of itself add to the efficiency of a blockade.

in these inventions, the simplest and most effective only having been described.

The following principles should govern their construction :

1. The case must be strong, and absolutely water-tight.

2. The machinery by which the charge is to be exploded should be simple, sure of action, not liable to corrosion or fouling from any cause, or to become disarranged or inoperative by action of the current.

3. Their discovery or removal by an enemy should be rendered difficult by the ordinary processes of dragging, sweeping, and such devices as "torpedo-catchers."

4. They should be easily, safely, and rapidly planted, and so arranged as to be safely removed, when necessary, by those acquainted with their construction and location.

5. They should be cheap, and as small as possible, so that the proper effect is produced by their explosion.

The practice of our officers during the late war, when entering channels in which the presence of torpedoes was suspected, was to drag or sweep for them in the following manner :

The ships' boats were provided with grapnels attached to long ropes and chains, and proceeded in advance of the vessel or vessels, dragging the grapnels over the bed of the channel, thoroughly raking the fair channel-way through which it was desired to pass. If a grapnel caught a torpedo it was hauled upon until its explosion occurred, or the torpedo dragged out of the path.

Boats acting in couples would each take one end of a line weighted in the centre with chain or kentledge, and, separating nearly its length, pull together at right angles to the line, the bight being thus swept over considerable surface. If this operation was carefully conducted it seldom failed to lead to the discovery, explosion, or removal of most of this species of torpedo. Many hundreds were rendered innocuous by these means during the war.

Where several vessels were operating together, they followed closely in the wake of the leading vessel, and nearly all stationed in inland waters were sooner or later provided with "torpedo-catchers," which, although occasionally inoperative to protect, very frequently saved vessels from destruction.*

A plan has been patented by which it is proposed to throw, by mortars arranged on a vessel specially adapted to the purpose, bombs arranged with grapnel-hooks, which on reaching the bottom are to be hauled upon by ropes or chains attached to them, the ends of which are retained on board. The plan, however, has never been successfully applied. Floating rafts, barges of considerable draft of water, and various other devices, have been suggested and employed with more or less success. All contact torpedoes are liable to be removed and overcome by ordinary ingenuity, if it is allowed full exercise by uninterrupted operations; but the results of their use during the war will not permit of any doubt as to their utility as part of the submarine defences of a water approach.

In waters commanded by an enemy, dragging and sweeping can only be carried on under cover of darkness. The application of calcium or magnesium lights to illuminate the enemy's positions, and to protect our iron-clads from the secret approach of torpedo boats, was frequently tried during the war, with great success. Similar arrangements could easily be made to light waters in which torpedoes are placed, and thus guard against their removal or displacement by an enemy.

There are two inventions for submarine war, which, properly speaking, cannot be called *torpedoes*, yet deserve to

---

* These were simple arrangements of spars and weighted nets, rigged out 20 ft. in advance of the vessel, the net extending below the keel, with spars at each lower corner to keep the net from being swept beneath the ship. Each commander exercised his own ingenuity in these contrivances; some of them were very clever and efficient.

be mentioned in this connection. We refer to submarine batteries composed of guns or mortars fired by electricity, or mechanical devices for producing contact explosions. A variety of similar plans have been patented, but the only ones which have been experimented upon are "Jones' Submarine Battery" and "Hunt's Submarine Gun." The former consists of a brass howitzer placed in a framework of wood and iron, its trunnions resting on rubber "packers." The whole is placed at the bottom of the channel, the gun pointing vertically. It is fired by contact; arms and levers, connected with friction-primers in a water-tight box, communicate fire to the charge. Loaded with two pounds of powder and a hollow shell, this gun was sunk in four fathoms water, and discharged by its apparatus into a heavy raft placed over it. The effects were extraordinary, considering the smallness of the charge; the raft was blown to pieces, and the gun (a 20-pounder) was uninjured.

"Hunt's Submarine Gun*" consists of a breech-loading rifled gun, attached to the side of a vessel at considerable distance below the surface. A water-tight tompion closed the muzzle for loading. The torpedo was arranged on the principle of a rocket, the original direction being given by the gun, and experiments made with it proved that it could be projected several hundred feet through the water. The inventor, Major E. B. Hunt, U. S. A., while conducting a series of experiments with his "battery," was killed by the accidental explosion of the torpedo, while attempting to adjust his apparatus, after it had been set in motion; the results known only to himself, are thus lost, no one having prosecuted further the experiments he commenced.

It may be now assumed:

First. That we have in either of the magnetic batteries described, a simple and certain method of exploding torpedoes at any distance from, and at the will of, the operator.

---

* This idea of *submarine guns* is an old idea of Fulton's, who made several experiments with one, and proposed to build a vessel armed with them.

Second. That practically simultaneous explosions of a number of torpedoes may be made with equal certainty.

Third. That the floating submerged torpedo can be so constructed as to fulfil all the conditions necessary to its action.

The question, therefore, as to the efficacy of the defensive torpedo system relates principally to our power so to combine and distribute electric and contact torpedoes, that a hostile fleet cannot come near enough to our ports to do material mischief, without incurring the hazard of disastrous explosions beneath the ships.

It is not enough, that as at Fort Fisher, Charleston and Mobile, torpedoes should be placed only in the channels immediately adjacent to the fortifications, with the view to prevent steam iron-clad ships from running by the defences; for, as we have seen, they failed of their object at Mobile. At Fort Fisher, the fleet was mainly instrumental in accomplishing the reduction of that work without incurring any danger from them; while at Charleston, although the inner harbor was made secure against our fleet by torpedoes, it nevertheless operated for two years against the enemy's positions without material losses from this species of defence.

From a careful inspection of the chart of either of the above-mentioned localities, it seems very clear that by a different arrangement of the fortifications, *with a view* to the employment of torpedoes as a system of defence, the chances of successful resistance would have been greatly increased.

Fort Fisher, for example, was so placed that, without entering into the channels immediately in its front, and which alone offered facilities for the successful application of the system, our fleet was able to concentrate upon it an overwhelming fire, which destroyed its artillery, and rendered the assault comparatively easy. Had the fort been placed so that, to make its fire effective, our fleet would have been compelled to pass over the bar, and enter upon the waters prohibited by the submarine defences, it would have been secure against any attack by a fleet however powerful. Such is the opinion of Vice-Admiral Porter, who says, "had Fort Fisher been built a mile further back, Wilmington could have defied us as long as the rebellion lasted."*

The effective range of modern artillery should, therefore, govern the distance from the fortifications where the torpedo system is to commence; and, according to the facilities afforded by the configuration of the shores, the width of the channels, and the location of the fortifications, defensive torpedoes will be more or less effective in repelling a naval attack.

There are few harbors in which torpedoes of both forms cannot be so placed that a fleet must pass or rest over them in order to attack its defences. Without great expense, they may be so distributed as to cover the channels of approach, and by leaving a passage free from "contact" torpedoes, permit ingress and egress of friendly vessels.

The difficulty presented in the application of electricity as an explosive agent, is the determination of the relative position of the ship and the torpedo, in order that the operator of the battery may know when to produce an effective explosion. By planting torpedoes in groups, so that the forces developed by simultaneous explosions shall surely destroy or disable an object within their limits, we are able to dispense with mathematical certainty in fixing the position of the ship; still the greatest precision is desirable.

To this end, it is necessary that each torpedo or group should be accurately laid down upon a chart of the harbor, and numbered in regular order. Several positions should be selected at such points within the defences, that lines bearing from at least two of them shall intersect at each torpedo or group as nearly at a right angle as possible. Let observers be placed at each of these positions, in telegraphic communication with the operator of the battery, each provided with a torpedo chart, and theodolites, plane-tables, or other instruments adapted to the accurate measurement of horizontal angles. The charts of observers should have marked upon

* Report Sec'y of Navy, 1865, p. 201.

them the point of observation and the lines of bearing only, so that in the event of the capture of one signal station with its apparatus, the enemy would not be advised of the localities of the torpedoes.

The operator and signal men being at their stations, let us suppose an enemy's fleet is approaching to attack. The telescopes of the instruments being carefully adjusted to the several lines of bearing, as soon as it is evident to an observer that any of the vessels will pass a particular line, the operator is warned by telegraph, and the instant the ship crosses the line, the fact is announced by specifying the number only of that line. If two or more observers coincide at the same instant in signalling the same number, the ship must then be at the point of intersection, or over the torpedo or group upon which the lines respectively bear. The operator, previously warned, then explodes the group thus signalled to him. Its effect will depend upon the promptness of the observers and operators, the accuracy with which the positions of the torpedoes have been determined, the lines of bearing plotted, and the instruments adjusted.*

Such an arrangement as is here suggested seems necessary to the effective use of electric torpedoes in very wide harbors, at considerable distances from the operator. In narrow channels, at short distances, it is not difficult to explode torpedoes at the proper instant as the vessel crosses the line of sight of the operator. Simple range stakes, as used by the rebels, in such cases serve every purpose.

The usual method of ascertaining the distance of a ship or other object at sea, depending upon triangulation, in which the height of the mast is assumed, and the angle subtended by the mast between the truck and water-line is measured by an instrument in the hands of an observer, is far too inaccurate to be used in determining the relative position of ships and torpedoes, even with the most carefully prepared tables.

* It is easy to conceive of mechanical devices by which the circuit would be closed by the coincidence of the instruments with which the angles are measured; and if the battery is constant, the explosion could thus be effected without depending upon the vigilance of an operator.

Numerous inventions for measuring distances upon water have been offered, principally for the use of artillerists; among them a camera obscura, with a graduated scale and vernia for measuring the distances on the image formed in the instrument, seems practicable, if the camera can be placed at a considerable height above the water-level.

The accompanying sketches show the torpedo mound, system of ranges, torpedoes and connections, at Fort Fisher, as they existed at the time of its capture.

FIG. 11.

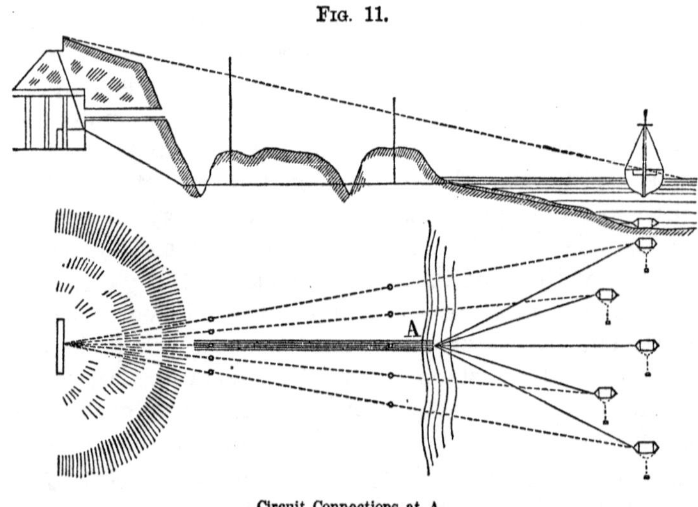

Circuit Connections at A.

FIG. 12.

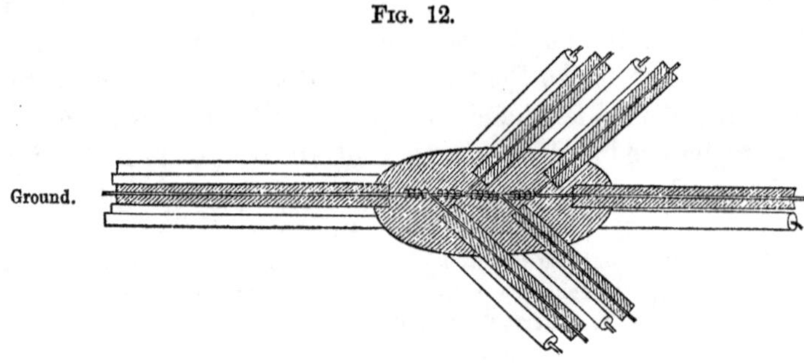

Two conducting wires were employed to each torpedo, which were of the form and size shown in Plate IX., Fig. 1. The wires were covered with tarred yarns, and weighted at intervals with sections of chain; being brought together at extreme low-water mark, one wire from each torpedo, numbered to correspond with the torpedo with which it was connected, was placed in a deep trench running to the mound; the other wires were severed at a point above high water, the ends bared of the gutta-percha insulator, and connected to one of the wires in the trench in the manner shown in Fig. 12. The connections, being carefully insulated, are then buried in the sand. The centre wire is carried within the mound and attached to one pole of the battery; the others are intrenched up to the parapet of the mound, where they are connected with metal circuit-closers, numbered to correspond with the torpedoes; a wire is brought from the other pole of the battery to the parapet, and connected with a metal plate beneath the circuit-closers. The battery being charged and the connections completed, an operator stationed on the parapet observes when a vessel crosses the line of bearing to a torpedo as shown by the range stakes, and, closing the corresponding circuit by pressing upon its key, produces the explosion of the particular torpedo over which the vessel is determined to be.

The point selected for the submergence of these torpedoes was at an extremely narrow part of the channel; the lightest draft vessels would have been compelled to pass over one or more of them in the endeavor to run by the ranges, while the destruction and sinking of one vessel in the channel would inevitably have barred the further advance of her followers.

When the torpedo cases are properly constructed, the powder contained in them is kept in perfect order, although submerged for a long time. Many of both forms, electric and contact, that were removed by our people at the close of the war, had been under water for more than a year, and in some instances more than two years. When examined, slight crystallization was discovered in places, but their effectiveness was unimpaired, and disasters frequently occurred in handling them.

With the lapse of time, the natural deposit of a muddy channel covers the torpedo and its wires. It seems practicable to bury them, in the first instance, in order that anchors may not accidentally foul them, and that the enemy may be unable either to discover their locality or destroy their connections by dragging or submarine operations.*

The art of submarine warfare is still in its infancy. Many interesting questions in regard to it are as yet unanswered by the results of such experiments as have been made, and have escaped from the jealous care of the persons or governments who have conducted or instituted them. It cannot, however, be doubted that practice and patient investigation will develop the full power of this novel element of defence, and to an extent not yet conceivable.

Gunpowder, closely packed in water-tight cases, has so far been employed as the explosive agent. It remains to be shown whether, by the employment of other more highly explosive compounds, as gun-cotton or nitro-glycerine, the effect of submarine explosions may not be rendered still more destructive and certain.

Gun-cotton is not injured permanently by damp, like gunpowder, nor is it so liable to absorb moisture. Large quantities can be exploded instantaneously, with a power more or less violent and active according to the strength of the case in which it is enclosed, its power being in exact proportion to the resistance it encounters.† The Austrians, as is well known, have ever been the firmest advocates for its adoption for military and mining purposes, and, so far as we are enabled to judge from their experience, it seems peculiarly well adapted to submarine operations. The only instance of which we have any knowledge of its application to this pur-

* The introduction of *defensive* torpedoes alone seems to necessitate the use of submarine boats and the adaptation of submarine illumination, in order to examine the bottom of a channel, with the view to the removal of torpedoes by the assailants as well as their examination and repair by the defence.

† Holley's Ordnance and Armor.

pose is in an experiment made at Venice, related in Holley's Ordnance and Armor. A barrel containing 400 lbs. was here placed near a sloop in ten feet of water, at eighteen feet distance, and exploded by electricity. The vessel was shattered to pieces, and the fragments thrown to a height of four hundred feet. From this experiment it would appear that the line of least resistance, ten feet, was practically ignored, and that the sudden and violent expansion of the gas created such a disturbance of the equilibrium as to break through the vessel's side in a horizontal direction, although at a distance of eighteen feet from the centre of explosion. With gunpowder the explosion would have been harmless.

In England, during the year 1863, a commission was appointed to report on the application of gun-cotton to warlike purposes. Baron Von Lenk, a major-general in the Austrian army, and the inventor of the system by which this material is made available for military purposes, attended the meetings of the commissioners, and gave them all the information in his power in regard to it. In answer to the question: "How is gun-cotton adapted for mining?" he replied: "The more accelerated effect of gun-cotton, and the possibility of enclosing in the same space more than double the quantity of gases, especially directs us to employ gun-cotton where it is desired to attain an energetic effect for mining purposes; for example, *to secure harbors by means of sea mines.*"

The reader is referred to the very interesting article on gun-cotton contained in the work already quoted, for further information in regard to the adaptability of this explosive agent for warlike purposes.

CHAPTER XII.

EXPERIMENTS IN SUBMARINE EXPLOSIONS.—SUBMARINE BLASTING.—MAILLEFERT SYSTEM.—CASE OF THE "MINNESOTA."—ABSOLUTE CONTACT UNNECESSARY.—"ALBERMARLE."—"TERPSICHORE."—CONDITIONS OF AN EFFECTIVE EXPLOSION.—AIR CHAMBERS.—WOOD & LAY'S TORPEDO.—EXPERIMENTS WITH IT.—ERICSSON'S TORPEDO.—MAJOR KING'S WILLET'S POINT EXPERIMENTS.—DESCRIPTION OF APPARATUS.—EFFECT OF AIR CHAMBERS.—INCREASING NUMBER OF POINTS OF IGNITION.—RELATIONS OF CHARGE, DEPTH, AND DISTANCE.—EXTENT AND FORM OF CRATER.—CONCLUSIONS.—THEORY OF SUBMARINE EXPLOSIONS.—NITRO-GLYCERINE.—MR. NORTH'S PRACTICE.—APPLICATION TO SUBMARINE OPERATIONS.—DYNAMITE.—CONCLUSION.

Very few reliable or satisfactory experiments have ever been made to determine the laws governing the explosive force of gunpowder, or other explosive compounds under water, and the results of such as have been made, have usually been kept secret for reasons connected with public policy.

As is well known, a Government commission, known as the "Torpedo Commission," has been organized in England, and for several years it has been engaged in investigating the bearing of the torpedo system upon naval warfare and the science of fortification. We can only judge of the importance of the results of its labors by the time which has been devoted to the investigation, and the carefulness with which the results are witheld from public scrutiny. In France also great attention has been given to the subject, and a torpedo school, for the education of a corps of submarine artillerists, has been established by the Government, whose pupils are being specially instructed in this new branch of military and naval science.* In fact there is scarcely a government in

* The French have probably made greater advances in submarine warfare than any other nation. They have in service a torpedo boat termed "Plongeur," but its principles and action are shrouded in secrecy.

Europe which is not actively engaged in preparations to develop the system to its fullest extent, and in due time we may expect the mantle of secrecy to be withdrawn, and an interchange of ideas upon this as upon other questions of public armament.

The amount of attention which early discussions of submarine explosions has excited, is very well illustrated by the following extract from an article on mining, in that work of general reference, the Encyclopædia Britannica:

> "It may be here observed that explosions under water have, in some instances, been proposed as a mode of attack in marine warfare; and it is presumed that explosions at considerable depths might occasion such an impression upon the water, and so disturb the equilibrium of the atmospheric pressure, as to be capable of sinking large ships or floating batteries."*

It would be supposed that the extensive application of gunpowder to the removal of obstructions to navigation, would have led, before this, to the determination of all the rules establishing the proper relations existing between the amount of the charge, depth of water, distance of object, and effect produced; but owing to the difficulties in the way of making observations, or other causes, submarine mining seems to be in a very crude state, and little that is reliable has been written or is known about it.

The practice has usually been to drill holes in the subaqueous rock, or other obstructing material, for the reception of the charge of powder, and to proportionate it by the same rule governing ordinary blasts in mines and quarries, which may be stated thus:

For ordinary blasts, in rocks of uniform consistence and cohesion, the charge of powder is proportioned to the cubes of the lines of least resistance. This line is the distance between the bore and the open side of the rock, measured in the direction in which the resistance is least. In chalk, the

---

* Enc. Brit. vol. iv. p. 757.

charge in pounds is found in practice to be in the proportion of $\frac{1}{32}$ of the cube of the line of least resistance in feet.

Recently Mr. Maillefert, a mining engineer, has introduced the practice of simply placing the charge of powder upon the surface of the subaqueous rock which he desires to remove, thus dispensing with the slow and laborious process of drilling, and the use of diving bells. He bases his calculations of effect upon the theory of resistance the water offers to the passage of bodies through it, which is as the square of the velocity and the mass of water displaced; hence the gas produced by the explosion would meet with such resistance in passing through the water to the surface, that the force would act in all directions, although in a different degree.

This plan has been found effective in cases where the proper proportion exists between the depth of water over the charge and the quantity of powder exploded, although it does not appear that Mr. Maillefert, or any other person, has stated what this proportion should be, or that engineers have given any great amount of attention to the subject; but the practice of drilling has been partially abandoned for the cheaper method above mentioned in cases of deep blasting. Where the water is shallow, or the bottom very hard rock, drilling is necessary to produce effective results.*

All of the instances where torpedoes were successfully applied during the late war are evidences of the vast power of submarine explosions, against all sizes of vessels, and at greatly varying depths. The most complete case, and which may be looked upon in the light of a great practical experiment, is that of the attack upon the "Minnesota" (p. 122). Here we have given: 1st, the quantity of powder exploded (53 lbs); 2d, the distance below the surface at which it was

---

* Mr. Maillefert had charge of the attempt to deepen the channel at Hell Gate, N. Y., some years ago, where he practised his system almost exclusively; but results do not seem to have proved its effectiveness. General Newton, who has charge of the renewed efforts now being made, has returned to the former practice, and, with the use of the "diamond drill," is confident of success.

exploded (6 feet, as shown by the centre of effect upon the ship's side); 3d, the fact that the charge was practically in contact with the ship at the moment of explosion, as it was ignited by a sensitive contact fuze; 4th, the extent of the injury resulting from the explosion.

The law governing the explosion of powder in any position, as generally stated and received, is that its destructive energy is mainly directed in the direction of the line of least resistance. In vacuo, much of its force is lost for want of resistance; in mid-air, the force is exerted practically alike in all directions, confined, as in a gun, in the direction of the bore; in blasts, in a line between the bore and the face, or open side of the rock. So, in water, the fluid yields, in the first instance, in all directions, to the sudden expansion, but most rapidly in that direction which offers the least resistance to the passage of the gas to the air, which ultimately determines the force of the explosion; hence, in order that an object shall receive the full force that the charge is capable of exerting under the circumstances, this line of least resistance must pass through it.

Applying this law to the case of the "Minnesota," we must conclude that the resistance due to the form and material of the hull at the point of explosion was greater than the resistance offered by the column of water immediately over the torpedo, and that the greater part of the force exerted escaped directly upwards. That this was actually the case is shown by the large column of water forced into the air. Hence it follows that to have secured the destruction or sinking of the ship, 53 lbs. of powder should have been exploded at a greater depth than 6 ft. It may, however, be inferred, judging by the actual effect of this explosion, that had the charge of powder been considerably greater, the explosion would have been equally effective, as the smaller charge exploded deeper in the water. The following general deductions may be made: 1. The deeper the torpedo is submerged when in contact with a ship, the smaller may be the charge, and, *vice versa*, the nearer it is to the surface the greater must be the charge, in order that its explosion may disable or sink the vessel. Numerous instances have occurred where large torpedoes have exploded harmlessly at the water-lines of ships. A very early one is recorded in the attempt upon the French shipping at Boulogne, with Fulton's torpedoes.

As is well known, absolute contact of the torpedo and ship is very far from being a necessary condition to her destruction, provided the requirements as to depth of submergence and quantity of powder are fulfilled.

The "Albemarle" was blown up by a torpedo which was at a considerable distance from her bilge at the moment of its explosion, and an examination of her injuries after she was raised showed that it was not beneath her bottom or floor, which was intact. A hole about five feet in diameter was made in her bilge and side, and the direction of the explosion, as shown by the interior injuries, was diagonal to the surface.

So, too, in an experiment made before a commission appointed by the Admiralty in England, in October, 1865, the "Terpsichore," frigate, was blown up with a torpedo exploded by electricity, which was dropped alongside of her from a boat, and was found to have been carried by the tide to a considerable distance from the plane of her side. The explosion tore through her frame and decks in a line diagonal to the surface, on a prolongation of the straight line joining the torpedo and the ship at its nearest point. The torpedo contained 170 lbs. of powder.*

The experiment at Venice, previously referred to, also illustrates this point, although the extraordinary effects produced by that explosion were due to the nature of the explosive material employed.

The general conclusions, then, to which we have come in regard to the application of torpedoes to ships would seem to suggest, as the conditions of success, *that whatever is the size of the charge the distance between the ship and torpedo should be*

---

* The electric torpedoes of the rebels, planted in very deep water, contained, as will be remembered, 2,000 lbs. of powder.

the least possible, while the depth to which it is submerged should be the greatest practicable. This gives as the best possible position for an effective explosion a point immediately beneath and in contact with a vessel at its lower part.

So situated, it may be reasonably concluded that a very moderate charge of powder would be effective against the frame of the strongest ship.

Since considerable discussion has arisen upon the value of an air chamber attachment to a torpedo, as for instance, in the form of torpedo shell, invented by Messrs. Wood and Lay (see Plate XI.), and adopted by Mr. Ericsson, in his Obstruction Remover, the advantages of the arrangement as claimed by the former are here given:

"The first part of this invention relates to the construction of a submarine shell or torpedo, which is composed of a casing of any desired form, and of any suitable material, so charged with gunpowder or other explosive substance, as to leave an air space in the shell, which space is separated from the charge by a yielding wad or diaphragm.

"The main object of this portion of the invention may be enumerated and expressed as follows:

"*First.* The concentration of the full force of the explosion, and the direction of that force in the desired course.

"*Second.* Sufficient buoyancy to enable the torpedoes to rise after they have been submerged.

"*Third.* The maintenance of the submerged shell in the proper position for producing the best effect.

"*Fourth.* A certainty of the entire charge being consumed, and the full force therefrom obtained, before the water can reach and injure the explosive compound.

"*Fifth.* A much more destructive effect than can be caused by the explosion of torpedoes as hitherto constructed."

Although the diaphragm, which is made of any suitable

material,* is packed sufficiently tight to maintain the explosion compressed within the desired limits, it is not so tightly secured to the interior of the casing as to prevent it from yielding and passing into the air-space the instant the explosion takes place.

In order that the claimed advantages of this submarine shell or torpedo may be thoroughly understood, it may be well here to give the following brief account of certain experiments made at Schenectady, New York, in obedience to orders from Rear-Admiral F. H. Gregory, U. S. N., the account being taken from the official report of Captain Charles S. Boggs, U. S. N., and Chief Engineer W. W. Wood, U. S. N.

"The dimensions of the experimental shells were as follows: Three feet in height, one foot in extreme diameter, cylindrical in form, and constructed of iron one-sixteenth of an inch thick, with a diaphragm inside dividing the interior into two compartments, the lower compartment containing the powder, and the upper portion acting as an air vessel to direct the course of the explosion.

"The shells, when exploded, were in a vertical position.

"Experiment No. 1.

"In this trial the shell contained 40 lbs. of powder, and was retained at the bottom of the river, at a depth of 10 feet, by a weight of 120 lbs.; the weight being detached, the shell rose to the surface in two seconds, and then exploded, raising a column of water, as nearly as could be determined, 175 feet high, some of the fragments of the shell being projected upwards to the height of probably 400 feet.

"The diameter of the column of water raised was about 8 feet, and caused but little disturbance immediately under the vortex of the explosion.

"Experiment No. 2.

"In this case the shell contained 60 lbs. of powder, and was moored to the bed of the river; a heavy raft of timber, 16 feet

* In the improved shell this diaphragm is made of wire gauze.

by 16 feet square and 10 inches in thickness, solid, well bolted, and secured, was placed over the shell, 3½ feet of water intervening between the raft and the top of the shell.

"When the shell was exploded the raft was blown to atoms, some of the pieces being raised to a vertical height of from 175 to 200 feet.

"The column of water in this case was concentrated and solid, reaching, apparently, a height of 200 to 250 feet, the fragments of the raft falling at no great distance from the point of explosion.

"EXPERIMENT No. 3.

"The shell in this case contained 50 lbs. of powder, and floated in the water, so that the upper extremity of the shell was about one foot beneath the surface.

"The column of water was projected about 250 feet vertically, and was 6 feet in its concentrated diameter.

"The shells were exploded by a line of about 125 feet in length, at which distance the operators stood without any inconvenience, and could have been in a boat 10 feet from the point of explosion without being in any danger, except from falling timber broken up by the explosion."

The cause of these most extraordinary results may be best explained by the following extract from the report :

"In torpedoes and submarine shells, as heretofore constructed, the explosions have been nearly equal in all directions.

"It is well known that powder exploded in vacuo loses much of its effect, and in torpedo cases filled entirely with explosive compound, rupture takes place instantly, when, in consequence of the water coming in contact with the powder, much of it remains unburnt, and its effect is dimished in the ratio of the quantity unburnt.

"The centre of gravity of the improved shell is so fixed that its vertical position at the time of contact and explosion is secured, and a diaphragm of slight resistance being placed in the shell, forms an air space, which directs the force of the explosive material in the shell, while it secures the means of causing it to rise rapidly when liberated, and of maintaining its vertical position in contact with the bottom of the vessel when exploded.

"The experiments prove very conclusively the correctness of this theory. The method of firing was by liberating a ball enclosed in a tube two inches in diameter, extending the length of the shell."

Mr. Wood adds to this report, in a pamphlet explanatory of the invention:

"From the foregoing experiments, it will be seen that the concentration of the force of the explosion is caused by the air chamber. The moment the ignition of the charge is effected, the first part to yield will be the diaphragm, and the disruption of the torpedo and the force of the explosion will be in the direction in which the diaphragm was moved in the first instance."*

A number of experiments were made in New York by Mr. Ericsson with his torpedo, particularly to test the value of the air chamber in giving direction to the force of explosion; fears having been entertained that the explosion of so great a quantity of gunpowder (700 lbs. No. 7 powder) would destroy the vessel or the raft to which it was attached. Planks were nailed on the rear of the raft, extending below the level of the torpedo; a steam-tug then pushed the torpedo against a row of piling; the charge was fired, tearing up the obstructions, and elevating into the air a huge mountain of water many feet high immediately in front, while the bulkhead of planks was not disturbed or a joint started.

The following official reports of a trial with this torpedo, made off Charleston, S. C., during the war, also show that, whether due to the air chamber or other causes, the explosion was not attended by any damage to the vessel from which it was fired:

---

* It is claimed by Mr. Lay, that he invented the torpedo apparatus and shell used by the United States during the late war, and that Mr. Wood's connection with it was in bringing it forward and to the favorable notice of the Government.

Pl. XIV.

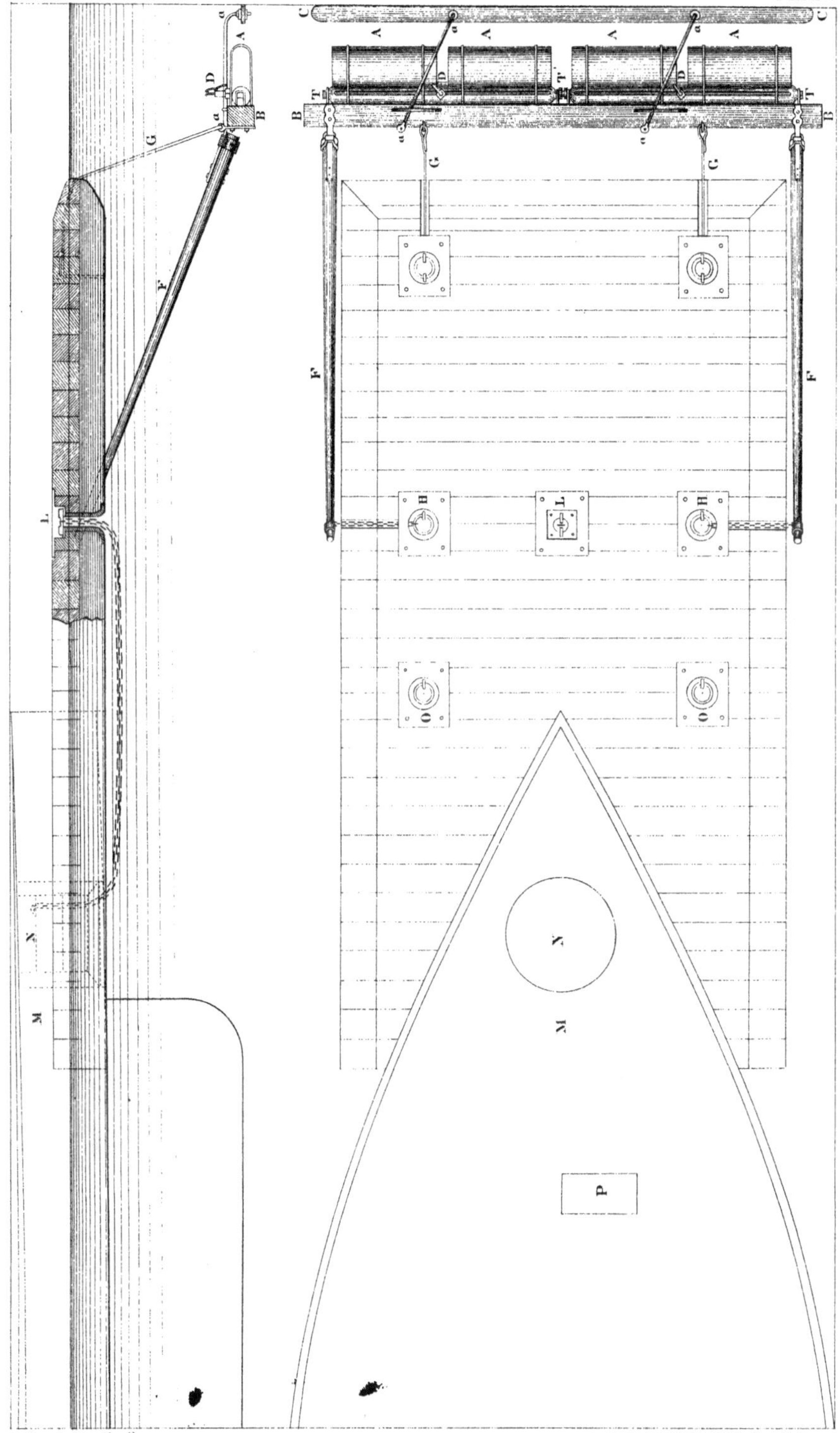

See Appendix C.

D. VAN NOSTRAND, Publisher.

"UNITED STATES IRON-CLAD 'PATAPSCO,'
"OFF MORRIS ISLAND, *November* 7, 1863.

"SIR,—I have the honor to report that after two trials, one of which failed on account of the damaged condition of the powder, we succeeded yesterday in exploding the torpedo designed by Mr. Ericsson. For the special purpose of removing fixed obstructions, I think it, like all that Mr. Ericsson undertakes, a complete success. The shock of the explosion was hardly perceptible upon the vessel.

"While I give my unqualified approval, resulting from this practical test in favor of this invention of Mr. Ericsson, I am constrained to believe that, for operations against iron-clads, or a moving force, the arrangement and attachment are too cumbersome and complicated. In my opinion, we require something, in the way of a torpedo, which can be managed with facility, and will not interfere with the steaming and manœuvring of the iron-clads.

"I am, Sir, yours respectfully,
"T. H. STEVENS,
"*Commander.*

"Rear-Admiral J. A. DAHLGREN,
"*Commanding South Atlantic Blockading Squadron.*"

"UNITED STATES MONITOR 'PATAPSCO,'
"OFF CHARLESTON, SOUTH CAROLINA, *November* 7, 1863.

"SIR,—I respectfully submit the following report of an experiment made yesterday of an obstruction remover, which was designed by Captain Ericsson. This obstruction remover consists of a cast-iron shell, or torpedo, about twenty-three feet long and ten inches in diameter, containing seven hundred pounds of powder. This is discharged by a trigger-board placed directly in front, and extending the entire length of the shell, adjusted on the plan of a parallel ruler. This board, by being pushed in contact with obstructions, will spring two locks placed equidistant on the torpedo, causing an explosion of the shell. These torpedoes are suspended from rafts carried on the bows of monitors, and held in position forward by two booms, which are firmly secured to the raft. There is also attached to the forward part of the torpedo a series of air vessels, so arranged as to cause the explosive power to be expended in that direction.

As this trial was only made to show the effect of the explosion on the monitor, and how much it interfered with the manœuvring of the vessel, it was carried on in deep water. The 'Patapsco,' the vessel on which the trial was made, had, on account of the foulness of her bottom, only a speed of about 3½ knots with the raft on. I should judge she was not to be driven more than three knots; and in making a circuit with the helm hard down, it takes at least half as much more room.

"In exploding the torpedo, which was suspended at a depth of thirteen feet, the shock was hardly perceptible on the 'Patapsco,' while the body of water displaced, and thrown upwards to a height of from forty to fifty feet, was really fearful. This body of water was thrown forward, and but a slight quantity of water fell upon the deck of the vessel. The raft was raised about two feet at the forward end, but sustained no material injury. In reference to the effectiveness of this arrangement for removing and destroying obstructions, such as spiles, chains, net-work, and torpedoes, which it can be brought in contact with, I believe it will be completely successful. The three rafts which are now at hand can have all the attachments made, except launching the torpedo overboard, so as to be ready for use at short notice.

"I am, very respectfully, your obedient servant,

"THOMAS J. GRIFFIN,
"*Inspector of Iron-clads,*
"*S. A. Blockading Squadron.*

"Rear-Admiral J. A. DAHLGREN,
"*Commanding S. A. Blockading Squadron,*
"*Off Charleston, S. C.*"

Perhaps the most systematic course of experiments ever made in this country, with a view to arriving at the laws governing the explosion of gunpowder under water, were made by Major W. R. King, U. S. Army, under the instructions of General Delafield, Chief of Ordnance, at Willet's Point, N. Y., in November, 1865. We give such extracts of his report as appear most striking, and which go to show that the advantages claimed by the inventor of the Wood & Lay torpedo are mainly imaginary.

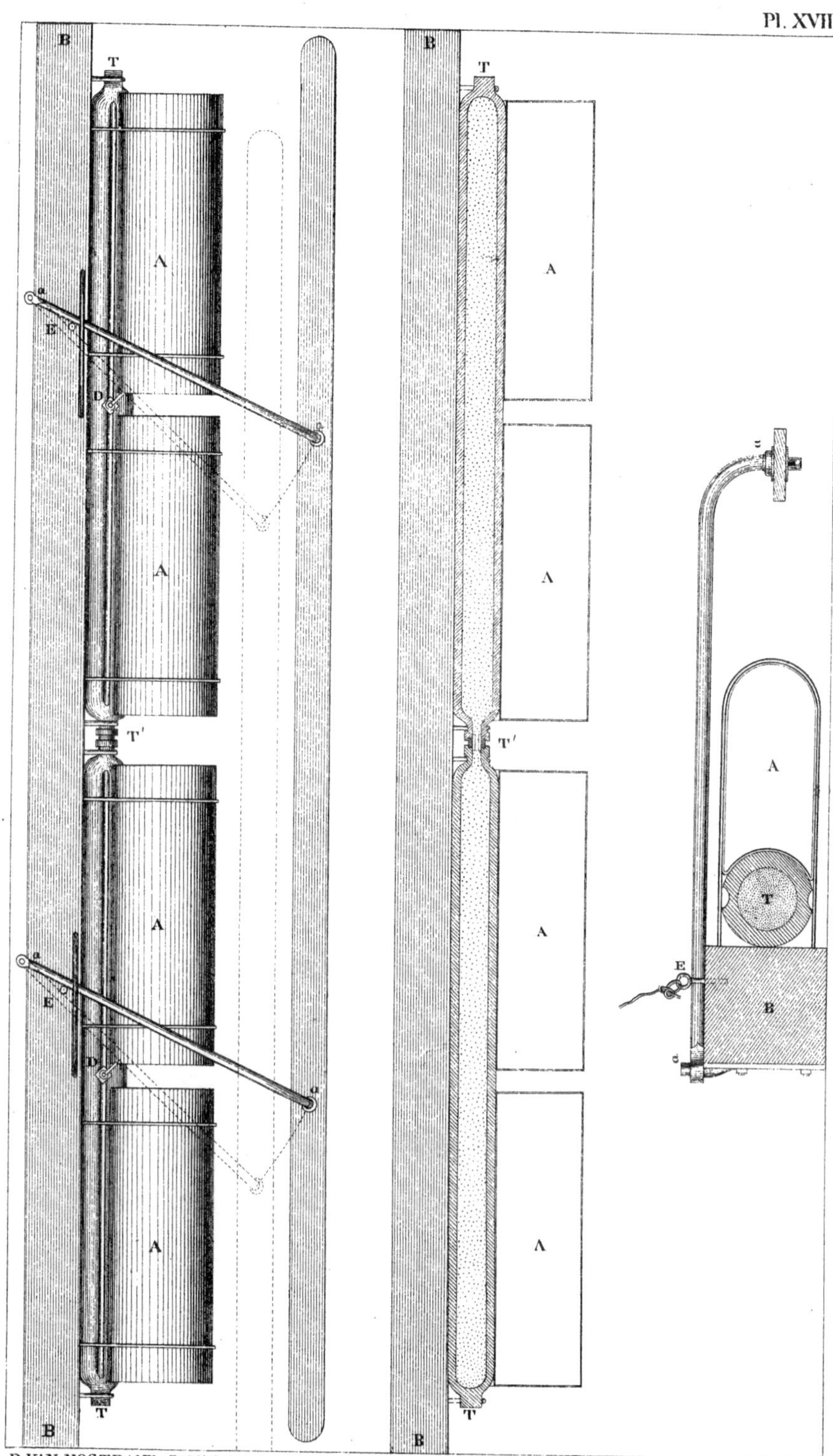

D. VAN NOSTRAND, Publisher.

"*Report of Experiments on the Force of Gunpowder, exploded under Water, made at Willet's Point, N. Y., November and December*, 1865.

"1. Apparatus, Preparations, etc.—Pressure Pistons.—These were in every way similar to those used by Major Rodman, of the Ordnance Department, and called 'internal-pressure pistons.' The discs or heads were made of different sizes, according to the distances at which they were to be placed from the charge. For convenience, they were made of the following areas : 0''.1, 0''.8, 2''.7, 6''.4, 12''.5, etc., increasing according to the cubes of the numbers 1, 2, 3, 4, 5, which were intended to represent their distances from the centre of the charge. Pl. XVII., Fig. 1, represents one of these pistons with an area of 2''.7, and shows the manner in which they were attached to the rings which held them in position. The pressure to be measured, coming in the direction indicated by the arrow-head, is transmitted to the cutter (*C*), which makes an indentation of a certain length in the copper disc (*D*), which length in inches, taken as an argument in the table of pressures, * to obtain the entire pressure in pounds, and the latter divided by the area of the piston-head, gives the pressure per square inch.

"*A A*, barrel of piston; *B B*, tangs for attaching barrel to rings; *P*, head of piston; *C*, cutter; *D*, copper disc; *R*, section of ring; *S S*, screws holding tangs to barrel.

"2. Rings.—These were made of iron ¾'' thick, bent edgewise, and of a width varying with their diameters, the widest being 4'', the narrowest, 2½''. Their diameters were 3', 5', 7', and 9' inside, and they were placed in different vertical planes, having a common intersection which passes through the common centre of the rings and charge.

"3. Derrick.—In order to lower the rings and their attachments to any desired depth, and raise them after the explosion, a floating derrick was improvised by substituting a boom for the hammer on an ordinary floating pile-driver. By this machine the ring could be lowered so steadily as not to derange the

* The table used was that constructed experimentally by Major Rodman, and given in his "Reports of Experiments on Metals for Cannon."

piston nor the insulated wire, by means of which the explosion was effected.

"4. Exploding Apparatus.—This consisted of one of Beardslee's magneto-electric machines. * * * As the object of the experiments herein reported was not to test the efficiency of the exploding apparatus, it is only necessary to remark in this connection that the machine worked well, and that the only failures which occurred were traceable to faults in the insulation.

"5. Cartridge.—Beardslee's cartridge was employed in all the experiments.

"6. Conducting Wire.—For this purpose a small cable, composed of seven small copper wires twisted together, and insulated by a single coating of vulcanized rubber, was used. The water was used to complete the circuit.

"7. Crater Gauge.—In the absence of a better one, the above-named is given to the apparatus represented in Figs. 2 and 3, Pl. XVI., Fig. 2 being one of the slides used, the spring (*s*) permitting it to move in one direction only.

"EXPERIMENTS.

"I. The object of the first series of experiments was to ascertain the effect of an air chamber in determining the direction of the explosion.

"For this purpose, four cylindrical cases of tin, 6″ in diameter and 3′ long, were arranged as shown by Fig. 4, Pl. XVI. The charge was ignited at the point *C*, the axis of the case being horizontal, and 5′ below the surface of the water for the first three explosions, and 10′ for the last.

"The results were as follows:

	Per Squre Inch.			
	1st Experim't.	2d Experim't.	3d Experim't.	4th Experim't.
	Lbs.	Lbs.	Lbs.	Lbs.
Pressure at A...........	2,100	2,508	2,100	1,500
Pressure at B............	1,500	1,833	1,100	900

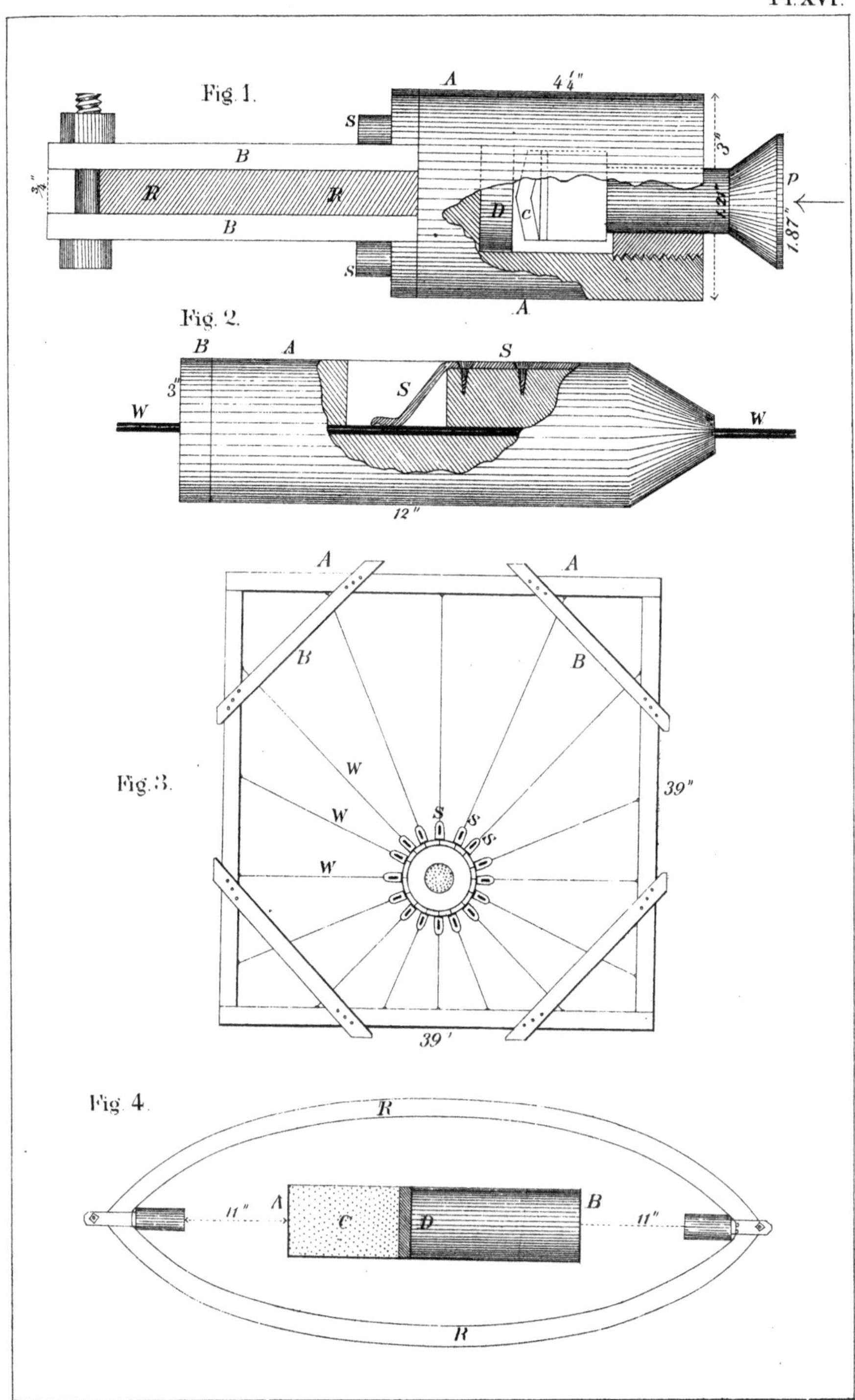

D. VAN NOSTRAND, Publisher.

Which shows an averaged loss of 35 per cent. by using the air chamber, as above described. During the first three experiments there was no wind, and the water was smooth ; during the last, slight wind and waves.

"II. The object of the second series of experiments was to ascertain the effect of increasing the number of points of ignition. Six tin cases, 6″ in diameter and 4′ 6″ long, containing 50 lbs. of powder, were arranged in pairs, one of each pair being ignited at a single point, and the other being ignited once in 6″ along its axis. Fig. 4, Pl. XVIII., shows the arrangement of one of the cases ignited at nine equidistant points.

"In the trial of the second pair of cases, two additional pistons were placed at the extremities of the conjugate axis of the ring, or directly above and below the centre of the charge. The results may be tabulated as follows, the numbers representing the pressure per square inch in pounds :

	First Pair.		Second Pair.		Third Pair.	
	Ignited at 9 points.	Ignited at 1 point.	Ignited at 9 points.	Ignited at 1 point.	Ignited at 9 points.	Ignited at 1 point.
	No. 1.	No. 2.	No. 3.	No. 4.	No. 5.	No. 6.
Pressure at A........	11,000	2,300	300*	1,325	15,562	2,700
Pressure at B........	11,000	2,300	1,832	4,500	11,540	8,332
Pressure at C........	....	....	180	2,300	.....	.....
Pressure at D........	....	....	180	3,000	.....	.....

"Charges Nos. 1 and 2 were exploded 4′ 6″ below the surface of the water, and threw a column of water 75 to 100 feet high, the mass of water moved being much larger in the former than in the latter case. Gentle wind and waves.

"Charge No. 3 was exploded at the surface of the water, as before mentioned, and although the report was very much louder

* This charge was exploded by the carelessness of an assistant just as it touched the water.

than either of the preceding explosions, the concussion at 50 feet distance was not greater than that of a 6-pounder field piece when fired with a blank cartridge. A man standing within 25 or 30 feet sustained no injury by the explosion.

"Charge No. 4 was exploded 10′ below the surface; column of water raised, only 5 or 6 feet.

"Charges Nos. 5 and 6 were exploded 10′ below the surface. Column of water raised from No. 5, 50 to 60 feet high; and from No. 6, 25 to 30 feet high. The indication of the piston at *B* in the last explosion was, doubtless, too great, and may be accounted for by the supposition that a piece of the case was driven against the piston head.

"Leaving the last record out of the computation, we have for the charges ignited at nine points an averaged pressure of 12,275 lbs. per square inch; and for those ignited at a single point, 2,632 lbs., or something less than one-fourth part of the former.

"From these results it is fair to presume that in the cases which were ignited at one point the *complete combustion* of the powder extended only about one foot (1′ 1′′) from the point of ignition; and applying this principle to a large spherical charge ignited at the centre (which are the most favorable circumstances under which large masses of powder can be exploded with a single point of ignition), we can form an approximate idea of what obtains in that case.

"Referring to Fig. 4, Pl. XVIII. *A B* represents one of the tin cases, *C* the point of ignition, and *C D* the portion of the charge which will be entirely consumed by igniting at *C*. From *C* as a centre, let two circles be described, one having a radius $C\,B=4'\,6''$, and the other a radius $C\,D=1'$ nearly. The former will represent a meridian section of a sphere, the volume of which will be 381.7 cubic feet, and the contents about 22,000 lbs. of powder. The latter will represent a corresponding section of a sphere of which the volume will be 4.19 cubic feet, and which will contain about 250 lbs. of powder. But the cylinder is not an aliquot part of a sphere, and in order to attain even an approximate result, we must ascertain what takes place in the cone of which *C E F* is a section. In this cone, when the surface of inflammation has reached *D d*, the mass of inflamed powder, consisting of grains in all stages of combustion, will be only one-third part of what it would be in the cylinder, while the resistance to be overcome by the expansive force of the gas is sensibly the same in each case, at that point, *D*. The inflammation will therefore have time to extend, in the case of the cone, to some point beyond *D*, before the expansive force of the gas can rupture and disperse the charge. From a rough calculation, it is found that the distance *d D'* will be something less than one-third of *c d*, or that the radius of the sphere entirely consumed will be about 1′ 4″. A sphere of this radius will contain about 572 lbs. of powder, which shows that only $\frac{1}{38}$ of the entire charge is consumed.

"III. The object of the third series of experiments was to determine the effect of increasing the *charge, depth* below the surface, and *distance* from the charge to the point where the effect was measured.

"For this purpose wooden shells (covered with paper and waterproof varnish), containing 10, 20, 30, 40, 50, and 60 lbs. of powder, were provided with electric fuzes, igniting them in the centre, and fired as hereinafter described. The pressure pistons were placed on two rings at right angles to each other, their diameters being 3′ and 5′ respectively, each ring containing four pistons.

"Although considerable discrepancies will be observed in the following results, a careful inspection is sufficient to discover very nearly what the true results are, and to establish beyond a doubt the practicability of obtaining by this method results sufficiently accurate for all practical purposes.*

"1.—10 *lbs. of Powder in* 5 *feet of water.*

	Inner Ring.	Outer Ring.
Right	....	1,088 lbs. per square inch.
Left	....	855 " " " "
Up	....	1,883 " " " "
Down	2,300 lbs.	†560 " " " "

* It was found impracticable to procure a sufficient number of rings and pistons (4 rings and 16 pistons), as was intended at the time of commencing these experiments.

† Piston blew out.

"2.—10 *lbs. of Powder in* 5 *feet of water.*

	Inner Ring.		Outer Ring.
Right	2,300 lbs.	....	650 lbs. per square inch.
Left	2,600 "	....	700 " " " "
Up	1,500 "	....	1,100 " " " "
Down	1,500 "	....	

"3.—10 *lbs. of Powder in* 10 *feet of water.*

	Inner Ring.		Outer Ring.
Right	2,000 lbs.	....	1,242 lbs. per square inch.
Left	2,000 "	....	525 " " " "
Up	.... "	....	700 " " " "
Down	1,916 "	....	

"Column of water about 20 feet high; but little mud raised.

"4.—10 *lbs. of Powder in* 15 *feet of water.*

	Inner Ring.		Outer Ring.
Right	1,834 lbs.	....	1,976 lbs. per square inch.
Left	2,000 "	....	1,477 " " " "
Up	2,600 "	....	1,911 " " " "
Down	1,916 "	....	578 " " " "

"Column of water raised 5 or 6 feet. Considerable wind and waves.

"5.—20 *lbs. of powder in* 5 *feet of water.*

	Inner Ring.		Outer Ring.
Right	5,572 lbs.	....	4,312 lbs. per square inch.
Left	4,857 "	....	
Up	5,429 "	....	5,312 " " " "
Down	4,857 "	....	2,107 " " " "

"Column of water 45 to 50 feet high. No wind, nor waves.

"6.—20 *lbs. of Powder in* 10 *feet of water.*

	Inner Ring.		Outer Ring.
Right	4,198 lbs.	....	2,495 lbs. per square inch.
Left	7,644 "	....	
Up	4,312 "	....	{ 1,348 " " " " 1,348 " " " "
Down	4,374 "	....	{ 2,495 " " " " 12,42 " " " "

"Column of water about 50 feet high. Inner ring broke loose at top.

"7.—20 *lbs. of Powder in* 15 *feet of water.*

Inner Ring.			Outer Ring.
Right only two pistons.....	....	....	1,750 lbs. per square inch. / 1,286 " " " "
Left, used on this ring....	....	....	2,500 " " " " / 1,500 " " " "
Up	4,350 lbs.	....	4,925 " " " "
Down.......	4,374 "	....	865 " " " " / 1,308 " " " "

"Column of water 10 feet high.

"8.—30 *lbs. of Powder in* 15 *feet of water.*

Inner Ring.			Outer Ring.
Right....	....	....	3,250 lbs. per square inch.
Left.........	....	....	3,120 " " " "
Up....	5,000 lbs.	....	Other pistons lost.
Down........			

"Column of water 10 to 15 feet high. Inner ring broke loose.

"9.—40 *lbs. of Powder in* 10 *feet of water.*

Inner Ring.			Outer Ring.
Right....	8,800 lbs. / 8,400 "	....	3,750 lbs. per square inch.
Left....	7,066 " / 7,000 "		
Up...........	6,500 " / 6,000 "	....	4,562 " " " "
Down	9,200 " / 6,830 "	....	2,230 " " " "

"Column of water 30 to 50 feet high.

"The *secondary cuts* which occurred in several cases, especially in the last, were probably due to the elasticity of the water.

"IV. The object of the fourth series of experiments was to determine *the extent and form of the crater* produced by a given charge, at a given depth below the surface of the water.

"For this purpose, the apparatus shown in Figs. 2 and 3, Plate XVI., was prepared, but owing to continued rough weather, only one experiment was made with it.

"The frame shown in Fig. 3 was raised to a vertical position by means of the derrick, and a small spherical case, containing 10 lbs. of powder, was secured at the centre of the ring, the slides (*s*, *s*, *s*) being in the positions shown in the drawing. The frame was then lowered in a vertical plane, until the centre of the charge reached a point 5′ below the surface of the water, when the explosion was effected.

"The result showed, as was anticipated, that the depth of water was not sufficient* with the given charge to prevent the upper slides from being thrown up to the ends of the wires with such force as to break the connection between several of the wires and the frame (A, A).

"Fig. 3, Plate XVIII., shows the relative positions of those slides which were not probably disturbed by the breaking of the wires, the distances given being measured from the centre of the charge (C). None of the slides were injured by the explosion, and none of the wires, which were of common telegraph size, were detached from the ring at the centre.

"Had it been practicable to repeat this experiment in *deeper water*, there is reason to believe that results could have been obtained much more accurate and satisfactory than are usually obtained in similar investigations.

"An experiment similar to that just described was made with 20 lbs. of powder in 5 feet of water, the ring and wires in this case being horizontal, and the latter, three in number, secured to piles instead of the frame before used. The slides were left at an averaged distance of 7 feet 8 inches from the centre of the charge.

"V. The last experiments consisted in exploding two charges of 10 lbs. each in 5 feet of water, to ascertain the proper corrections which were necessary in order to reduce the indications of the pistons of various areas to the same standard, the latter being assumed as the indications of the pistons with an area of one-tenth inch.

"For this purpose, two pistons of each size were placed on the same horizontal ring (where the indications would have been sensibly equal), and from the discrepancies in the actual results (doubtless owing to the varying weight of the cutter and piston-head as compared with the area of the latter), the proper corrections were obtained and applied to these experiments.

* Owing to the shallowness of the water and other causes this could not be corrected without considerable delay.

"*Conclusions.*

"Although the number of experiments made was not sufficient to justify any very arbitrary conclusions, especially in regard to details, some general deductions may be made which are not only the most reliable information we have on the subject, but sufficiently accurate for all practical purposes.

"The results of the first series of experiments indicate that an air chamber should *not* be interposed between the charge and the object to be destroyed. It is as easy to place the charge near the object as to place an air chamber there, and in addition to the increased effect of the former arrangement, we have, by placing the air chamber below the charge, an additional security against moisture reaching the powder.*

"The results of the second series of experiments give an idea of the immense loss by the dispersion of the charge, when the latter is large, and contained in cases which offer but slight resistance to rupture. Two remedies suggest themselves for this defect: one, to ignite the charge at many points simultaneously, a method which is practicable but not economical; and the other, to make the strength of the case so nearly equal to the ultimate force of the contained charge that a very large percentage of the latter must be consumed before rupture takes place.

"The vast saving of powder which may be effected by this last method is apparent from the results of ordinary rock blasting. In illustration of this, let us suppose an ordinary 12-pdr. shell, containing a bursting charge of about half a pound of powder, to be in contact with any vessel below the water-line. The explosion of this shell will exert a force upon the bottom of the vessel at least equal to the force required to rupture the shell, and since a shell of this description will penetrate hard wood or even thin iron plates without breaking, this force must be greater

* By reference to the descriptions of Messrs. Wood & Lay's torpedo, and the advantages claimed for it by the inventors, it will be noticed that the contrary is asserted. It does not seem that the experiments on either side warrant any very decided opinion on the subject. The experiments with Captain Ericsson's torpedo would seem to show, however, that direction is given to the explosion by the air chamber attachment.

than the resistance offered by the vessel within the space acted upon.*

"It may, therefore, be concluded with a reasonable degree of certainty, that half a pound of powder properly applied will sink any vessel of ordinary construction; and as a ship totally disabled is as harmless as one blown to atoms, the only object in increasing the charge is to insure the impossibility of plugging the orifice, or of overcoming the leak by the use of pumps. For this purpose 20 or 30 pounds of powder, or even a smaller quantity, would probably answer.

"A very interesting and useful series of experiments might be made by using strong iron shells, of various sizes, in a manner similar to that in which wooden shells were used in the third series of experiments herein described, or with the 'crater gauge.' In order to prevent the fragments of shells injuring the apparatus, their direction could be determined within certain limits by turning creases in the surfaces of the shells, and placing these creases in the same planes with the rings.

"From the third series of experiments, leaving out those indications which were probably produced by causes other than the direct action of the inflamed powder, we have the following averaged results, the numbers representing the pressure per square inch at the ends of the nearest pistons, or 1′ 2″ from the centre of the charge:

Charge of 10 lbs...............2,385 lbs.
" " 20 " ....4,700 lbs.
" " 30 " ....Not definitely ascertained.
" " 40 " ....7,500 lbs.

"The relation between the weight of a charge and the pressure by it, at or near the surface, may be represented as shown by Fig. 1, Pl. XVIII. The abscissas of the curve representing the charge in pounds, the ordinates will give the corresponding pressure per square inch. The only part of this curve which is of any practical importance, is that in the vicinity of the origin (A), which corresponds to small charges. Representing the pressure due to charges which are so small, or which are ignited

* This, of course, implies that the side of the vessel shall be but a few inches in thickness as is generally the case below the water line. [NOTE.—The reasoning here applied does not in our judgment prove the proposition.]

at so many points as to be entirely consumed, by an ordinate equal to the abscissa which represents the weight of the charge, we have for all such charges, ordinates terminated by the straight line (A B) which makes an angle of 45° with the co-ordinate axes, and passes through the origin (A). By reference to the above mean pressures, we find those due to 10 lbs. charge (2,385 lbs.), 20 lbs. charge (4,700 lbs.) and the 50 lb. charges ignited at nine points, and *entirely consumed* (12,275 lbs.), will give the ordinates of three points, very nearly, in the line (A B), and that those corresponding to charges of 30 lbs. (not definitely ascertained), 40 lbs. (7,500 lbs.), etc., give the ordinates of points of a curve tangent to A B at A. Although no points of this curve, other than those above given, were determined by these experiments, it may be assumed with mathematical certainty, that it constantly recedes from the tangent, until finally it becomes parallel to the axis of X, or in other words, it has an asymptote parallel to that axis.

"To determine the exact distance of this asymptote from the axis, would be a problem more curious than useful, and would involve an immense expenditure of powder; but it is evident that it must cut the tangent at some point beyond C, since it has been shown that 22,000 pounds of powder, ignited at the centre, will give a pressure greater than that due to the *complete combustion* of 500 lbs.

"By carrying out the design of the third series of experiments, all useful information in regard to the curve in question could be obtained, and its equation would be a practical formula for ascertaining the charge necessary to produce a given effect.

"*Theory of Submarine Explosions.*

"The relation between the 'pressure and distance' from a given charge will give a curve similar to (a a', b b', c d,) Fig. 2, Plate XVIII., the ordinates representing the pressures corresponding to the distances represented by the abscissas.

"As soon as the pressure from the inflamed charge becomes greater than the resistance offered by the case containing it, the latter is ruptured, and the surface of the expanding gas moves in the direction of the least resistance towards X, the pressure increasing until a point (B) is reached, where the density of the gas $(\frac{W}{V})$ is a maximum. (For small charges, and for all charges contained in very strong cases, the maximum pressure will be exerted near the surface of the case.) From this point the pressure decreases very rapidly until it becomes sensibly zero. When the surface of the gas has reached a certain point (*P*), the pressure and resistance are in equilibrio, but the expansion will continue until the living force acquired in passing over the distance (*O P*), to that point, is overcome by the continued resistance of the water. The point at which this takes place, as given by the crater gauge in the third series of experiments, was for 10 and 20 lbs. respectively, 6′ 6″, and 7′ 8″, from the centre of the charge. At this point the expansion ceases, and the elasticity of the water, aided by its weight, forces the displaced water back towards (*A*) the centre of the explosion; the gas in the mean time making its escape to the surface of the water, either in a single volume, or broken up into small bubbles, according to the distance it has to pass through the water, and being equally condensed in volume by the cooling effect of the latter.

"Since this movement takes place simultaneously on all sides of the crater, the water meeting at the centre, it would appear that a second concussion must result, and that, under certain circumstances, this would be greater than the first. This is precisely what was observed to take place in all the preceding experiments. The first effect of the explosion appeared to be a violent tearing asunder of the case and water, and after a momentary pause, greater than that due to the difference of velocity of sound in air and water, a concussion was felt similar to that produced by a heavy wave striking a steamer under the guard, followed by a jet of water projected from the crater, and of a height and diameter depending upon the size of the charge and its depth below the surface. It was noticed that in 20 or 25 feet of water, a greater quantity of mud was brought to the surface when the charge was from 5 to 10 feet deep than when it was placed nearer to the bottom, and that the boiling motion of the water was more violent and prolonged under the same circumstances.

"If *W* represents the *weight of powder consumed* at any given time, and *V* the space it then occupies, $\frac{W}{V}$ is therefore a measure for the density of the gas, and, leaving *temperature* out of

Fig. 1.

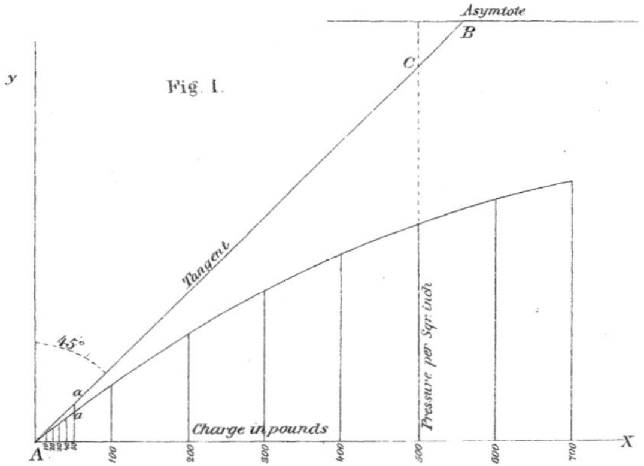

Asymtote

Tangent

Pressure per Sqr. inch

Charge in pounds

45°

100 200 300 400 500 600 700

Fig. 2.

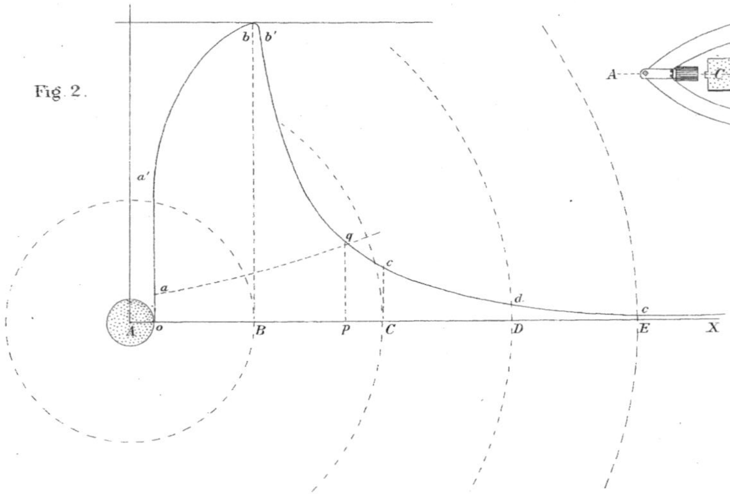

Fig. 3.

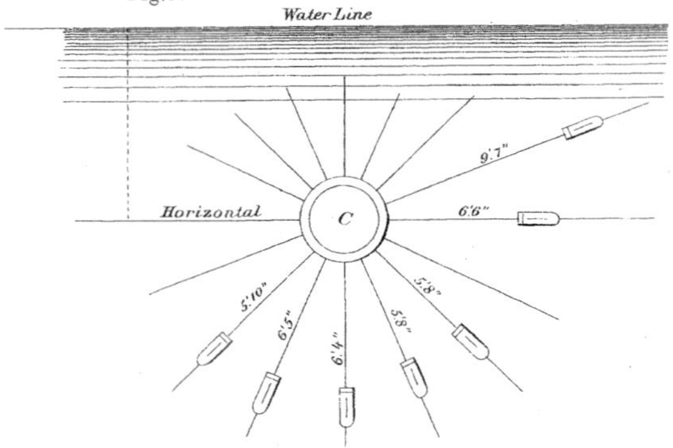

Water Line

Horizontal

9'.7" 6'.6" 5'.8" 5'.8" 6'.4" 6'.5" 5'.10"

Fig. 4.

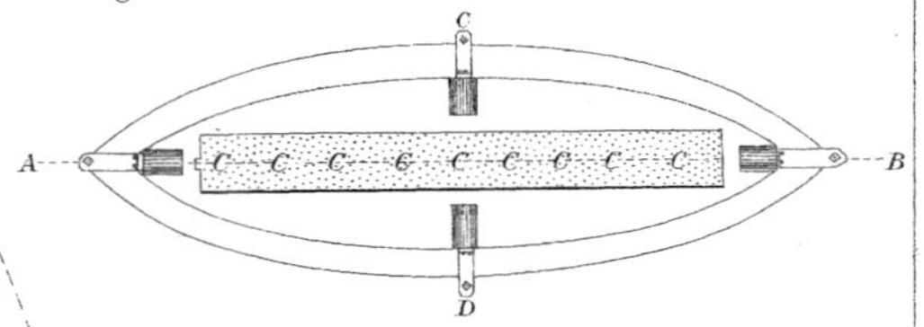

Fig. 5.

VOL. 381.7 Cubic Ft.
Cont.g 22000 lbs. of Powder

419 Cu. Ft.

250 lbs.

572 lbs.

$\frac{22000}{572} = 38+$

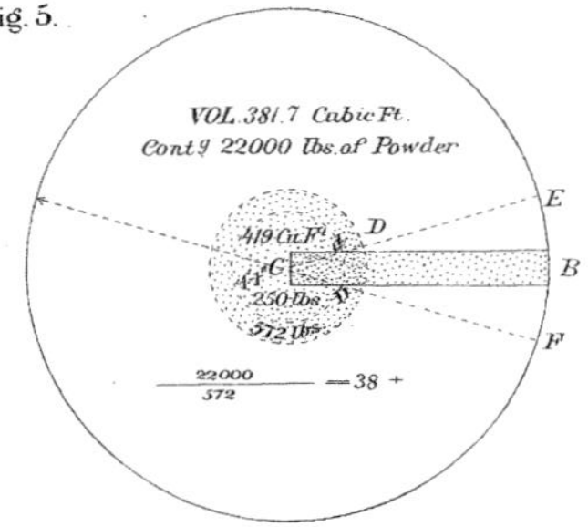

D. VAN NOSTRAND, Publisher.

the account, it will vary *directly* with the *elastic* force of the same.

"Since W soon becomes constant, and V increases with the cube of the distance from the centre, it might be concluded without experiment or computation, that in submarine explosions, where the gas is free to expand in all directions, a great loss of force must result from any attempt to destroy an object beyond the distance (A B) where $\frac{W}{V}$ is a maximum; or, since the charge should be confined in a strong case to insure its complete combustion, as concluded from the third series of experiments, it may be assumed that a reasonable economy would require the object to be very near the point O, or the surface of the charge."

Nitro-glycerine, so recently introduced in mining and blasting operations, is certainly the most powerful explosive substance yet discovered, and, where unlimited effect is desired, will probably supersede all other compounds. Its application is comparatively new, and, consequently, generally unknown. No experiments appear to have been made with it to test its effect under water,* but it has been recommended by those who, by practice in mines, quarries and other engineering operations, have become familiar with its use, as specially adapted for submarine blasting. General Newton, of the U. S. Engineers, in his report upon the obstructions at Hell Gate, New York, particularly recommends its use on the score of economy, and it may be reasonably inferred that, if peculiarly adapted to such purposes, it would be also advantageously used in submarine warfare.

The most reliable information we have been able to procure on the subject of the treatment and comparative force of nitro-glycerine is contained in an able and interesting paper read before the American Society of Civil Engineers

---

* The principal difficulty to be encountered in the use of nitro-glycerine for submarine blasting is the fact that it congeals readily at high temperatures; and in various experiments made with it during winter weather, it has been found a difficult matter to explode charges with magnetic fuzes, and, upon examination as to the cause of failure, the compound has been found to be frozen by being submerged in water of a temperature of about 40° Fahr.

on the 4th of March, 1868, by Edward P. North, C. E., from which the following extracts are taken:

"I have been led to introduce to your notice the subject of this paper (nitro-glycerine, or Nobel's blasting oil), because its application to blasting is comparatively new, and, consequently, not generally known. As over three-fourths of a ton has been used on the New Canaan Railroad, of which I am now in charge, I may, perhaps, be able to convey some ideas of information and interest. It may be as well here to give a little sketch of nitro-glycerine, and to compare it with powder and gun-cotton.

"Some Prussian sporting powder, analyzed by Professor Bunsen, of Heidelberg, contained:

Nitrate of potassa	KO, NO^5	78.99
Sulphur	S	9.84
Carbon	C	7.69
Hydrogen	H	0.41
Oxygen	O	3.07
		100.00

On burning it, he found as residue	68.06
And the gas amounted to	31.38
	99 44

"The residue consisted of:

Sulphate of potassa	KO, SO^3	42.27
Carbonate of potassa	KO, CO^2	12.64
Hyposulphite of potassa	KO, S_2, O_2	3.27
Sulphide of potassium	KS	2.13
Sulpho-cyanide of potassa	K Cy, S_2	0.30
Nitrate of potassa	KO, NO^5	3.72
Sulphur	S	0.14
Carbon	C	0.73
Carbonate of ammonia	NH^4, O, CO^2	2.86
Residue		68.06

"The gas consisted of:

Nitrogen	N	9.98
Carbonic acid	CO_9	20.12
Carbonic oxide	CO	0.94
Hydrogen	H	0.02
Hydro-sulphuric acid	H, S	0.18
Oxygen	O	0.14
		31.38

"Gun-cotton was discovered by Prof. Schonbein, about 1846, and its manufacture was almost immediately commenced, but never with financial success till lately. It is now being made in England by Prof. Abel and Messrs. Thomas Prentice & Sons, a very interesting account of whose process can be found in the last volume of 'Engineering,' pages 408, 431, and 467.

"Nitro-glycerine was discovered in 1846, by Sobrero, but nothing was done with it till 1863, when Alfred Nobel patented its application to blasting. Gun-cotton and nitro-glycerine are made, the one from cotton, and the other from glycerine, treated with nitric and sulphuric acid, the action of the sulphuric acid being, in each case, to intensify the action of the nitric. In the case of gun-cotton, cotton which has a formula of C_{12}, H_{10}, O_{10}, is dipped into a mixture of three parts of sulphuric acid and one of nitric acid, by weight. Some of the oxygen in nitric acid goes to the hydrogen, forming water, and the formula stands $C_{12}, H_7, 3(NO_4), O_{10}+6HO$, three parts of the hydrogen in the cotton being replaced by three parts of nitrous acid. On its explosion, it is resolved into gases, namely:

		By volume.	By weight.
Carbonic oxide	CO	28.95	29.97
Carbonic acid	CO^2	20.82	33 86
Light carburetted hydrogen	C^2, H^4	7.24	4.28
Hydrogen	H	3.16	0.24
Nitrogen	N	12.67	13.16
Carbon	C	1.82	1.62
Steam	HO	25 34	16.87
		100.00	100.00

—leaving no residue. As to its relative strength, the article on 'Engineering' already referred to says it is ten times stronger than powder. According to Von Lenk, in blasting, one pound of gun-cotton is equal to 6.274 pounds of powder. According to a commission appointed by the French Government, the explosive power of gun-cotton depends, in a measure, on the degree of compression, and, in the mean, is about three times that of gunpowder. When uncompressed, it will burn more freely than gunpowder, but by compression its rate of burning can be brought below that of gunpowder.

"Gun-cotton, according to Prof. Abel, when well made, can

be kept for a long time without undergoing change, and can be transported as safely as powder ; but when impure and acid, a gradual decomposition takes place, the result of which is an explosion.

"Nitro-glycerine is made by treating glycerine, which has the formula C_6, H_5, N_3, O_{18}, with nitric and sulphuric acids, as in the case of cotton, and the chemical reactions are nearly the same, it being in both a case of the substitution of nitrous acid for a part of the hydrogen. By explosion, according to an article in the London *Mechanics' Magazine*, September, 1865, one volume of oil is converted into 429 volumes of carbonic acid, 554 volumes of steam, 39 volumes of oxygen, and 236 volumes of nitrogen—1,298 volumes in all, for one volume of liquid oil, being thus, theoretically, five times more effective than its bulk in gunpowder ; but by the greater amount of heat generated by the explosion, and the consequent higher tension of the gases, it is really thirteen times more effective by bulk, and eight times by weight, than the same. The United States Blasting Oil Company, in a pamphlet published by them, assert that nitro-glycerine has thirteen times the strength of powder by volume, and ten times by weight. It is a lightish yellow, oily liquid, with a specific gravity of 1.6, nearly insoluble in water, not volatile, taking fire at 360° F., and freezing at from 40° to 36° F. When impure and acid, it decomposes spontaneously, with an escape of gas and the formation of oxalic C_4 O_6 2 HO, and glyceric C_6 H_6 O_8, acids. Under these circumstances, it is liable to explode. * * * As I advised the use of nitro-glycerine, I, of course, took a great deal of interest in its success, loading and firing a great many of the holes myself. * * * In one cut, which in its deepest part was about twelve feet, the rock was mostly feldspar and mica, in large crystals ; but it was very wet, springs forcing themselves up through the bore-holes, so that they could not be puddled. *Here the fact that nitro-glycerine was entirely unaffected by water* rendered it particularly valuable. The mode of procedure was this : a single hole was put down to grade about the centre of the cut, a foot or two further back from the face than the depth of the cutting, so as to have the line of least resistance a vertical one ; from five (5) to eight (8) pounds of nitro-glycerine was poured in ; a tin cartridge, about 4 inches long and $\frac{3}{4}$ in diameter, filled with powder, into which a water-proof fuze (Buckford's) was introduced, was put into the nitro-glycerine, and the hole filled with water.

"These charges were very effective, in some instances loosening over 100 cubic yards, so that it could be readily barred out, while that immediately around the charge was burned to a soft, white powder. The quarrymen said it had turned to lime. About fifty per cent. of the rock was usually so fine as to be readily thrown into carts without sledging or block-holing, while that farthest from the charge was in masses of two or three cubic yards."

Mr. North thus refers to an apparent difficulty in securing an explosion in a "dry cut":

"As this cut was perfectly dry, and the water had to be brought from some distance, water-tamping was dispensed with. The same cartridges were at first used as in the wet cut, only the fuze was cut short off, and they were dropped into the hole after being lighted. This was found objectionable, as, there being nothing to confine the gases generated by the explosion of the powder, they would sometimes fail to produce either heat or concussion enough to explode the nitro-glycerine, though they would ignite it and cause it to boil and smoke till sometimes, after about ten minutes, the glycerine would either go out or go off, which produced delay, as the men did not like to go and drop in another cartridge. A large copper cap, known as Nobel's patent cap, that fitted closely over the end of the fuze, and contained percussion powder, was also used, but failed for lack of power or heat. The plan finally adopted was to pour in the glycerine, and then put down a light wad of hay or dry grass, on which some powder was poured, with which the fuze was connected. The hole was then filled with loose sand and fired. After having seen many holes fired with and without tamping, I doubt if tamping is of much more use than to insure the explosion of the glycerine.

"The effect of nitro-glycerine differs from that of powder, in consequence, I suppose, of its greater force and quickness of explosion, in that powder, when fired, when the line of least resistance is a vertical one (the bore also being vertical, and the rock homogeneous), will form a tolerably uniform crater, with the sides sloping according to the hardness of the rock. When the line of least resistance is a horizontal one, and not too long, the rock being solid, the powder will throw out what is before it, leaving the back uncracked, and no sign of action below the bottom of the hole.

"Nitro-glycerine, on the contrary, in the first case, will form a well, and if the rock is not too hard, the bottom diameter will be greater than the top. Nor, as far as I have seen, will the action ever be concentrated on the line of least resistance, but will extend back from the hole and downward to a greater or less distance, according to the hardness of the rock. I think that this action of nitro-glycerine, in connection with the fact that its explosive force is uninfluenced by the presence of water, will tend to its being the only explosive agent used in all subaqueous operations; for, with any depth of water, it will be unnecessary to drill holes—only to sink a flask of nitro-glycerine upon the rock and fire it.

"Mr. Myers, our contractor, who has had a great deal of experience in blasting operations, says, that in hard, dry ledges, he thinks fully double speed could be made with glycerine than with powder, and in wet ledges, fully four times the speed with the same force of men. * * * A hole can be loaded and fired in much less time with nitro-glycerine than with powder, and, as a matter of economy, he would prefer to pay $1.12½ per pound for nitro-glycerine, to having powder given to him for hard dry ledges, or to having $10 per keg given to him for all the powder he would use in blasting wet ledges. He also thinks nitro-glycerine much safer than powder.

"From the fact that nitro-glycerine explodes with so much violence that it would burst any cannon, its strength cannot be ascertained as that of powder can.

"In regard to the relative safety of gunpowder, gun-cotton, and nitro-glycerine, I think the last-named is the safest agent. I do not wish to be understood to underrate the disastrous effects that would, probably, and have occurred from an accidental explosion; only to say that I think, with properly made, unfrozen nitro-glycerine, the cans packed in plaster of Paris, as the law requires it, it is safer than powder. I speak of its being unfrozen, because during the use of it on this road, from last September until the middle of January, the only instance in which any glycerine was exploded without the aid of powder was a small frozen piece that was crushed between two stones. Nitro-glycerine was placed in the hands of six different foremen, and by them in the hands of the men; was carried unprotected in sixty-pound cans up and down the line, frozen and unfrozen, in dump-carts; and was generally treated with the recklessness with which Irishmen treat powder. And as blasting material is usually used on roads, it must be the safest of the three; for as there is no necessity of any tamping but water-tamping, if a charge miss fire there is no solid tamping to cut out—at the danger of the driller's life—as with powder; for if water has been used, another cartridge can be dropped in in a minute; or if sand has been used, a portion of it can be scraped out, and a small charge of glycerine poured in and fired on top of the old charge. Besides which, gun-cotton will ignite and explode, not only from a light spark, but from a flame, thus making it the most dangerous of the three; while powder, though it cannot be ignited without the aid of a spark, or something red-hot, can be ignited by any spark, such as one flying from drills or from rocks falling; and nitro-glycerine cannot be exploded, even if ignited, unless confined, and in that case a spark could hardly reach it.

"*Experiments made at Stockholm, 28th September*, 1865.

"*First Trial.*—A quantity of nitro-glycerine was poured on a flattened stone; a red-hot iron bar was then made to wear along the surface of the nitro-glycerine without igniting it, and finally placed into the blasting oil, spread on the stone, which, after being warmed, partly took fire, and burned with a flame, but without exploding. After removing the iron bar, some undecomposed oil remained on the stone.

"*Second Trial.*—A cavity in a stone was filled with nitro-glycerine; a burning wood shaving was introduced, and on stirring it, the nitro-glycerine burned with a flame, but without exploding. The combustion ceased as soon as the shaving was consumed.

"*Third Trial.*—Several glass bottles were filled with nitro-glycerine; these bottles were thrown with great force from a height against a rock below. The bottles were shattered, but without, however, exploding the oil.

"*Fourth Trial.*—On the suggestion of some of the gentlemen present, three bottles filled with this agent were heated in warm water to 50° Celsius, or 120° Fahr. These bottles, thrown with a great force against the rocks, shattered likewise, without causing an explosion of the blasting oil.

"*Fifth Trial.*—Two flasks of tinned iron (of the same kind as those used by the Nitro-glycerine Company) filled with nitro-glycerine were packed into a wooden box, as is customary in forwarding them. After having screwed down the cover, this box was thrown from a height of nine or ten feet upon a rock below, and without any result.

"*Sixth Trial.*—A cartridge of tinned iron filled with nitro-glycerine was placed in a kettle of boiling water, without producing any result.

"In regard to the accidents that have occurred, the one in New York almost surely occurred from the nitro-glycerine having leaked into the sawdust in which it was packed, and oxidation and combustion followed, as surely as if oil had been put on the same sawdust, and it put in a warm place, only the combustion was rather more rapid. I have been informed that the accident at the express office in San Francisco occurred from the same cause. As there is now a law against transporting nitro-glycerine in glass, or in any mode except in tin cans, packed with plaster of Paris in wooden boxes, we will probably have no more such accidents.

"At Aspinwall, a case of nitro-glycerine was dropped into the hold of the steamship; few of us would have cared to have been on the deck when a barrel of gunpowder was treated in the same way. At Bergen, red-hot iron was brought in contact with tin and solder that melts at from 360° to 475° F., and nitro-glycerine would be of little use as a blasting material if it had not proved disastrous. At the risk of reiteration, I will sum up the advantages possessed by nitro-glycerine over gunpowder and gun-cotton.

"1*st.* That, being of greater strength, there is a great saving in drillers' wages, as fewer holes have to be made, and the charge of glycerine can be put into the rock much more compactly. For instance, if, to break up a certain rock, 1 foot of depth in the bore-hole was required with glycerine, 13 feet would be required with powder, which would necessitate 6 feet of additional drilling if but one hole was used; but 13 feet of powder could not be exploded in a 2-inch or 2¼-inch hole so that it would be effective, on account of the slowness with which it burns; so that additional holes would have to be drilled, with in each an allowance of at least ⅜ of the depth for tamping. With gun-cotton there would not be so much difference.

"2*d.* That nitro-glycerine is not injured, either permanently or temporarily, by water or moisture, which enables us to use water-tamping, a great saving of time and risk of life, impossible with either of the others; and it can be stored in damp cellars, or under water, without the necessity of drying it before using, as in the case of gun-cotton, or having it ruined, as with gunpowder.

"And lastly, the difficulty of exploding it renders it the least dangerous to human life."

The effect of submarine explosions of this compound will soon be fully tested in the course of the efforts now being made to deepen the channel of East River at Hell Gate, under the able superintendence of General Newton, U. S. Engineers, who has determined to give nitro-glycerine a full trial.

The objections to the use of nitro-glycerine seem to be in a fair way of removal by the ingenuity of those whose attention has been specially drawn to the subject, and several methods of altering the form while preserving the explosive force of the compound, have been discovered, which, if successful, will render this a much more effective agent of destruction than in its present condition.

An English scientific journal says:

"Some fifteen months ago, M. Nobel, the well-known manufacturer of nitro-glycerine, introduced to the public a modified form of that powerful explosive, to which he gave the name of 'dynamite.' This substance, which in appearance greatly resembles coarse brown sugar, consists of nitro-glycerine, absorbed by fine particles of silicic acid or a silicious earth, and it differs from nitro-glycerine in its ordinary liquid state in several very important particulars. In the first place, if ignited by an ordinary flame it does not explode, but merely burns away rapidly, but quietly; and in the second place, it cannot be exploded in bulk by percussion applied in any ordinary manner. We say that it is not exploded in bulk by any ordinary manner. We say that it is not exploded by percussion when in bulk; because small isolated particles can be exploded by severe percussion as, for instance, by placing them on an anvil and striking them with a hammer; but even in this case the particles, when ignited, would not communicate their ignition to a bulk of dynamite close at hand.

"In ordinary working M. Nobel employs to ignite the dynamite a fuze terminating in a copper cap, which contains a powerful charge of fulminate of mercury, and which is imbedded in the charge. When this cap is ignited by the fuze not only is a great heat generated, but also an extreme local pressure, and it appears that it is only by this combination of heat and pressure that the explosion of the dynamite can be effected. When a charge has to be fired by electricity the copper cap has still to be used, the cap being ignited by the electric agency, and it, in its turn, exploding the dynamite.

"Already dynamite has been brought into use for quarrying purposes to a considerable extent in Sweden and in other parts of the Continent. Recently M. Nobel performed a series of very interesting experiments with it in the neighborhood of Glasgow. The first experiments were intended to show the powerful character of the explosive, and at the same time prove that it could not be caused to explode by ordinary flame. For these purposes a paper cartridge, containing rather less than one-half ounce of dynamite, was placed upon a two-inch oak plank, and fired by means of a fuze and fulminating cap, as already mentioned, the effect being that the plank was splintered, and was, in fact, completely pierced at the point on which the cartridge had rested. A second experiment was made, with similar results, and M. Nobel then placed a larger cartridge on the ground and ignited it by ordinary flame, when the dynamite was found to burn quietly without any explosion whatever. To prove that material of the same quality was used in the different experiments, a cartridge was, at the suggestion of one of the gentlemen on the ground, cut in halves, one-half being exploded by a fuze and cap, while the other was ignited by ordinary flame, and was, as before, found to burn without explosion.

"The next experiment was made to show that the dynamite could not be exploded even by violent concussion. For this purpose a small deal box, containing rather more than eight pounds of the material, was twice thrown from the top of a cliff sixty feet high on to the stones below ; but even by this severe treatment no effect was produced. At the same time a similar box, containing eight and one-third pounds of dynamite, was placed on a fire and allowed to remain until, the box being burned through, the dynamite was ignited and burned away without any explosive action whatever.

"The next experiment consisted in exploding on the top of a block of granite—measuring two feet nine inches by two feet six inches by two feet—a quarter of a pound of dynamite, the explosive material being merely covered down with a thin layer of clay and some sand placed over it. Notwithstanding the very slight confinement to which the dynamite was thus subjected, the effect of the explosion was to completely shatter the granite block, the latter being found to be cracked in every direction. The action of dynamite under the above circumstances is strikingly dissimilar to that of gunpowder, and it is altogether very remarkable. The experiment on the granite block was followed by one which showed in a still more striking manner the enormous explosive force of dynamite. A cylindrical block of wrought iron, ten and a half inches in diameter and twelve and a half inches long, was taken, and a hole one inch in diameter, which had been bored right through its centre, was charged with dynamite. As the block was placed in a vertical position, the lower end of the hole was closed by the ground on which the block stood, while at the upper end the charge, which completely filled the hole, was merely covered down, after the fuze had been inserted, with a little sand. On the explosion taking place, it was found that not only had the block been completely split in two, but that one of the halves, weighing about one hundred and fifty pounds, had been projected with considerable force against a bank about seventy feet distant. The section of the iron torn asunder by this explosion was about one hundred and nineteen inches, and an inspection of the fragments showed the material to have been of very fair quality, and to have been free from flaws.

"The next two experiments were of a different character, and were made to show the action of the dynamite in actual work. For this purpose a hole, fifteen feet deep and two inches in diameter, had been bored in one part of the quarry, at a distance of about twenty feet from the working face, and this hole had been charged with twelve pounds of dynamite, and tamped with five feet of sand. The explosion of this charge did not bring down the mass between the hole and the face, but the ground was thoroughly broken up by cracks extending from the hole in every direction throughout a circle about twenty feet in diameter. A second charge of about four pounds of dynamite was then fired in another hole fifteen feet in depth, and situated about eight feet from the working face; and in this case also the results were very similar to those above mentioned, but the cracks, of course, did not extend so far.

"To show that the dynamite was equally effective below water, M. Nobel next placed a cartridge containing a charge in a bucket of water, and fired it by the aid of the usual fuze and fulminating cap, the result of the explosion being the entire disappearance of the bucket, water and all. Two one-and-a-half ounce cartridges of dynamite were next fired in holes bored in the face of the quarry, and in each case the quantity of the chalk brought down was, for such small charges, very considerable. Next a cartridge, suspended from a line extending across the quarry, was fired, to show, by the loudness of the explosion, the value of the dynamite for detonating signals; and finally the experiments were brought to a conclusion by firing some gunpowder in contact with dynamite, the result being that the latter was merely ignited and burnt, but not exploded.

"The experiments of which we have above given an account

tend to show that dynamite is destined to hold a very prominent place among the explosives used for all purposes where a violent disruptive force is required. Dynamite contains seventy-six per cent. by weight of nitro-glycerine, and its power is estimated by M. Nobel as ten times that of gunpowder, while its cost is at present about four times that of the latter material, and is likely to be shortly reduced. For quarrying work it is likely to prove especially valuable, as it can be used with but very little tamping, or, indeed, without any tamping whatever, its explosive force being in the latter case but very slightly impaired."

Whatever may be the practical difficulties in the way of the employment of this new adaptation of explosions to purposes of war, who can doubt but that they will be eventually overcome? The attention of military and naval engineers of all countries is steadily devoted to the consideration of the subject, and although working in secret, and mostly withholding the results of their investigations from public scrutiny, enough has been permitted to escape them to prove that its next application in actual warfare will be fraught with gravest consequences to the combatants. No longer trammelled by the humanitarian ideas which have made the system obnoxious to the sense of the warlike nations, it must advance under the guidance of able and intelligent minds to the first position amongst the recognized engines of war.

"The ram will be the future umpire of naval combats," says Admiral Tegethoff, in his report of the battle of Lissa. How powerful and terrible an auxiliary to the ram will the torpedo become, remains for the future to prove!

APPENDIX A.

Annals of Philadelphia and Pennsylvania, edition 1844, *pages* 335, 336, 2*d vol.*

AMUSING INCIDENTS.

Among the amusing and facetious incidents of the war, which sometimes cheered the heart amidst its abiding gloom, was that of the celebrated occurrence of the "Battle of the Kegs," at Philadelphia. It began at early morn, a subject of general alarm and consternation, but at last subsided in matter of much merry-making among our American whigs, and of vexation and disappointment on the part of the British. When the alarm of explosion first occurred, the whole city was set in commotion. The housekeepers and children ran to their houses generally for shelter, and the British everywhere ran from their shelters to their assigned places of muster. Horns, drums and trumpets sounded everywhere to arms with appalling noise, and cavalry and horsemen dashed to and fro in gay confusion.

The kegs which gave this dire alarm were constructed at Bordentown, and floated down the Delaware for the purpose of destroying the British shipping which all lay out in the stream moored in a long line, the whole length of the city. The kegs were charged with gunpowder, and were to be fired and exploded by a spring-lock, the moment the kegs should brush against the vessel's bottom. The kegs themselves could not be seen—being under water; but the buoys which floated them were visible. It so happened, however, that at the very time (on January 7th, 1778) when the scheme was set in operation, the British, fearing the making of ice, had warped in their ships to the wharves, and so escaped much of the intended mischief. The crew of a barge attempting to take one of them up, it exploded and killed four of the hands and wounded the rest. Soon all the wharves and shipping were lined with soldiers. Conjecture was vague, and imagination supplied many "phantoms dire." Some asserted the kegs were filled with armed rebels, that they had seen the points of their bayonets sticking out of the bung-holes. Others, that they were filled with inveterate combustibles, which would set the Delaware in flames and consume all the shipping. Others deemed them magic machines which would mount the wharves and roll all flaming into the city! Great were the exertions of officers and men, and incessant were the firings, so that not a chip or stick escaped their vigilance. We are indebted to the facetious muse of Francis Hopkinson, Esq., for the following *jeu d'esprit* upon the occasion. I give an extract:

Those kegs I'm told the rebels hold,
Packed up like pickled herring;
And they've come down to attack the town
In this new way of ferrying.

The soldiers flew, the sailors too,
And, scared almost to death, sir,
Wore out their shoes, and spread the news,
And ran till out of breath, sir.

"Arise, arise!" Sir Erskine cries;
"The rebels, more's the pity,
Without a boat, are all afloat
And ranged before the city."

The royal band now ready stand,
All ranged in dread array, sir.
With stomach stout to see it out,
And make a bloody day, sir.

Such feats did they perform that day,
Among those wicked kegs, sir,
That years to come, when they get home,
They'll make their boast and brag, sir.

[To the son of the same gentleman we have since been indebted for our two national songs, "Hail Columbia," and "Columbians all, the present hour."]

APPENDIX B.

FULTON'S OPINION OF ELECTRIC TORPEDOES.

Sir,—Every friend of the torpedo is encouragement to me to persevere to their actual practice. I thank you for the hints, and will be much obliged by any communication you will have the goodness to make of your thoughts or means of using them. Some years ago, I investigated the mode and practicability of firing by electricity under water; the difficulties are, to preserve long wires from being torn or broken—the enemy might float up a few logs or old boats with graplins and tear away the wires, and thus render the torpedo useless.

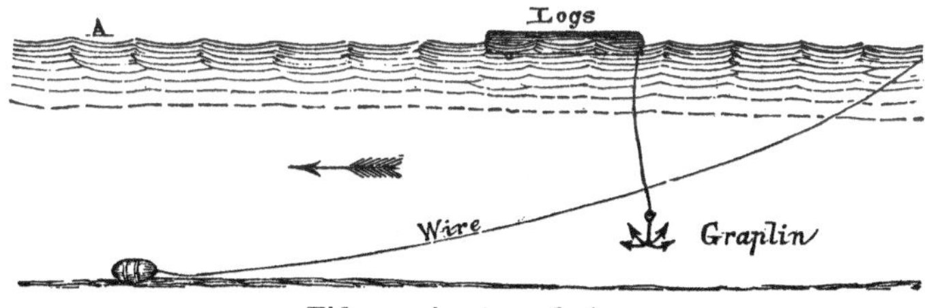

Tide running towards A.

Another difficulty is to know when the vessel is over the torpedo, for she *must be over it.*

Although a man at A can tell when a vessel cuts the visual line B, the post F being his guide, he could not tell whether she was over the torpedo C or D or not, they also lying in the same line.

It will give you some pleasure when I assure you that I believe I possess sufficient mechanical means to put torpedoes under the bottom of an enemy in our harbors or some miles at sea and all that I want is, men practised to this new mode of warfare, which can be had if Mr. Bradley's bill passes into a law But in addition to the modes I possess, there are hundreds yet undiscovered for applying torpedoes, hence I thankfully receive any communications from their friends. If successful their benefit to America will be immense, for I still assert, and every reflection confirms my opinion, that these submarine mines must go to the annihilation of military navies, and consequently produce the liberty of the seas, relieve us of all the trouble and expense of our foreign negotiations, and turn the whole genius and resources of our people on the useful arts. Everything therefore, should be done to prove their value. The embarrassments which Com. Rodgers threw in my way was no defeat of torpedoes, it was only a defeat of the mode I then practised As a brick wall one foot thick will stop a musket bullet, but not a 24-pound shot, as well might it be said that defeating the musket bullet proved gunpowder not so good as bows and arrows.

I am, very respectfully,
Your obedient servant,
ROBERT FULTON.

WILLIAM BRENTS, Jr., Esq.
Near Aquia, Virginia.

APPENDIX C.

*Description of Ericsson's Torpedo and "Obstruction Remover."**

PLATES XIV., XVII.

Plate XIV.—Elevation and plan showing the method of attaching the raft with its appendages to the bow of a "monitor" for which it was specially designed. For accounts of experiments with this torpedo see pp. 198, 199.

T. T'. T. *The torpedo shells,* consisting of two cast-iron shells, screwed together with a water-tight joint at T', each shell being 11½ feet long, 10 inches in diameter, and containing 350 lbs. No. 7 gunpowder.

A. A. A. A. *Copper air chambers,* 20″ × 10½″, fitted to anterior portions of shells *to give direction* to force of explosion. For arrangement of air chambers, and method of attaching the same to torpedo shells, see Plate XVII.

B. B. *Square timber* to which the torpedo and air chambers are bolted and strapped, as shown in Plate XVII.

C. C. *Trigger-board,* moving parallel to B. B., to which it is connected by arms *a*, *a*, which, when the trigger-board is pushed against obstructions, press upon triggers.

D. D. *Triggers,* connected with locks and percussion primers contained within the torpedo shells.

E. E. *Safety pins,* to be withdrawn by lanyards at proper time.

---

* The drawings of this apparatus were kindly furnished by Captain Ericsson, but were subsequently mislaid, and not recovered until too late for insertion with detailed description in the appropriate place of the text.

F. F. *Booms* to support apparatus and maintain it in proper position in advance of raft.

G. G. Lines by which the apparatus is lowered, raised, and kept at proper depth below the surface.

H. H. Ring bolts let into the deck of the raft, through which chains are passed to secure ends of booms.

K. *Raft,* of framed timber, its after part formed to receive the wedge-shaped bow of a monitor. Dimensions of raft 38′ × 20′, including overlap on bow of monitor; distance between forward edge of raft and bow 25′. Torpedo distant from bow, when exploded, 30 feet.

L. *Hole in raft* through which the bight of a chain is passed and toggled, the ends being taken underneath the raft and "overhang" of the monitor to the anchor well, in order to secure the raft firmly into position.

M. *Bow and overhang* of monitor.

N. *Anchor well* of monitor.

O. O. Ring bolts for lashings to further secure raft in position.

P. Anchor-room hatchway.

Plate XVII.—Shows the arrangement and construction of the torpedo on a larger scale.

In tolerably smooth water this apparatus worked well, and could be handled with safety to the vessel carrying it, and while it in some measure interfered with the celerity of movement and speed of the vessel, there was never a doubt but that under certain circumstances it would prove efficient in clearing away any obstructions that could be placed in a fair channel way.

At Charleston, the only place where its use was attempted, our monitor fleet lay just within the outer bar, where all preparations for the attack of 7th of April, 1863, had to be completed. Here at all times a swell set in over the bar, causing considerable motion to the vessels at anchor, and rendering the attempts made to attach the apparatus exceedingly hazardous. As before stated (p. 87), the monitor "Weehawken" was fitted with it, but, for reasons already alleged, the attack was finally made without testing the torpedo. This vessel, however, carried the raft through the action, to which the familiar name of "Boot-jack" was given, with grapnels and nets attached to it to catch buoyant torpedoes. A heavy swell ensuing soon after the engagement, the raft was converted into a battering ram, and Commodore Rodgers was compelled to cast it off to prevent it from doing serious injury to his vessel.

Inasmuch as all preparations for the defence of harbors must now include obstructions by which a steam iron-clad fleet shall be prevented from entering, or detained under fire of batteries until destroyed or compelled to return, the question as to the means of overcoming such obstacles becomes a serious one for naval engineers. The Ericsson Obstruction Remover, while open to several objections in practice, contains the elements of success, and in some modified form will be sure to take its place amongst the new engines of war to which the further development of the torpedo and obstruction systems will give rise.

NAVAL BOOKS.

A TREATISE ON ORDNANCE AND NAVAL GUNNERY. Compiled and arranged as a Text-Book for the U. S. Naval Academy, by Commander EDWARD SIMPSON, U. S. N. Fourth edition, revised and enlarged. 1 vol., 8vo. Plates and cuts. Cloth. $5.

"As the compiler has charge of the instruction in Naval Gunnery at the Naval Academy, his work, in the compilation of which he has consulted a large number of eminent authorities, is probably well suited for the purpose designed by it—namely, the circulation of information which many officers, owing to constant service afloat, may not have been able to collect. In simple and plain language it gives instruction as to cannon, gun-carriages, gunpowder, projectiles, fuses, locks and primers; the theory of pointing guns, rifles, the practice of gunnery, and a great variety of other similar matters, interesting to fighting men on sea and land."—*Washington Daily Globe.*

GUNNERY CATECHISM. As applied to the service of Naval Ordnance. Adapted to the latest Official Regulations, and approved by the Bureau of Ordnance, Navy Department. By J. D. BRANDT, formerly of the U. S. Navy. Revised edition. 1 vol., 18mo. Cloth. $1.50.

"BUREAU OF ORDNANCE—NAVY DEPARTMENT,
Washington City, July 30, 1864.

"MR. J. D. BRANDT,—

"SIR:—Your 'CATHECHISM OF GUNNERY, as applied to the service of Naval Ordnance,' having been submitted to the examination of ordnance officers, and favorably recommended by them, is approved by this Bureau. I am, Sir, your obedient servant,

"H. A. WISE, Chief of Bureau."

ORDNANCE INSTRUCTIONS FOR THE UNITED STATES NAVY. Part I. Relating to the Preparation of Vessels of War for Battle, and to the Duties of Officers and others when at Quarters. Part II. The Equipment and Manœuvre of Boats, and Exercise of Howitzers. Part III. Ordnance and Ordnance Stores. Published by order of the Navy Department. 1 vol., 8vo. Cloth. With plates. $5.

THE NAVAL HOWITZER ASHORE. By FOXHALL A. PARKER, Captain U. S. Navy. 1 vol., 8vo. With plates. Cloth. $4.00. Approved by the Navy Department.

THE NAVAL HOWITZER AFLOAT. By FOXHALL A. PARKER, Captain U. S. Navy. 1 vol., 8vo. With plates. Cloth. $4.00. Approved by the Navy Department.

GUNNERY INSTRUCTIONS. Simplified for the Volunteer Officers of the U. S. Navy, with hints to Executive and other Officers. By Lieutenant EDWARD BARRETT, U. S. N., Instructor of Gunnery, Navy Yard, Brooklyn. 1 vol., 12mo. Cloth. $1.25.

'It is a thorough work, treating plainly on its subject, and contains also some valuable hints to executive officers. No officer in the volunteer navy should be without a copy."—*Boston Evening Traveller.*

CALCULATED TABLES OF RANGES FOR NAVY AND ARMY GUNS. With a Method of finding the Distance of an Object at Sea. By Lieutenant W. P. BUCKNER, U. S. N. 1 vol., 8vo. Cloth. $1.50.

NAVAL LIGHT ARTILLERY. Instructions for Naval Light Artillery, afloat and ashore, prepared and arranged for the U. S. Naval Academy, by Lieutenant W. H. PARKER, U. S. N. Third edition, revised by Lieut. S. B. LUCE, U. S. N., Assistant Instructor of Gunnery and Tactics at the United States Naval Academy. 1 vol., 8vo. Cloth. With 22 plates. $3.

ELEMENTARY INSTRUCTION IN NAVAL ORDNANCE AND GUNNERY. By JAMES H. WARD, Commander U. S. Navy, Author of "Naval Tactics," and "Steam for the Million." New Edition, revised and enlarged. 8vo. Cloth. $2.

"It conveys an amount of information in the same space to be found nowhere else, and given with a clearness which renders it useful as well to the general as the professional inquirer."—*N. Y. Evening Post.*

MANUAL OF NAVAL TACTICS; Together with a Brief Critical Analysis of the principal Modern Naval Battles. By JAMES H. WARD, Commander U. S. N. With an Appendix, being an extract from Sir Howard Douglas's "Naval Warfare with Steam." 1 vol., 8vo. Cloth. $3.

NAVIGATION AND NAUTICAL ASTRONOMY. Prepared for the use of the U. S. Naval Academy. By Prof. J. H. C. COFFIN, Fourth edition, enlarged. 1 vol., 12mo. Cloth. $3.50.

SQUADRON TACTICS UNDER STEAM. By FOXHALL A. PARKER, Captain U. S. Navy. Published by authority of the Navy Department. 1 vol., 8vo. With numerous plates. Cloth. $5.

"In this useful work to Navy officers, the author demonstrates—by the aid of profuse diagrams and explanatory text—a new principle for manœuvring naval vessels in action. The author contends that the winds, waves, and currents of the ocean oppose no more serious obstacles to the movements of a steam fleet, than do the inequalities on the surface of the earth to the manœuvres of an army. It is in this light, therefore, that he views a vast fleet—simply as an army; the regiments, brigades, and divisions of which are represented by a certain ship or ships."—*Scientific American.*

OSBON'S HAND-BOOK OF THE UNITED STATES NAVY. Being a compilation of all the principal events in the history of every vessel of the United States Navy, from April, 1861, to May, 1864. Compiled and arranged by B. S. OSBON. 1 vol., 12mo. Cloth. $2.50.

HISTORY OF THE UNITED STATES NAVAL ACADEMY. With Biographical Sketches, and the names of all the Superintendents, Professors, and Graduates; to which is added a Record of some of the earliest votes by Congress, of Thanks, Medals, and Swords to Naval Officers. By EDWARD CHAUNCEY MARSHALL, A. M. 1 vol., 12mo. Cloth. Plates. $1.

NAVAL DUTIES AND DISCIPLINE: With the Policy and Principles of Naval Organization. By F. A. ROE, late Commander U. S. Navy. 1 vol., 12mo. Cloth. $1.50.

"The author's design was undoubtedly to furnish young officers some general instruction drawn from long experience, to aid in the better discharge of their official duties, and, at the same time, to furnish other people with a book which is not technical, and yet thoroughly professional. It throws light upon the Navy—its organization, its achievements, its interior life. Everything is stated as tersely as possible, and this is one of the advantages of the book, considering that the experience and professional knowledge of twenty-five years' service, are crowded somewhere into its pages."—*Army and Navy Journal.*

MANUAL OF THE BOAT EXERCISE at the U. S. Naval Academy, designed for the practical instruction of the Senior Class in Naval Tactics. 18mo. Flexible Cloth. 75c.

MANUAL OF INTERNAL RULES AND REGULATIONS FOR MEN-OF-WAR. By Commodore U. P. LEVY, U. S. N., late Flag-Officer commanding U. S. Naval Force in the Mediterranean, &c. Flexible blue cloth. Third edition, revised and enlarged. 50 cents.

"Among the professional publications for which we are indebted to the war, we willingly give a prominent place to this useful little Manual of Rules and Regulations to be observed on board of ships of war. Its authorship is a sufficient guarantee for its accuracy and practical value; and as a guide to young officers in providing for the discipline, police, and sanitary government of the vessels under their command, we know of nothing superior."—*N. Y. Herald.*

TOTTEN'S NAVAL TEXT-BOOK. Naval Text-Book and Dictionary, compiled for the use of the Midshipmen of the U. S. Navy. By Commander B. J. TOTTEN, U. S. N. Second and revised edition. 1 vol., 12mo. $3.

"This work is prepared for the Midshipmen of the United States Navy. It is a complete manual of instructions as to the duties which pertain to their office, and appears to have been prepared with great care, avoiding errors and inaccuracies which had crept into a former edition of the work, and embracing valuable additional matter. It is a book which should be in the hands of every midshipman, and officers of high rank in the navy would often find it a useful companion."—*Boston Journal.*

LUCE'S SEAMANSHIP: Compiled from various authorities, and Illustrated with numerous Original and Selected Designs. For the use of the United States Naval Academy. By S. B. LUCE, Lieutenant-Commander U. S. N. In two parts. Fourth edition, revised and improved. 1 vol., crown octavo. Half Roan. $7.50.

LESSONS AND PRACTICAL NOTES ON STEAM. The Steam-Engine, Propellers, &c., &c., for Young Marine Engineers, Students, and others. By the late W. R. KING, U. S. N. Revised by Chief-Engineer J. W. KING, U. S. Navy. Twelfth edition, enlarged. 8vo. Cloth. $2.

STEAM FOR THE MILLION. A Popular Treatise on Steam and its Application to the Useful Arts, especially to Navigation. By J. H. WARD, Commander U. S. Navy. New and revised edition. 1 vol., 8vo. Cloth. $1.

THE STEAM-ENGINE INDICATOR, and the Improved Manometer Steam and Vacuum Gauges: Their Utility and Application. By PAUL STILLMAN. New edition. 1 vol., 12mo. Flexible cloth. $1.

SCREW PROPULSION. Notes on Screw Propulsion, its Rise and History. By Capt. W. H. WALKER, U. S. Navy. 1 vol., 8vo. Cloth. 75 cents.

POOK'S METHOD OF COMPARING THE LINES AND DRAUGHTING VESSELS PROPELLED BY SAIL OR STEAM, including a Chapter on Laying off on the Mould-Loft Floor. By SAMUEL M. POOK, Naval Constructor. 1 vol., 8vo, with illustrations. Cloth. $5.

HARWOOD'S LAW AND PRACTICE OF UNITED STATES NAVAL COURTS-MARTIAL. By A. A. HARWOOD, U. S. N. Adopted as a Text-Book at the U. S. Naval Academy. 8vo. Law binding. $4.

"It is believed to be the first treatise this side of the Atlantic which has essayed to deal with the subject of navy law by itself. That there is much of military jurisprudence common to both is well known; also, that the distinguishing laws and regulations of each arm of the service make of necessity the Court-Martial usage of each a distinct and particular one. An exposition of the law and practice of Naval Courts only has long been a want in the service; that it has been dealt with thoroughly and understandingly in this treatise will not be questioned. It is obviously a practical book."—*Washington Star.*

NAUTICAL ROUTINE AND STOWAGE. With Short Rules in Navigation. By JOHN McLEOD MURPHY and WM. N. JEFFERS, Jr., U. S. N. 1 vol., 8vo. Blue cloth. $2.50.

NAVY REGISTER OF THE UNITED STATES FOR 1868. 8vo. Paper. $2.

SYSTEM OF NAVAL DEFENCES. By JAMES B. EADS. With illustrations. 4to. Cloth. $5.

TREATISE ON THE MARINE BOILERS OF THE UNITED STATES. By H. H. BARTOL. Illustrated. 8vo. Cloth. $1.50.

DEAD RECKONING; Or, Day's Work. By EDWARD BARRETT, U. S. Navy. 8vo. Flexible cloth. $1.25.

SUBMARINE WARFARE, DEFENSIVE AND OFFENSIVE. Comprising a full and complete History of the invention of the Torpedo, its employment in War, and results of its use. Descriptions of the various forms of Torpedoes, Submarine Batteries and Torpedo Boats actually used in War. Methods of ignition by Machinery, Contact Fuzes, and Electricity, and a full account of experiments made to determine the explosive Force of Gunpowder under Water. Also a discussion of the offensive Torpedo system, its effect upon Iron-Clad Ship systems, and influence upon Future Naval Wars. By Lieut.-Commander JOHN S. BARNES, U. S. N. With illustrations. 1 vol., 8vo. In press.

TREATISE ON GRAND MILITARY OPERATIONS. Illustrated by a Critical and Military History of the Wars of Frederick the Great. With a summary of the most important principles of the Art of War. By BARON DE JOMINI. Illustrated by Maps and Plans. Translated from the French by Col. S. B. HOLABIRD, A. D. C., U. S. Army. In 2 vols., 8vo, and Atlas. Cloth, $15; Half-Calf or Half-Morocco, $21; Half-Russia, $22.50

"It is universally agreed that no art or science is more difficult than that of war; yet by an unaccountable contradiction of the human mind, those who embrace this profession take little or no pains to study it. They seem to think that the knowledge of a few insignificant and useless trifles constitute a great officer. This art, like all others, is founded on certain and fixed principles, which are by their nature invariable; *the application of them* only can be varied."

In this work these principles will be found very fully developed and illustrated by immediate application to the most interesting campaigns of a great master. The theoretical and mechanical part of war may be acquired by any one who has the application to study, powers of reflection, and a sound, clear common sense.

Frederick the Great has the credit of having done much for tactics. He introduced the close column by division and deployments therefrom. He brought his army to a higher degree of skill than any other in manœuvring before the enemy to menace his wings or threaten his flanks.

SCOTT'S MILITARY DICTIONARY. Comprising Technical Definitions; Information on Raising and Keeping Troops; Actual service, including makeshifts and improved *materiel*, and Law, Government, Regulation, and Administration relating to Land Forces. By Colonel H. L. SCOTT, Inspector-General U. S. A. 1 vol., large 8vo, fully illustrated. Half-Morocco, $6; Half-Russia, $8; Full-Morocco, $10.

"It is a complete Encyclopædia of Military Science, and fully explains everything discovered in the art of war up to the present time."—*Philadelphia Evening Bulletin.*

"It should be made a text-book for the study of every volunteer."—*Harper's Magazine.*

CAVALRY; ITS HISTORY, MANAGEMENT, AND USES IN WAR. By J. ROEMER, LL.D., late an Officer of Cavalry in the Service of the Netherlands. Elegantly illustrated, with one hundred and twenty-seven fine wood-engravings. In one large octavo volume, beautifully printed on tinted paper. Cloth, $6; Half-calf, $7.50.

SUMMARY OF CONTENTS.—Cavalry in European Armies; Proportion of Cavalry to Infantry; What kind of Cavalry desirable; Cavalry indispensable in War; Strategy and Tactics; Organization of an Army; Route Marches; Rifled Fire-Arms; The Charge; The Attack; Cavalry versus Cavalry; Cavalry versus Infantry; Cavalry versus Artillery; Field Service; Different Objects of Cavalry; Historical Sketches of Cavalry among the early Greeks, the Romans, the Middle Ages; Different kinds of Modern Cavalry; Soldiers and Officers; Various systems of Training of Cavalry Horses; Remounting; Shoeing; Veterinary Surgeons, Saddlery, etc., etc.

WHAT GENERAL M'CLELLAN SAYS OF IT.

"I am exceedingly pleased with it, and regard it as a very valuable addition to our military literature. It will certainly be regarded as a standard work, and I know of none so valuable to our cavalry officers. Its usefulness, however, is not confined to officers of cavalry alone, but it contains a great deal of general information valuable to the officers of the other arms of service, especially those of the Staff."

NOLAN'S SYSTEM FOR TRAINING CAVALRY HORSES. By KENNER GARRARD, Captain Fifth Cavalry, Bvt. Brig.-Gen. U. S. A. 1 vol., 12mo, cloth. 24 lithographed plates. $2.

COOKE'S CAVALRY TACTICS; or, Regulations for the Instruction, Formations, and Movements of the Cavalry of the Army and Volunteers of the United States. 100 illustrations, 12mo. Cloth, $1.

PATTEN'S CAVALRY DRILL. Containing Instructions on Foot; Instruction on Horseback; Basis of Instruction; School of the Squadron, and Sabre Exercise. 93 Engravings. 12mo, paper. 50 cents.

ELEMENTS OF MILITARY ART AND HISTORY. By EDWARD DE LA BARRE DUPARCQ, Chef de Bataillon of Engineers in the Army of France, and Professor of the Military Art in the Imperial School of St. Cyr. Translated by Brigadier-General GEO. W. CULLUM, U. S. A., Chief of the Staff of Major-General H. W. HALLECK, General-in-Chief U. S. Army. 1 vol., 8vo, cloth. $5.

"I read the original a few years since, and considered it the very best work I had seen upon the subject. General Cullum's ability and familiarity with the technical language of French military writers, are a sufficient guarantee of the correctness of his translation

"H. W. HALLECK, Major-General U. S. A."

"I have read the book with great interest, and trust that it will have a large circulation. It cannot fail to do good by spreading that very knowledge, the want of which among our new, inexperienced, and untaught soldiers, has cost us so many lives, and so much toil and treasure.

"M. C. MEIGS, Quartermaster-General U. S. A."

"Barre Duparcq is one of the most favorably known among recent military writers in France. If not the very best, this is certainly among the best of the numerous volumes devoted to this topic. Could this book be put into the hands and heads of our numerous intelligent but untrained officers, it would work a transformation supremely needed. We can say that no officer can read this work without positive advantage and real progress as a soldier. General Cullum is well known as one of the most proficient students of military science and art in our service, and is amply qualified to prepare an original text-book on this subject."—*Atlantic Monthly.*

"The work contains a History of the Art of War, as it has grown up from the earliest ages; describes the various formations which have from time to time been adopted; and treats in detail of the several arms of the service, and the most effective manner of employing them for offensive and defensive purposes. It is fully illustrated with diagrams displaying to the eye the formations and evolutions which find place in ancient and modern armies. Though the book is especially designed for the instruction of officers and soldiers, the non-professional reader cannot fail to perceive the clearness of its statements and the precision of its definitions."—*Harper's Monthly.*

THE PRINCIPLES OF STRATEGY AND GRAND TACTICS. Translated from the French of General G. H. DUFOUR. By WILLIAM P. CRAIGHILL, Captain of Engineers U. S. Army, and Assistant Professor of Engineering, U. S. Military Academy, West Point. From the last French edition. Illustrated. In 1 vol., 12mo, cloth. $3.

"General Dufour is a distinguished civil and military engineer and a practical soldier, and in Europe one of the recognized authorities on military matters. He holds the office of Chief of the General Staff of the Army of Switzerland."—*Evening Post.*

"This work upon the principles of strategy, the application of which we have sorely stood in need of in all our campaigns, comes from an acknowledged authority. It was General Dufour who successfully arrayed the Federal Army of Switzerland against secession, and 'subdued' the rebellious Cantons."—*Boston Journal.*

ARMY OFFICERS' POCKET COMPANION. Principally designed for Staff Officers in the Field. Partly translated from the French of M. de Rouvre, Lieutenant-Colonel of the French Staff Corps, with Additions from standard American, French, and English authorities. By Wm. P. Craighill, First-Lieutenant U. S. Corps of Engineers, Assistant Professor of Engineering at the U. S. Military Academy, West Point. 1 vol., 18mo, full roan. $2.

"I have carefully examined Captain Craighill's Pocket Companion. I find it one of the very best works of the kind I have ever seen. Any army or volunteer officer who will make himself acquainted with the contents of this little book will seldom be ignorant of his duties in camp or field.
"H. W. HALLECK, Major-General U. S. A."

"I have carefully examined the 'Manual for Staff Officers in the Field.' It is a most invaluable work, admirable in arrangement, perspicuously written, abounding in most useful matters, and such a book as should be the constant pocket-companion of every army officer, Regular and Volunteer.
"G. W. CULLUM, Brigadier-General U. S. A.,
"Chief of General Halleck's Staff, Chief Engineer Department Mississippi."

MAXIMS AND INSTRUCTIONS ON THE ART OF WAR. A Practical Military Guide for the use of Soldiers of all Arms and of all Countries. Translated from the French by Captain Lendy, Director of the Practical Military College, late of the French Staff, etc., etc. 1 vol., 18mo, cloth. 75 cents.

HISTORY OF WEST POINT, and its Military Importance during the American Revolution; and the Origin and Progress of the United States Military Academy. By Captain Edward C. Boynton, A. M., Adjutant of the Military Academy. With numerous Maps and Engravings. 1 vol., octavo. Blue cloth, $6.00; half mor., $7.50; full mor., $10.

"Aside from its value as an historical record, the volume under notice is an entertaining guide-book to the Military Academy and its surroundings. We have full details of Cadet life from the day of entrance to that of graduation, together with descriptions of the buildings, grounds, and monuments. To the multitude of those who have enjoyed at West Point the combined attractions, this book will give, in its descriptive and illustrated portion, especial pleasure."—*New York Evening Post.*

"The second part of the book gives the history of the Military Academy from its foundation in 1802, a description of the academic buildings, and the appearance to-day of this always beautiful spot, with the manner of appointment of the cadets, course of study, pay, time of service, and much other information yearly becoming of greater value, for West Point has not yet reached its palmiest days."—*Daily Advertiser.*

WEST POINT LIFE. A poem read before the Dialectic Society of the United States Military Academy. Illustrated with twenty-two full-page Pen and Ink Sketches. By a Cadet. To which is added, the song, "Benny Havens, Oh!" Oblong 8vo., cloth, bevelled boards, $2.50.

GUIDE TO WEST POINT AND THE U. S. MILITARY ACADEMY. With Maps and Engravings. 18mo., cloth, $1.

BENTON'S ORDNANCE AND GUNNERY. A Course of Instruction in Ordnance and Gunnery; compiled for the use of the Cadets of the United States Military Academy, by Col. J. G. BENTON, Major Ordnance Department, late Instructor of Ordnance and Gunnery, Military Academy, West Point. Third Edition, revised and enlarged. 1 vol., 8vo, cloth, cuts, $5.

"A GREAT MILITARY WORK.—We have before us a bound volume of nearly six hundred pages, which is a complete and exhaustive 'Course of Instruction in Ordnance and Gunnery,' as its title states, and goes into every department of the science, including gunpowder, projectiles, cannon, carriages, machines, and implements, small-arms, pyrotechny, science of gunnery, loading, pointing, and discharging firearms, different kinds of fires, effects of projectiles and employment of artillery. These severally form chapter heads, and give thorough information on the subjects on which they treat. The most valuable and interesting information on all the above topics, including the history, manufacture, and use of small-arms, is here concentrated in compact and convenient form, making a work of rare merit and standard excellence. The work is abundantly and clearly illustrated."—*Boston Traveller.*

ELECTRO-BALLISTIC MACHINES, AND THE SCHULTZ CHRONOSCOPE. By Lt.-Col. S. V. BENÉT. 1 vol., 4to, illustrated, cloth, $3.

A TREATISE ON ORDNANCE AND ARMOR. Embracing Descriptions, Discussions, and Professional Opinions concerning the Material, Fabrication, Requirements, Capabilities, and Endurance of European and American Guns for Naval, Sea-Coast, and Iron-Clad Warfare, and their Rifling, Projectiles, and Breech-Loading; also, Results of Experiments against Armor, from Official Records. With an Appendix, referring to Gun-Cotton, Hooped Guns, etc., etc. By ALEXANDER L. HOLLEY, B. P. With 493 Illustrations. 1 vol. 8vo, 948 pages. Half roan, $10. Half Russia, $12.

"The special feature of this comprehensive volume is its ample record of facts relating to the subjects of which it treats, that have not before been distinctly presented to the attention of the public. It contains a more complete account than, as far as we are aware, can be found elsewhere, of the construction and effects of modern standard ordnance, including the improvements of Armstrong, Whitworth, Blakeley, Parrott, Brooks, Rodman, and Dahlgren; the wrought-iron and steel guns; and the latest system of rifling projectiles and breech-loading.

THE ARTILLERIST'S MANUAL. Compiled from various Sources, and adapted to the Service of the United States. Profusely illustrated with woodcuts and engravings on stone. Second edition, revised and corrected, with valuable additions. By Gen. JOHN GIBBON, U. S. Army. 1 vol., 8vo, half roan, $6.

This book is now considered the standard authority for that particular branch of the Service in the United States Army. The War Department, at Washington, has exhibited its thorough appreciation of the merits of this volume, the want of which has been hitherto much felt in the service, by subscribing for 700 copies.

"It is with great pleasure that we welcome the appearance of a new work on this subject, entitled 'The Artillerist's Manual,' by Capt. John Gibbon, a highly scientific and meritorious officer of artillery in our regular service. The work, an octavo volume of 500 pages, in large, clear type, appears to be well adapted to supply just what has been heretofore needed to fill the gap between the simple manual and the more abstruse demonstrations of the science of gunnery. The whole work is profusely illustrated with woodcuts and engravings on stone, tending to give a more complete and exact idea of the various matters described in the text. The book may well be considered as a valuable and important addition to the military science of the country."—*New York Herald.*

HAND-BOOK OF ARTILLERY. For the Service of the United States Army and Militia. Ninth edition, revised and greatly enlarged. By Col. JOSEPH ROBERTS, U. S. A. 1 vol., 18mo, cloth, $1.25.

The following is an extract from a report made by the committee appointed at a meeting of the staff of the Artillery School at Fort Monroe, Va., to whom the commanding officer of the School had referred this work:

* * * "In the opinion of your Committee, the arrangement of the subjects and the selection of the several questions and answers have been judicious. The work is one which may be advantageously used for reference by the officers, and is admirably adapted to the instruction of non-commissioned officers and privates of artillery.

"Your Committee do, therefore, recommend that it be substituted as a text-book."

(Signed,) I. VOGDES, *Capt. 1st Artillery.*
(Signed,) E. O. C. ORD, *Capt. 3d Artillery.*
(Signed,) J. A. HASKIN, *Bvt. Maj. and Capt. 1st Artillery.*

INSTRUCTIONS FOR FIELD ARTILLERY. Prepared by a Board of Artillery Officers. To which is added the "Evolutions of Batteries," translated from the French, by Brig.-Gen. R. ANDERSON, U. S. A. 1 vol., 12mo, 122 plates. Cloth, $3.

"WAR DEPARTMENT,
"WASHINGTON, D. C., March 1, 1863.

"This system of Instruction for Field Artillery, prepared under direction of the War Department, having been approved by the President, is adopted for the instruction of troops when acting as field artillery.

"Accordingly, instruction in the same will be given after the method pointed out therein; and all additions to or departures from the exercise and manœuvres laid down in the system, are positively forbidden.

"EDWIN M. STANTON,
"Secretary of War."

PATTEN'S ARTILLERY DRILL. 1 vol., 12mo, paper, 50 cents.

HEAVY ARTILLERY TACTICS.—1863. Instruction for Heavy Artillery; prepared by a Board of Officers, for the use of the Army of the United States. With service of a gun mounted on an iron carriage. In 1 vol., 12mo, with numerous illustrations. Cloth, $2.50.

"WAR DEPARTMENT,
"WASHINGTON, D. C., Oct. 20, 1862.

"This system of Heavy Artillery Tactics, prepared under direction of the War Department, having been approved by the President, is adopted for the instruction of troops when acting as heavy artillery.

"EDWIN M. STANTON,
"Secretary of War."

EVOLUTIONS OF FIELD BATTERIES OF ARTILLERY. Translated from the French, and arranged for the Army and Militia of the United States. By Gen. ROBERT ANDERSON, U. S. A. Published by order of the War Department. 1 vol., cloth, 32 plates. $1.

GILLMORE'S FORT SUMTER. Official Report of Operations against the Defences of Charleston Harbor, 1863. Comprising the descent upon Morris Island, the demolition of Fort Sumter, and the siege and reduction of Forts Wagner and Gregg. By Maj.-Gen. Q. A. GILLMORE, U. S. Volunteers, and Major U. S. Corps of Engineers. With 76 lithographic plates, views, maps, etc. 1 vol., 8vo. Cloth, $10; Half-Russia, $12.

"General Gillmore has enjoyed and improved some very unusual opportunities for adding to the literature of military science, and for making a permanent record of his own professional achievements. It has fallen to his lot to conduct some of the most striking operations of the war, and to make trial of interesting experiments in engineering and artillery which were both calculated to throw light upon some of the great points of current discussion in military art, and also to fix the attention of spectators in no ordinary degree.

"His report of the siege of Fort Pulaski thus almost took the form of a popular scientific treatise; and we now have his report of his operations against Forts Wagner and Sumter, given to the public in a volume which promises to be even more attractive at bottom, both to the scientific and the general reader, than its predecessor.

"The volume is illustrated by seventy-six plates and views, which are admirably executed, and by a few excellent maps; and indeed the whole style of publication is such as to reflect the highest credit upon the publishers."—*Boston Daily Advertiser.*

SUPPLEMENTARY REPORT to the Engineer and Artillery Operations against the Defences of Charleston Harbor in 1863. By Major-General Q. A. GILLMORE, U. S. Volunteers, and Major U. S. Corps of Engineers. With Seven Lithographed Maps and Views. 1 vol., 8vo. Cloth. $5.

SIEGE AND REDUCTION OF FORT PULASKI, GEORGIA. Papers on Practical Engineering. No. 8. Official Report to the U. S. Engineer Department of the Siege and Reduction of Fort Pulaski, Ga., February, March, and April, 1862. By Brig.-Gen. Q. A. GILLMORE, U. S. A. Illustrated by maps and views. 1 vol., 8vo, cloth. $2.50.

PRACTICAL TREATISE ON LIMES, HYDRAULIC CEMENTS, AND MORTARS. Papers on Practical Engineering, U. S. Engineer Department, No. 9, containing Reports of numerous experiments conducted in New York City, during the years 1858 to 1861 inclusive. By Major-General Q. A. GILLMORE, U. S. Volunteers, and Major U. S. Corps of Engineers. With numerous illustrations. One volume, octavo. Cloth. $4.

SYSTEMS OF MILITARY BRIDGES, in Use by the United States Army; those adopted by the Great European Powers; and such as are employed in British India. With Directions for the Preservation, Destruction, and Re-establishment of Bridges. By Maj.-Gen. GEORGE W. CULLUM, Lieut.-Col. Corps of Engineers, United States Army. 1 vol., octavo. With numerous illustrations. Cloth. $3.50.

www.ingramcontent.com/pod-product-compliance
Lightning Source LLC
LaVergne TN
LVHW010227110826
845151LV00004B/1208